NUCLEAR NATIVITY

NUCLEAR NATIVITY

Rituals of Renewal and Empowerment in the Marshall Islands

Laurence Marshall Carucci

NORTHERN ILLINOIS UNIVERSITY PRESS
DEKALB 1997

Published by the Northern Illinois University Press, DeKalb, Illinois 60115

Manufactured in the United States using acid-free paper

Library of Congress Cataloging-in-Publication Data

Carucci, Laurence Marshall, 1949–

Nuclear nativity: rituals of renewal and empowerment in the Marshall Islands / Laurence Marshall Carucci.

p. cm.

Includes bibliographical references and index.

ISBN 0-87580-217-6 (alk. paper)

1. Ethnology—Marshall Islands—Enewetak Atoll. 2. Rites and ceremonies—Marshall Islands—Enewetak Atoll. 3. Christmas—Marshall Islands—Enewetak Atoll. 4. Ethnopsychology—Marshall Islands—Enewetak Atoll. 5. Enewetak Atoll (Marshall Islands)—Social life and customs. I. Title.

GN671.M33C37 1997

305.8'0099683—dc20 96-30262

CIP

Credits for permissions appear in the Acknowledgments.

For Mary Helena, im barāinwōt aolep riWūjlan im riĀne-wetak ro mōttaō

Jān jinoe in, komuij ar bōke iō āinwōt juon riWūjlañ im kadeļọñ iō ilo bwij in Lianjebel. Komuij ar enajidiki iō āinwōt juon ri aelōñ en im kwalok aolep meļeļe ko rēļap ilo book i aduij. Kin eṃṃol eo aō eļap jān jọñen i maroñ ba, ij karọọlwōj wōt mōttan eñtaan ke aō im mōttan ṃṃākūtkūt ko aduij im naan kane amuij ilo juon ien eo eļap an aorōk im kaṃōņōņō. Etan ien en, Kūrijmōj. Eļap wōt amuij eṃṃol.

CONTENTS

ILLUSTRATIONS

PREFACE

The research on which this book is based was conducted during repeated visits to Wūjlañ and Āne-wetak Atolls in the Marshall Islands over the past twenty years. The primary research on Wūjlañ was supported by a grant from the National Science Foundation and extended from August 1976 through September 1978. Two full cycles of Kūrijmōj were celebrated during these years on Wūjlañ. An additional year of research on Āne-wetak in 1982–1983 allowed me to participate in the entire celebration, and several months of research in the Marshall Islands in 1990–1991 provided an opportunity for me to be part of the festivity during its culminating weeks. These periods of inquiry on Āne-wetak were supported by two separate grants from the National Endowment for the Humanities. Several shorter trips to Āne-wetak Atoll between 1989 and 1996 allowed me to reassess the celebration of Kūrijmōj and to remain aware of its innovative features. The Enewetak/Ujelang Local Government Council, as part of its Agricultural Rehabilitation Program, has funding these research and nutrition assistance endeavors. Further investigative inquiries on the northern Marshall Islands in association with the National Academy of Science as well as a 1995 research project on Kuwajleen Atoll, provided me with opportunities to gain some comparative perspective on the celebration as it exists in other parts of the Republic of the Marshall Islands. Finally, small grants from Montana State University helped me transform the current work into a publishable treatise.

Through the years a large number of people, both within the Marshall Islands and elsewhere, assisted in my quest for facility in and understanding of Marshallese language, culture, and daily practice. On Wūjlañ and Āne-wetak, every mature resident, and others younger, helped me along the way, and I hope that the entire community will accept my sincere thanks. In particular, however, I would like to express my gratitude to these community members, and preserve the memory of several now deceased: Welli, Aluwo, Luta, Jimeon, Tamar, Taina, Eliji, Kārlain, Onil, Lioni and her family, Ioanej and Bila and their family, Joseph and Metalina along with members of their family, Ken and Maji as well as Jakioj, Lombwe and Line, Hertej and Mary along with Benji, Obet and Ruth as well as Anej, Tira and Prujila, Drui and Benjamin and their family, Jemej and Netoui, Majao and Pimiko as well as Jakjen, Erine and Jitiam, Yojitaro and Jobi (and family), Balik and Tomko, Enōk and Median along with Hezra and Lenty, Ruth and Jormea, Paul and Akiko, Atela and Jonni along with Jinet, and Harry, Joniten, Kōen, and Ālaber. In even greater measure, my own family-by-adoption provided constant understanding and daily support: in particular, mama Biola, Yula and Mahten, Tallenja and Tellōñ.

In Mājuro, and other parts of the former Trust Territory of the Pacific Islands, I owe my gratitude to many others, most notably among them, Oscar DeBrum, Dwight Heine, Dick Cody, Tony DeBrum, Carmen Bigler, and Alfred Capelle. Ishmael John, senator and long-time representative of the Enewetak/Ujelang community, provided important guidance during my first days in the Marshall Islands and has continued to support my work since that time. Various members of the Peace Corps gave me assistance in the 1970s, and the College of the Marshall Islands (particular Hilda Heine Jetñil) has helped me pursue my work in Mājuro more recently. Equally, Micronesian Legal Services (former legal representatives of the residents of Wūjlañ), particularly Ted Mitchell, Tom Matsom, Judy Knape, and Donald Capelle, provided considerable opitulation during my years of work in the 1970s. More recently, Davor Pevec, current legal representative for Āne-wetak/Wūjlañ people, has supported and encouraged my interactions with the community.

Research librarians at the University of the South Pacific, Suva, Fiji and the Trust Territory of the Pacific Islands Library on Saipan, Mariana Islands; librarians at Bernice Pauahi Bishop Museum Library and the Pacific Collection at the University of Hawai'i; the Hawai'ian Historical Society; and the Hawai'ian Mission Children's Society have all been generous in their support of historical research for this project. I am especially grateful to Renee Heyum, Cynthia Timberlake, Betty Kam, and Karen Peacock. My indebtedness to my good friends, Lela Goodell and Barbara Dunn, is greater yet. Also in Hawai'i, Drs. Leonard Mason, Robert C. Kiste, Jack A. Tobin, Byron Bender, and Geoffrey White have each offered assistance at various times. Marshall Islands researchers from other parts of the globe, particularly Michael Rynkiewich, Nancy Pollock, and William Alexander, provided important information about the practice of Kūrijmōj elsewhere in the Marshall Islands.

Dr. Marshall Sahlins at the University of Chicago served as director for my initial research in the Marshall Islands, and his comments, along with those of Drs. David M. Schneider, Michael Silverstein, George W. Stocking, Jr., and Valerio Valeri helped me both to formulate and rethink various sections of this book. The comments of Drs. Mac Marshall and Katherine P. Ewing, as well as those of Michael Brown and an anonymous Northern Illinois University Press reviewer were also most helpful. The detailed comments of Dr. Lin Poyer have been of incalculable benefit to readers. Vera Marshall Carucci aided in editing earlier versions of this manuscript, and Mary H. Maifeld, Jocelyn DeHaas, Terry Wolfgram, Kate Maxfield, and Vranna Lynn Hinck helped at various points with typing and editing. Mr. John R. Jensen assisted in transforming my maps into elegant digitized documents. The director and editors at Northern Illinois University Press also worked diligently to bring this book into being. Dan Coran and Susan Bean have been particularly helpful, though everyone at the press has been supportive. To these persons, and other close relatives and friends, I owe a great deal of gratitude. Without financial support from the National Science Foundation, the National Endowment for the Humanities, the University of Chicago, and the Enewetak/Ujelang Local Government, the research on which this book is based would not be a reality. Without the inspirations, suggestions, and assistance of the above named individuals and collectivities, this work would be far less than it has turned out to be. While my own name appears on the cover of the book, it is by far a combined effort.

ACKNOWLEDGMENTS

Quotations from Gerald Knight, *Man This Reef,* are used by permission of the author.

Quotations from the Elizabeth A. Murphy and Ruth E. Runeborg translation of Augustin Kramer and Hans Neverman, *Ralik Ratak* (Walter de Gruyter & Co., Berlin and New York, 1938) are used by permission of Murphy and the publisher.

Quotations from Claude Lévi-Strauss, "Father Christmas Executed" in *Unwrapping Christmas,* edited by Daniel Miller (Oxford University Press, 1993) are used by permission of the publisher.

Quotations from Nancy Pollock, "A Pragmatic View of Marshallese Christmas Ritual" are used by permission of the author.

Typological Conventions for the Spelling of Marshallese Words
(following Abo, Bender, Capelle, and DeBrum 1976)

Marshallese Transcription	Phonetic Equivalent	Approximate English Enunciation (or description)
a	[ɑ]	father (a low back unrounded vowel)
ā	[æ]	cat (a low front vowel)
b	[b^{ɯ}]	butter (a heavy bilabial stop)
d	[ɹ]	a trilled "d" (a light retroflex trill)
e	[e] or [ɛ]	append (a mid front vowel)
i	[i]	intent (a high front vowel)
j	[ţ^{y}] or [c]	wished or French je suis (light dental or alveolar stop or affricate)
k	[k] or [k^{w}]	hike or poke (a velar stop)
l	[l^{y}]	illicit (a light lateral)
ļ	[l^{ɯ}] or [l^{w}]	lamb (a heavy lateral)
m	[m^{y}]	imprecise (a light bilabial nasal)
m̧	[m^{ɯ}]	mature (a heavy bilabial nasal)
n	[n^{y}]	knit (a light dental nasal)
ņ	[n^{ɯ}] or [n^{w}]	nova (a heavy bilabial nasal)
n̄	[ŋ] or [ŋ^{w}]	singer (a velar nasal)
o	[o] or [ɔ]	propane (a mid back rounded vowel)
o̧	[ɒ]	caught (a low back rounded vowel)
ō	[ə] or [ʌ]	but (a middle or mid back unrounded vowel)
p	[p^{y}]	importune (a light bilabial stop)
r	[r^{ɯ}] or [r^{w}]	Spanish burro (a heavy retroflex trill)
t	[t^{ɯ}]	tentative (a heavy dental stop)
u	[u]	true (a high back rounded vowel)
ū	[ɯ]	a high middle/high back unrounded vowel
w	[w]	without (a rounded velar glide)
y	[y]	yellow (an unrounded palatal glide)

NUCLEAR NATIVITY

Introduction

In December 1947 the residents of Āne-wetak (Enewetak),[1] a strategically situated atoll approximately 3,000 miles southwest of Hawai'i, were informed that they would have to leave their homeland in order to allow the United States to use the atoll for nuclear testing (see figures 1 and 2). They did not want to depart, but they believed they had little choice. Military authorities indicated that the tests would lead to peace and freedom for all humankind (cf. Kiste 1974: 28).

In retrospect, Āne-wetak people say they knew the value of peace, for missionaries had taught them to be good Christians (an attribute they use to point out their affinities with Americans and their differences from their own "heathen" past and from certain other islanders). What is more, the apocalyptic battle of World War II allowed them to consider the consequences of nonagreement and to further appreciate the value of peace. These wartime experiences also led them to fear the Americans, who controlled a force so great that Āne-wetak people understood the power in superhuman terms (Carucci 1989). Indeed, during Project CATCHPOLE, the Allied offensive to capture Āne-wetak, they had witnessed the massacre of more than 3,200 Japanese and had themselves survived continual bombing, rifle fire, and grenades. Residents on Āne-wetak islet faced what military historians term a relatively light showering of shells from naval vessels, including 1,098 eight-inch and 4,348 five-inch rounds, whereas Ānjepe, "some 220 acres[,] . . . shuddered under 497 16-inch, 954 14-inch, 673 8-inch, and 4,641 5-inch projectiles" (Shaw, Nalty, and Turnbladh 1966: 205) (see figure 3). On Meden, local people and occupying Japanese forces "staggered under the blows of American warships, planes, and howitzer batteries. . . . [The ships alone] slammed 143 16-inch, 751 14-inch, 896 8-inch, and 9,950 5-inch shells into an area of 200 acres" (Shaw, Nalty, and Turnbladh 1966: 211). More than 30 percent of Āne-wetak and Meden residents died during the battles. Local people remember the battles as terrifying events. In contrast, the times of peace, and unlimited food and supplies provided afterward by naval support forces seem idyllic. When military personnel asked the Āne-wetak people to leave their home atoll less than four years after the battle, how could they endanger their newfound wealth and peacefulness?

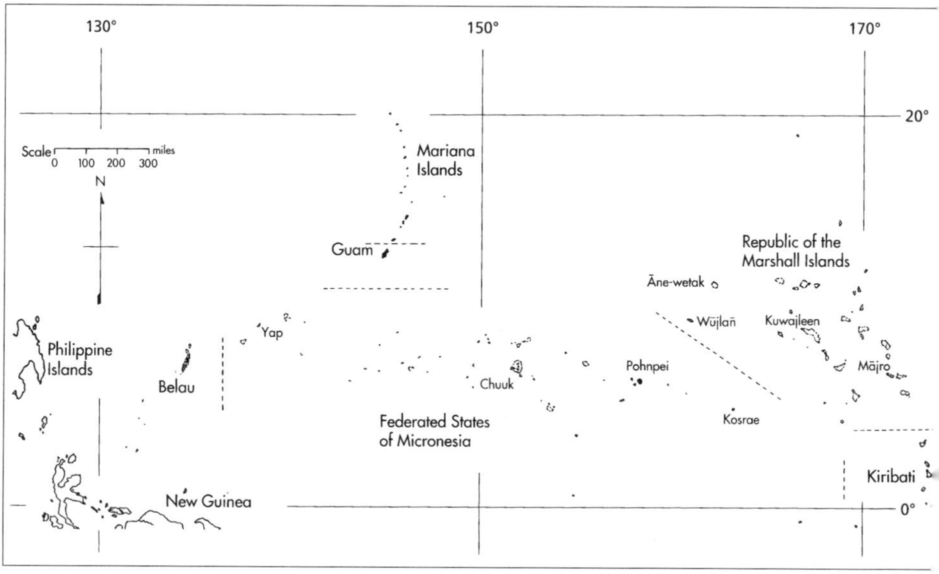

Figure 1. Atolls and islands of the Central Western Pacific. (Cartography by L. M. Carucci, after Kiste 1974)

Caught between trust and fear, the residents left their villages on the tiny outer islets of Āne-wetak in sadness and boarded a military vessel in search of a "new and pleasant" atoll (Tobin 1967: chap. 2; Tobin 1973). For most, curiosity turned to disappointment when they found that they were to be relocated on Wūjlañ (Ujelang), a tiny, coral-strewn atoll they knew well from the pre–World War I German era (see figure 4). Thinking back, the ambivalence they had about Americans typified their talk about Wūjlañ, located 130 miles from their primordial home. They were told that their stay would be short, however, and they believed they had no option but to agree to live in exile under American protection.

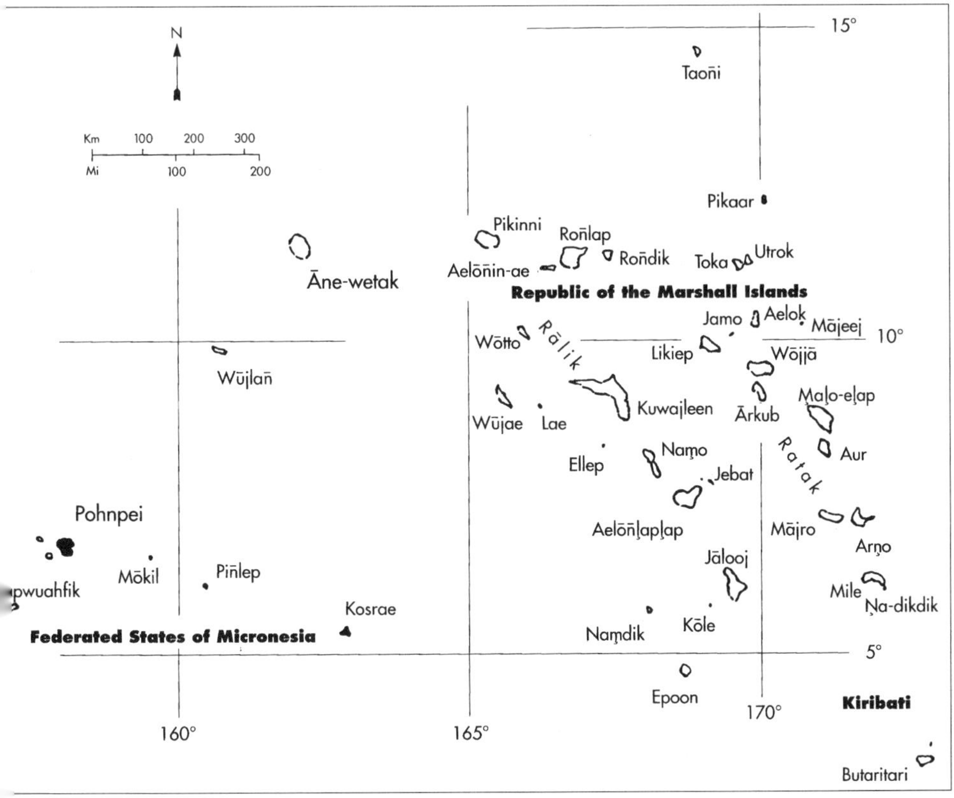

Figure 2. The environs of Āne-wetak and Wūjlañ Atolls, including the Republic of the Marshall Islands, eastern segments of the Federated States of Micronesia, and northernmost Kiribati. (Cartography by L. M. Carucci)

According to the residents' recollections, they reached Wūjlañ less than two weeks after they were first asked to leave their native land. They gathered to celebrate on Christmas Day in a simple, corrugated-steel sanctuary in the solemn seclusion of what, with their migration, had become the Marshall Islands' most isolated inhabited outpost. They prayed for God's grace and, with mixed sentiments, sang the tunes prepared on Āne-wetak for this special day. Normally infused with joy, the entire event is recounted as "a *Kūrijmōj* thrown off in sadness." Most people longed for a time in the near future when they could return home: they remained on Wūjlañ for the next thirty-three years.

With the move to Wūjlañ, the atoll dwellers committed themselves to a life of hardship. Wūjlañ had been ravaged by typhoons and colonial tycoons in the latter half of the nineteenth century (Tobin 1967: 35 et seq.; Hezel 1983: chap. 11). At the end of the Japanese era, the atoll became an abandoned copra (dried coconut) plantation, planted with aging coconuts from German times and strewn with coral waste. A small Japanese military contingent (eighteen men) was "exterminated" when United States Army personnel

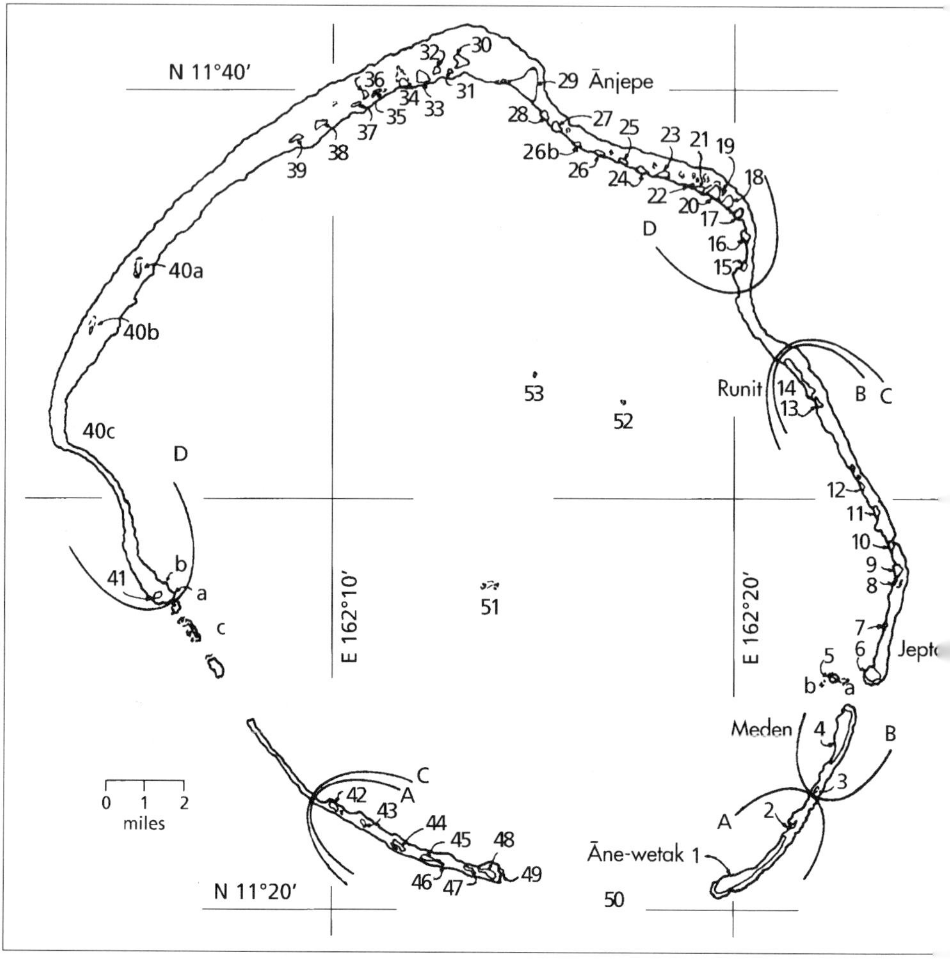

Figure 3. Āne-wetak Atoll. A/B = ancient Āne-wetak division/ancient Wūrrin division. C/D = pre–World War II Āne-wetak half/Ānjepe half. The islets of the atoll are (1) Āne-wetak, eoon-ene; (2) Bokwan-rātok; (3) Bok-eḷap; (4) Meden; (5) Jādool; (5a) Bōke; (5b) Jālouit; (6) Jeptaan; (7) Jinme; (8) Bokwan-mankolo; (9) Ananij; (10) Āne-doul; (11) Jinedoul; (12) Bokwan-iōñ; (13) Āne-laṃōj; (14) Runit; (15) Būlae; (16) Aḷampel; (17) Loojwa; (18) Pijle; (19) Jālik; (20) Aoṃaṇ; (21) Ālele-doon; (21a) Wa-kāmeej; (22) Bok-tūr; (23) Luuj-joor; (24) Aej; (25) Ālle; (26) Bok-eṇ-eḷap; (26a) Taiwel; (27) Kiden-eṇ; (28) Mij-eṇ-kadek; (29) Ānjepe; (30) Bokwōn; (31) Bokwan-jǫ-iwǫj; (32) Bok-aidik; (33) Deldelbwij; (34) Āllokḷap; (35) Looj; (36) Kuruno; (37) Bokwan-watmān; (38) Bokwan-pako; (39) Bokwā-luo; (40a) Boko-ṃaan; (40b) Boko; (40c) Watalā-iōñ (reef section); (41) Pik-eṇ; (41a) Win-bar (coral head); (41b) Jawin-bar (coral head), To-pedped (shallow pass); (42) Kiden-eṇ (rālik); (43) Debwe-iu-eṇ; (44) Bok-eṇ; (45) Mūt; (46) Mūt-dikdik; (47) Bokwōn-kkun; (48) Iukiden; (49) Likin-jābuoj; (50) Eoon-ili (wide pass); (51) Li-jā-iōñ, Li-jā-rōk (coral heads); (52) Dekā-tiṃoṇ (coral head); (and 53) Ḷañ-eṇ-uwe (coral head). Lagoon and ocean waters are common property, held equally by both halves. Only island spaces and selected reefs are held and improved by clan members. (Cartography by L. M. Carucci)

came to "clean up" the atoll in mid-April 1944 (Morison 1951: 314; Shaw, Nalty, and Turnbladh 1966: 219), but Wūjlañ remained largely untouched until Pikinni (Bikini) people chose it as a residence site after their unsuccessful relocation on Roñdik Atoll—a move that cleared Pikinni Atoll for Project CROSSROADS, phase one of the nuclear-testing program (Wasserman and Solomon 1982; Firth 1987). A last-minute decision in Washington sent Āne-wetak residents to Wūjlañ instead. Already disenchanted, Pikinni people became even more desultory when doomed to Kōle, a small, coral pinnacle in the Southern Marshalls, hundreds of miles from their home (Kiste 1967, 1976; Kirch 1984 [on coral atoll types]).

The unwelcome news of relocation delivered by American military authorities to the Āne-wetak people late in 1947 was not the first disappointment encountered in contacts with the outside world. They had eluded early European involvements, although many captains caught sight of the atoll and some disembarked for brief visits. Violence erupted in many Marshallese landfalls; mayhem was common on Wūjlañ, in many early contacts with Pohnpei, and even on Pikinni (Appleton 1834; Hezel 1983: chaps. 1–2; Peterson 1990). But Āne-wetak folks, shy and unassuming, claim that their forefathers "ran like

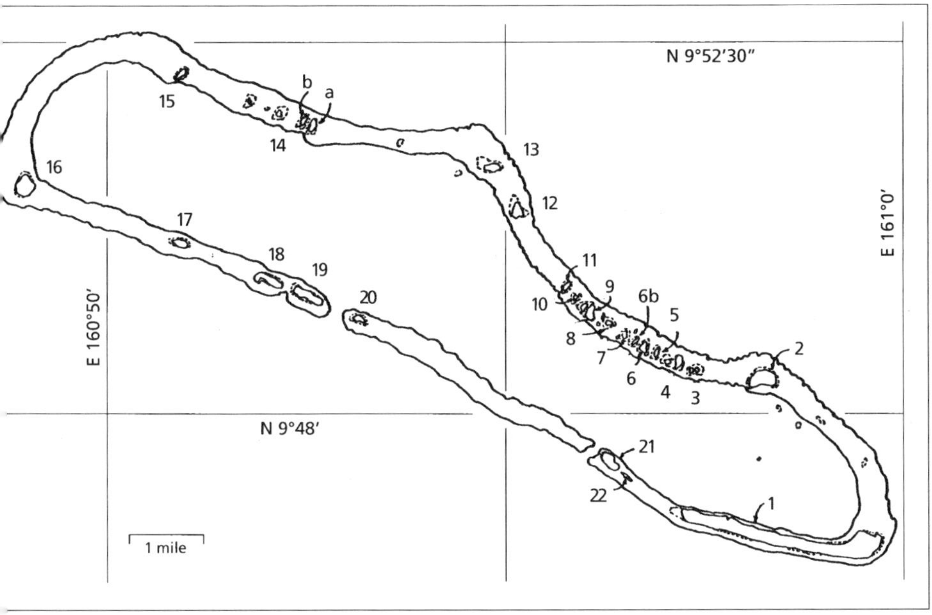

Figure 4. Wūjlañ Atoll. The islets are (1) Wūjlañ; (2) Ra-ej; (3) Mājro; (4) Ṃoriṇa; (5) Maroṃ; (6) Maroṃlap; (6a) Maroṃdik; (7) Bokwōn-eḷap; (8) Kideneṇ; (9) Kilọkwōn; (10) Wūjae; (11) Bokwōn-ibeb; (12) Bokwōn-juaakak; (13) Jedko; (14) Bokwōn-āneeḷlap-eṃen; (14a) Reeaar; (14b) Rālik; (15) Bokoṃ; (16) Kalo; (17) Kiden-eṇ (rālik); (18) Āne-ṃanōt; (19) Ane-ḷap; (20) Nōḷḷe; (21) Pietto; (22) Āne-raj. (Cartography by L. M. Carucci)

cats and rats and hid under palm fronds in the bush" when foreign vessels appeared. Ships' logs say congenial contacts were made on the atoll known first, perhaps, as Los Jardines and later as Brown's Range; exchanges took place, and water and coconuts were loaded on board (Sharp 1960: 19–23; Hezel 1983: 16–17).

As explorers, whalers, copra traders, and missionaries began to frequent the Marshall and Caroline Islands, Āne-wetak remained distant and relatively unknown to Europeans. During German times (1885–1915) the lengthy sail from Āne-wetak to Jālooj, the economic and political center of the Marshall Islands, and to Pohnpei, the Eastern Carolines hub (see figure 1), made it an infrequent stop for Europeans. A few residents were shipped out to work the copra plantation on Wūjlañ, but, accustomed to fishing, they found tending coconuts unpleasant and claim that the German overseers were disappointed in their lackadaisical attitudes toward work. Residents speak humorously of the difficulties German entrepreneurs encountered in convincing Āne-wetak folks to plant their atoll in coconuts. The coconut seedlings provided great quantities of *iu* (sprouted coconut), a delicious staple that locals preferred to eat rather than plant. Not until the latter half of the 1920s did the mission, which was first established on Epoon in the Southern Marshalls in 1857, reach distant Āne-wetak. After a retrenchment on Kosrae to avoid medical problems, disputes with resident traders, and disagreements with German authorities (Pease 1887), Kosraean-trained mission teachers finally reached Āne-wetak well after Japan gained control of the Western Pacific.

During Japanese colonial times, trade ships from Pohnpei became a familiar sight. A small, privately run trade station was established on Āne-wetak. Late in the 1930s two other small stores were opened, and local residents began to spend as much time making copra as they did fishing. Students were taken to school in Pohnpei, and a weather station was built on Āne-wetak islet. People were happy to have access to goods, although, in contrast to their subsequent treatment during the American era, they consider themselves to have been physically abused by the Japanese and underpaid for their labors.

Early in the 1940s, after Japan built a military installation on Āne-wetak as part of its expansionist plans in the Pacific region, the lives of the Āne-wetak people began to change drastically. They became conscript laborers for the Japanese, and within a short time an airfield was constructed on Ānjepe (where the "northern half" of the Āne-wetak people lived). The Japanese were not yet prepared for war when American reconnaissance vessels appeared in the area. Coconut trees were cut down and their disguised trunks aimed skyward in hopes that the Americans would count them as artillery. As undeniable reports of American forces reached the atoll, people became frightened. Japanese officers tried to convince the locals to support their cause, but the Āne-wetak people were concerned for their own safety and for that of their children.

When the Americans took Kuwajleen, enlisted Japanese on Āne-wetak foretold their unavoidable demise. The villagers knew there was no hope. Reconnaissance planes appeared, submarines were spotted, and on January 31, 1944, a carrier strike on Ānjepe sent resident islanders fleeing to small outer islets. On the morning of February 17, American ships entered Āne-wetak lagoon, and the holocaust began (Bickett 1965). Local people found the destruction unimaginable. All vegetation disappeared, and the main islets were turned to rubble. Having received permission to flee, Ānjepe people watched from a distance as their home was leveled. Upcoming days of battle would leave residents on the southern islets, Āne-wetak and Meden (see figure 3), with far more traumatic memories. Without a continuous reef to small outer islets, they had no place to flee. Many Meden inhabitants died with the Japanese in a ruthless massacre (Carucci 1989: 83–84).

The Americans secured the atoll within a week (Hough 1947: 202). Residents' memories of life after the battle are relatively pleasant, even though they were relocated onto small islets in the northern half of Āne-wetak Atoll. Āne-wetak inhabitants enjoyed the attention paid them by navy personnel, but, more than anything else, they were awed by the power and goods that Americans controlled. In a matter of weeks the atoll was transformed into a major transshipment and air-reconnaissance base, a task the Japanese had failed to complete in more than a year. Food support also continued after the war, so, for the Āne-wetak people, it was as though the conflict had never ended. From settlement villages on Pijle and Aoṃaṇ they were moved to a temporary tent-village on Meik Islet, Kuwajleen, while Āne-wetak-based crews completed all preparations and initiated atomic tests on Pikinni Atoll, 140 miles from Āne-wetak. The year after they returned to their homeland, Āne-wetak residents were relocated to Wūjlañ. This time, their understanding of "temporary" gradually became tinged with the taste of eternity.

After an exile of thirty-three years on Wūjlañ Atoll, the Āne-wetak people returned home. But the land that awaited them in 1980 was not the land they had left in 1947: its external form and internal content had been transformed. Wūjlañ residents assumed their homeland had vanished in 1952 when they were shipped from Wūjlañ halfway to Kosrae to see the roots of their atoll shaken by the world's first thermonuclear explosion. Subsequent attempts by the United States to buy the atoll gave them the idea that there was nothing to which to return. Dreams of repatriation were renewed, however, when Pikinni people began to seek a return to their home atoll in the late 1960s. Fortuitously, a medical evacuation took a few Wūjlañ residents through Āne-wetak to refuel on their trip to the Marshalls. Although the atoll that the medical sojourners saw had been radically reshaped, Āne-wetak did indeed exist. When word reached Wūjlañ that Pikinni's repatriation requests had received a positive review in Washington, local people began to pray for their own return.

Repeated requests finally made the plight of the Wūjlañ people newsworthy (*Pacific Daily News,* May 30, May 31, August 1, and August 29, 1973), and a few members of the Wūjlañ community were allowed to return to Āne-wetak for the first time in twenty-five years. They found a scene of massive transformation. The rusting, skeletal structure of a city that had housed thousands overburdened the radioactively clean islands. Americans had swarmed over the atoll prior to 1958, when more than forty-five announced nuclear tests had been conducted. Subsequently, the atoll served as the target area for intercontinental ballistic missiles launched from California (HOE n.d.: 59 et seq.). Finally, a series of "cratering experiments" in the 1970s used high-explosive charges of five to five hundred tons to replicate the effects of nuclear weapons under differing detonation conditions. A court injunction brought these tests to a halt in 1974.

Further discussions led to agreements to return atoll lands to the Āne-wetak people by September 1976, to clean up radioactive and World War II wastes, and to build houses for the people's repatriation (completed by 1980). Although the cleanup efforts were far more successful than those on Pikinni were, even today large segments of Āne-wetak remain uninhabitable, planting programs are years behind schedule, and plans to monitor radiation levels in humans and the environment have been politically compromised. Monetary compensation for damages to land have made arguments about land boundaries and landownership a local compulsion; yet, at the same time, some resettlement goals have been accomplished (cf. Enewetak Master Plan 1973).

Thirty years on Wūjlañ brought many hardships, long periods of famine, a polio epidemic, a period when rats were so plentiful they nibbled on the exposed digits of sleeping children, and, almost ironically, rapid population growth. Exile also brought changes in approaches to health, education, and government and witnessed a transformation of the Āne-wetak people *(ri Āne-wetak)* into the people of Wūjlañ. Ownership of Wūjlañ Atoll was granted in 1976 to help compensate the Āne-wetak people for the permanent loss of Runit and for restricted use of other sections of the atoll. But the formal rights only reinforced a common cultural identification that had transformed the displaced Āne-wetak residents into Wūjlañ people (Carucci 1992).

The return to Āne-wetak was, for many, a move to an entirely new setting, known only through the romanticized images of the elders. Rapid population growth had changed the internal dynamics of the community and altered its self-image. The small, insecure group of 138 that had moved to Wūjlañ in 1947 was filled with fears of extinction.[2] Overwhelmed with its own youthfulness in 1990, when the population exceeded 1,000, the community was no less certain of its future.[3] The move to Wūjlañ had brought experiences of food shortage, because the atoll's 25.5 square miles of lagoon and 0.67 square miles of land compared poorly with Āne-wetak's 387.9 square miles of lagoon, a concomitantly large reef space, and 2.75 square miles of land (Enewetak Master Plan, vol. 1, sec. 2–9). Yet currently, Āne-wetak people inhabit less than half the land space on the atoll and, due to their dependence on scarce fuel for outboard-motor boats, often have access to only a fraction of Āne-wetak's reef and lagoon space. Without additional fuel or a return to outrigger canoes, voyages to distant locations on the atoll in search of land or sea foods are out of the question.

The people have found a temporary solution to this dilemma. Until the local land foods that form the staples of an atoll diet (including coconuts, breadfruit, pandanus, and arrowroot), become largely productive, Āne-wetak residents are supported by food supplied by the U.S. Department of Agriculture and an agricultural support fund. Although the current means of making a living is commonly idealized, people remain insecure about their future. They question whether the slowly recovering environment will be able to catch up to an ever-increasing population. Indeed, the pages that follow elaborate on a local cultural solution to this insecurity, a celebration of Christmas learned from the missionaries, elaborated on Wūjlañ, and further shaped on Āne-wetak. This festive form actively engages the deities themselves in order to ensure ongoing plenty for those on earth.

A FIRST ENCOUNTER WITH KŪRIJMŌJ

Late in August 1976 I entered the field expecting to study processes of change in kinship, land tenure, and exchange. But like Renato Rosaldo's *Ilongot Headhunting* (1980), the focal event of this manuscript grew out of the field experience. It imposed itself on my sensibilities and forced me to rethink my intentions. The initial imposition came about six weeks after I had settled on Wūjlañ, as I walked briskly back to the village with a bundle of coconut spathes collected to kindle a small cooking fire. Suddenly I was ambushed by a group of local women shouting, *"Karate, Karate!" "Take them. Take those things."* After the uproar subsided, they grabbed the spathes and ran off, leaving behind on the path a batch of Marshallese doughnuts and a bewildered anthropologist.

In the weeks that followed this incident, many of my naive preconceptions about fieldwork were shattered. I had hoped to learn about Wūjlañ culture while maintaining my independence since I did not want to be a burden. But, at some level, ethnographic research is always emburdening, a fact that Wūjlañ people knew and accepted. They also had little time for demonstrations of independence, since the mythos of individual identity occupied a space some distance from the core of the Wūjlañ worldview. In coming weeks, the elderly head of the family with whom I shared a land parcel would adopt me as a member of her family. As part of that group, I would be able to construct a much more social persona, a self relevant to Wūjlañ. While my mother-to-be was worried about my health, I believe the adoption also was her attempt to integrate me into one of the fundamental social units in the community. At the same time, the socially constructed persona she had helped to shape would be easily used for her own symbolic purposes. My adoption would also help me to understand Wūjlañ life, not in some generic way, but in a fashion that had its own biases and its own set of constraints and opportunities (Carucci 1995b). Nevertheless, when the women ambushed me these negotiations of identity had not yet transpired, and, without a place to seek understanding, I returned to my small house very confused.

Munching greasy doughnuts coated lightly with peanut butter (in lieu of the rice I had planned to cook), I contemplated what had gone awry. My father-to-be, who resided on the same land parcel, stopped by, listened to my story, and smiled as though he had already heard the tale. In broken Marshallese, interspersed with English, I tried to re-create the mayhem. I told him of the spathes (he had taught me how to gather and bundle them), the women, the doughnuts. He roared with laughter. But I did not understand, and I felt imposed upon. If this was some sort of game, as I surmised from his explanation, it was a bad one. If it was a form of fighting (as he pantomimed), then greater stealth should be required. I suggested sneaking into the village by night with kindling. Again he laughed heartily. In the end, he brought me kindling from his own pile. As when I had first arrived and displaced his son's family from my current abode, I felt badly for the imposition.

Pieces were missing. My framework for interpretation was all wrong. As he suggested, I was a white person, an American, and this battle was Marshallese. But there was not time to learn the language, to discover the rules of the culture (as I then expected to be able to do), and to experience this lived reality. I felt dejected. The task was insurmountable.

Ex post facto the incident makes me chuckle each time I think of it. In typical Marshallese style, the women were building a suitable context in order to incorporate me into the festivities known as *Kūrijmōj*. They led me into this four-month celebration for their own humorous purposes, but they also, I believe, knew that involvement would require me to fulfill my purported interest in language and cultural information.

They took my interest in building these understandings seriously, and they grasped the requirements of my project better than I did at the time. Studying helped, as did working with selected local teachers, but to really learn, they believed, I would have to become involved. Others suggested that I should interact more, but I wanted to be able to do so in Marshallese. The women forced me to make a decision. With reluctance, I began to participate in the daily events of celebration in the hope that I could improve my language abilities and elicit information on families while engaged in other activities.

That was a turning point in my research. I left behind Regenstein Library and the hallowed corridors of the University of Chicago. I hit the streets—more accurately, the village path—cut the pages of my notepads in half, and wrote myself a reminder to send for pocket notebooks. I went into the village and became the nuisance I had feared. Fishing, sailing, making copra, celebrating—in time my ineptitude disappeared and feelings of guilt subsided. Michael Silverstein's lectures on context-specific significance became more than theoretical murmurs. Fused with my own heavily participatory biases, I was forced to refashion his classroom dicta into a modus operandi—a way of listening, observing, coding, constructing.

After having participated in the celebration for four years, I realize that the Wūjlañ women were correct. The only way to really learn about Wūjlañ people's lives was to experience, to enact, to become an active part of those lives.

Nothing less than inundation in and experiencing of them would suffice. Whatever knowledge I have been able to gain came through participation, through intersubjective understandings worked out in interactional contexts.

SEARCH FOR A (PRESENTATIONAL) METHOD

In *Naven,* Gregory Bateson began to experiment with the mass of interpretations that constitute anthropology's public facade (1958: epilogue). His view of Iatmul ceremonial practice involves the reader in some of the layers of festive and interpretational practice. Certainly, Bateson's descriptive material (1958: 6–22) is thick description (Geertz 1973: chap. 1), not an objective account. The picture one forms of the Iatmul in *Naven* is substantially different from other ethnographies of the day. Bateson poses a few of the questions addressed in David M. Schneider's *A Critique of the Study of Kinship* (1984). In my reading, Bateson suggests that although the world may not be knowable in any terms other than one's own, such knowledge is still worth our consideration, not as fact but as meta-account, as an attempt to visualize other people and to come to know ourselves.

In the chapters that follow, I employ the heuristic method Bateson adopted in *Naven* to present an overview and analysis of *Kūrijmōj.* Chapter 1 contains a description of the ceremony based on the several times I witnessed and recorded it. Each subsequent chapter then posits different, additional aspects of *Kūrijmōj,* each a new pathway to understanding, inspired by the ways in which one or more local people explained their ritual movements to me. Although these pathways reflect local logics, each chapter is of my own fashioning and integrates the differentially motivated explanations of *Kūrijmōj* posited by local residents.

Because the ritual is richly productive, the perspectives of these chapters in no way exhaust the array of interpretations. Instead, I have fashioned a few into critical guideposts that allow outsiders to situate Wūjlañ and Āne-wetak actions within contexts of interpretation that local people take for granted. Each represents an abstraction from what was expressed and enacted by community members during *Kūrijmōj.* Ancient lore, daily actions, and value-laden statements about how life should be lived are all brought to bear on this complex ritual event. If a definitive continuity is sacrificed by segmenting the text into seemingly disparate interpretative frames, the cumbersomeness serves as an iconic reminder that anthropology itself is a multifaceted and highly interactive process, without a single set of meanings or interpretations (Marcus and Fischer 1986). Bateson's experimental approach in *Naven* allows us to glimpse his method. My approach, I hope, will make us more sensitive to how indigenous discourses and practices reflect back on the theory and methods from which an analytic framework derives.

As a study of ritual, I also hope to dissuade readers from the belief that these events, though deeply embedded and routinized, are set structural forms with set meanings. Certainly, some themes are frequent components of indigenous arguments about the ancient past, but even these meanings change as the members of the Wūjlañ and Āne-wetak community alter their interpretation of their own past for purposes of current social empowerment. But *Kūrijmōj* on Wūjlañ and Āne-wetak is such a central part of village activities that it dynamically constitutes a newly fashioned social world even as it unsuccessfully replicates its own past. Āne-wetak people then rely on that verified past for purposes of historical reference and current empowerment. Thus its form, as well as its interpretations, are multifaceted. As Rosaldo notes in relation to the emotions associated with Ilongot headhunting, analytical depth and cultural elaboration do not line up as concisely as anthropologists have contended. Unelaborated experiences may be more emotionally salient and culturally central than the most highly elaborated text (Rosaldo 1989: 12 et seq.). The different facets of *Kūrijmōj* explored in chapters 2–6, therefore, reflect not only the most frequent views of the celebration but equally the wide array of directions that different participants found important. My hope is that these diverse perspectives help the reader see the ritual in a broader context of interpretation.

At the same time, renderings of the celebration presented here are not randomly selected. It is certainly my aim that the presentational style will allow readers with dissenting interpretations to reformulate the material along new lines. Nonetheless, as Eco has noted (1990), not all readings of a text are equally valuable or, in local terms, equally viable. The pathways to understanding contained in these chapters, though not exhaustive, are those suggested by local residents precisely because they have cultural and historical legitimacy and value. Although the meanings of *Kūrijmōj,* like its overt forms, are constantly changing, I would hope that those with alternative interpretations attempt to maintain sympathy with the range of logics that make the most sense to Wūjlañ and Āne-wetak people.

As a Marshall Islands event, *Kūrijmōj* is far different from "Christmas," the New England religious festival American-educated mission teachers first brought to Āne-wetak. To say that the celebration is syncretic is fairly obvious and not very informative. Indeed, both the Christianity and the Christmas introduced to islanders were equally syncretic on their arrival. More important, *Kūrijmōj* provides a workshop for anthropologists who are interested in the way meaning is fashioned in social practice precisely because it is dialectically syncretic and syncretically dialectic. The pagan and doctrinaire are inseparably appropriated to construct an indigenous history and then are reappropriated to formulate the conditions of that historically significant existence. At one moment, the Christian becomes the present set against the uninterrupted *durée* of the past, but then, in opposition to fears of inconsequentiality, elements of practice resurface to challenge the singularity of a unified Christian or Marshallese identity.

At moments, primordial themes analogous to those in related Pacific societies give the festive period a unifying structure, but overall unity is constantly fractured by foreign elements—American, Japanese, German, or

Spanish in origin—that are reshaped to situationally construct differences with others. My initial biases led me to focus on the structural continuities, the widespread Malayo-Polynesian notions that provide an undercurrent of ideas worked out in various logically coherent combinations in specific Pacific societies. Wūjlañ and Āne-wetak actions and utterances are, from one perspective, a specific spatial and temporal manifestation of this historical mosaic. Indeed, in some instances local discourses and ritual practices legitimately can be interpreted as analogues of general Pacific patterns because the Wūjlañ and Āne-wetak people use such similarities as evidence that "we are all Pacific people" or "we are all Marshallese." But at other times differences denote the experiences of a group searching for a distinct identity and are used to construct and express cultural uniqueness vis-à-vis others.

Kūrijmōj is by far the most prolonged ritual activity on Wūjlañ and Āne-wetak Atolls. It occupies people's time for nearly one-third of each year. Its complexity and constantly changing character present challenges to both description and analysis. Nevertheless, my idealism leads me to hope that living through these experiences allows me to capture in my constructions of their way of life some of the critical categories that local people use to understand their world. I have little doubt that the significant symbols discussed in the text are real to Āne-wetak/Wūjlañ people, but at the same time, in writing about them, I assist in the process of making them into overly empowered concretions derived from many biased glimpses of a social practice in constant flux and change (Bourdieu 1991).[4]

What is the aim of this celebration? As I hope will become clear, there are many intentions, each suited to its own arena of performative meaning. Nevertheless, at its most general and important level, this complex Wūjlañ/Āne-wetak celebration seeks prosperity and the well-being of local people, exudes a message of love and seeks compassion, and pursues happiness in games and playful trickery. Although condescending European or American Christians may criticize elements of the performance as being outside their own Christian ethics, this festivity needs no apologies to be accepted, for it is a wholesome realization of the manner in which the world is symbolically constructed by impassioned members of a social order seeking viability and recognition. *Kūrijmōj* not only seeks the renewal of life; simultaneously, it *is* life in the process of its actualization or becoming.

My approach to this study is to describe the ritual forms of *Kūrijmōj* as they recur from year to year and to elaborate on a few of the variations. This is the primary work of the first chapter. The second chapter begins to explore the connections between the ritual forms and the major cultural contrasts that Wūjlañ and Āne-wetak people use to orient their activities on a day-to-day basis. Although these cultural contrasts are presented as reified prototypes all too reminiscent of Durkheim's social facts, in actuality they are constructs that are definitionally relative in a cosmological sense (see, for example, Schrempp 1992). But part of the work of *Kūrijmōj* is to transform the arbitrary into the factual, to make the categories seem comfortably real (Geertz

1966). Therefore, I present these cultural contrasts as fully reified social categories, much as they are discussed by local people.

Chapter 2 begins with an outline of the exchanging scenario that governs the activities of *Kūrijmōj*. I then attempt to show the various contexts in which the scenario is applied. The first is the recruitment phase that each songfest group must pursue in order to attract new members. The second is the exchange among opposed equals that typifies many of the inter-*jepta* (songfest group) activities of *Kūrijmōj*. Last comes the exchange among beings of unequal rank. As Sahlins suggests (1985: chap. 3), in any society in which the principles of rank and egalitarian ideals coexist (and Wūjlañ is one such society), there will be locations where the principles come into conflict. I suggest that *Kūrijmōj* provides a context in which specific applications of the principles of exchange are employed to mediate these conflicting principles of rank and egalitarian relationship to the benefit of local people.

The close relationship between food and sexuality has been explored by a number of Pacific researchers, including Annette Weiner (1976), Anna S. Meigs (1984), and Miriam Kahn (1986); chapter 3 and the initial section of chapter 4 follow up on a few of the ritual realizations of these processes in Wūjlañ *Kūrijmōj*. Chapter 3 shows how the relative meanings of Āne-wetak and Wūjlañ foods are employed by local people as if they had set, prototypical values. Even though this overly reifies a certain set of meaning relations among foods, it allows me to show how these ideals are metaphorically manipulated to send a variety of symbolic messages during *Kūrijmōj*.

Chapter 4 begins with a description of the generic feasting format, one most often apparent in first-birthday celebrations, in order to show precisely how the generic model can be reshaped in certain ways for a variety of celebratory purposes. Each of these ritual practices, I suggest, involves an array of signifying relationships that tell us something important about the meanings of *Kūrijmōj*. The second half of chapter 4 describes the locally fashioned ritual games, *karate* and *kalbuuj*. Not only do these games represent important elements of Wūjlañ and Āne-wetak identity, they also point clearly to the counterpoint, gendered relationships that are humorously employed during *Kūrijmōj* in order to denote their significance for the perpetuation of meaningful social life.

Chapter 5 deals with the ways in which the celebration of *Kūrijmōj* uses an array of supportive devices from the symbolically coded atoll environment to convey important elements of meaning during the performances, and chapter 6 sees the lengthy ritual as an emotively powerful event that relies on a variety of highly saturated channels of important sensory signifiers used to attract and overwhelm its participants.

Chapter 7 summarizes the ritual journey, pointing out the critical fashion in which *Kūrijmōj* is used to construct and convey an important set of meanings for its participants. At the same time, I discuss many recent changes in the celebration that have accompanied the community's repatriation on Āne-wetak Atoll. Clearly, the celebration situates Wūjlañ and Āne-wetak people in the universe at large, giving identifiable form and meaning to what might otherwise be experienced as cosmic confusion. This sense of order has its social intents, not unconnected with the cosmogenic but, often, elaborating on them. In addition to this Geertzian sense of order, however, the celebration is used to accomplish things, as Stanley J. Tambiah would remind us (1973). The things that are accomplished have to do with empowerment at the *jepta* level and at the community level as well as at other important levels of daily activity (Foucault 1970, 1980; Bourdieu 1977: 15, 187 et seq.). For *Kūrijmōj* as a ritual contest, the relative empowerment of songfest group members is most important, but, in part, this empowerment must be transformed into a more important set of communal exchanges and meanings. At the communal level, the celebration positions Wūjlañ and Āne-wetak people vis-à-vis surrounding island groups by contending that "our celebration is the best of all." And as the most important extension of this task, *Kūrijmōj* places living Āne-wetak residents in a direct and ongoing relationship with God, with ancestors, and with other sacred and superhuman beings in order to ensure that the sacred forces generated during *Kūrijmōj* will be returned manyfold to local people in the year to come.

CHAPTER ONE

Kūrijmōj on Wūjlān

On Wūjlañ and Āne-wetak, as throughout the Marshall Islands, *Kūrijmōj* is the focal point of the yearly cycle. The celebration relies on historically and culturally validated representations or symbols and, at the same time, constitutes them as entities to be taken for granted and "lived." Indeed, an important value of performance is that it makes itself real by becoming its own enacted form. Thus, although the past is brought into being in a certain ethnohistorical form to order the present, its historical value can only be understood in relation to its current use as a source of personal and group empowerment.

Marshall Islanders' views of their own ancient past as well as their views of the sequence of colonial interactions with the West and East are firmly rooted in the performative present of *Kūrijmōj*. Although ceremonial forms of action are often set off from the ordinary by inversions of daily actions, the lengthy period of ritual reordering that makes up the liminal activities of *Kūrijmōj* (Turner 1969: 94 et seq.) makes sense only in terms of its contrast to the mundane. The culturally and historically defined set of symbols Āne-wetak and Wūjlañ people feel to be of central significance provide the largest meaningful context for the local understanding of *Kūrijmōj*. However, it is the performative manipulation of these symbols as sources of empowerment for local people that provides the grounding for this extended ritual. But this ground is itself shifting in ways that reflect an active convolution of perspectives on the celebration by different Wūjlañ and Āne-wetak social actors at different moments in time.

Even though it is impossible to capture the uniquely situated perspectives each participant has about *Kūrijmōj* (voices that also vary through time), I hope to explore the range of meaningful constitutive uses to which *Kūrijmōj* is put by its socially varied participants. In adding another analytic layer to the dialectic of meaning construction, appropriation, and use, I necessarily simplify that which, in its performative richness, is inexhaustibly complex. Equally, in giving literary expression to samples that represent the range of interpretations of *Kūrijmōj,* I empower and legitimize certain of these images and, thereby, alter their representational value (Bourdieu 1991: chaps. 3–4). As "thick description" this initial chapter carries precisely this burden of unequal representation, of personal ethnographic bias, of categorical incompatibility, and of literary condensation and transformation vested in the reformulation of enacted and performative forms (Clifford 1983; Fabian 1990: 279 et seq.). Anthropologists and other social analysts cannot escape these dilemmas of representation. Nevertheless, it would be unconscionable not to try to develop innovative approaches to deal with them.

In a very real sense *Kūrijmōj is* the Wūjlañ/Āne-wetak style of life, for community activities throughout the year are oriented toward this event. A short period exists between the latter part of January and mid-February or early March when festivities are far from folks' minds. People then pursue other projects and catch up on work that was left undone during the height of celebration. Late winter is when the community is most likely to experience famine, so residents commonly work hard to help with family foraging. Many begin producing copra as a cash crop that promises a modest reward when supply boats finally set sail for the isolated western isles. Others focus on subsistence tasks. Most critically, however, community members must act in morally acceptable ways, for when typhoons and famines strike, their causes will be found in the inadequacies and inappropriate enactments of *Kūrijmōj* or in objectionable actions in the new year.

The wet season, April through September, provides relief from the potential retributions of nature and nature's god and is a time to rebuild houses and boats or canoes, clear brush from agricultural lands, gather pandanus and breadfruit, and dry pandanus fronds for mats. Major community projects take place at this time: school repairs, work on the wharf, and large tasks such as the construction of the concrete church. Life during these months is easy compared with that of late winter. By early winter, however, October through the winter solstice, each day grows shorter. Ceremonial activities increase, with more prayers and more days spent in church. As the sun slips ever southward, somber signs of scarcity are hardly noticed amid songs, speeches, and secret plans. What better way to approach scarcity than with largesse and dreams of a better day?

Talk of the upcoming *Kūrijmōj* begins as soon as Easter passes. Thoughtful women reserve rolls of dry pandanus leaves and leaves dried on an open hearth to make mats and handicrafts for the upcoming festivities. Men begin to talk of the pigs they will set aside for the celebration. For families who want to elevate their rank in the community, a pig must be large yet young enough to be tender and juicy (or very greasy, as Marshallese would say). Typically, however, contingencies intervene. By December, many men must borrow pigs from relatives to replace others butchered for unexpected burials or larger-than-expected first-birthday celebrations *(keemem)*. And many women scramble to secure more pandanus leaves to replace those used to make mats for other occasions. Originally, however, each person intends to set aside materials in advance for the greatest, most extravagant Marshallese Christmas.

At the time of the midsummer harvest, a few Wūjlañ breadfruit may be made into preserved breadfruit paste, *bwiro*. Women clean and mash the breadfruit, while men prepare huge pits where it will age in large, covered containers or leaf storage liners. In its fermented form the fruit can last for perhaps two years, but few families will have any remaining to enhance December's food baskets, for breadfruit are few in the Northern Marshalls, and the desire for *bwiro* is fervent.[1]

During the summer, large numbers of money cowries, *Cypraea moneta*, are collected on the reef by women and children. Baskets full of small, live cowries are brought home, buried in the sand, and unearthed months later to be cleaned, polished, and punctured with awls. Once readied, the shells are strung into necklaces or, in combination with pandanus and coconut fibers, are made into valuable, multicolored handicraft items to be used as adornment at *Kūrijmōj* or to be sold to raise money for the festive event.

As the late months of summer bring the return of temperate trade winds the community cannot wait for the celebration to begin. "Christmas," Marshallese style, refers not only to December 25, *roñoul lalim raan*, it denotes the full festive time, from late September or early October until mid-January. Like *Tijemba* (December), *Kūrijmōj* also refers to the frenzied period when ritual activity reaches a maximum. But these times would have less significance and would carry less meaning were they not part of that larger period of rejoicing and fun. Whereas the climactic days of celebration overwhelm individuals with a continuous array of group activities and sensory stimuli, the early days entice each community member into full participation through anticipation of long-awaited excitement. Beginning and end are equally important to the creation of festive furor.

The celebration begins with the formation of *jepta*, the members of which design songs and dances. People dedicate virtually all of their time to these groups as they move along the path toward the new year. The course is simultaneously exhilarating and exhausting. To prevent disorientation, I offer a brief glimpse of the course to be followed. Once some songs are learned, the groups begin competitive visitations and exchanges known as kaṃōḷo. These songfest competitions are hard enough to plan and carry out successfully, but to increase the difficulty, ritual games—*karate* and *kalbuuj*—are employed to destroy the best-laid plans of competing groups. With the beginning of Advent, each songfest group presents its songs in front of the church. Then, on December 25, all of the groups, including separate women's (Rādikdoon) and children's (Naan Aorōk) groups, display their full array of foods, songs, and dances, present their piñatalike money tree to the minister, and engage in a set of antics to humor, honor, and disrupt the performances of other groups. The scene is repeated on New Year's Sunday, while New Year's Eve has its own set of Halloween-like performances. Competitive games occupy New Year's Day, followed by a week of solemn, morally proper demeanor to begin the new year.

The gradual move toward this flurry of ritual activity accelerates during summer months, when seasoned song composers move into action. Ditties from past performances throughout the Marshalls and the Eastern Carolines are dredged up, and as cohorts from songfest groups of old hum savory tunes in reminiscence, skilled musicians recombine phrase and verse to author new works. All look forward with anticipation to the upcoming celebration, when the lyrical cries of adolescent males, "It is now practice time," bring participants together. As the festive time approaches, young boys, out to draw attention to their carefree manipulation of public humor, mimic the older "policemen" who call members together each evening. But it is the gathering together that the young men yearn for, because such times provide prime opportunities to impress young paramours who, prior to the celebration, may exist only in fancied form. *Kūrijmōj* is also a time for great joking rivalries focused on fishing, food gathering, cooking, singing, and dancing. It is a time "to create happiness," when youthfulness abounds, when the liveliness of life itself is honored, when love and generosity are given manifest form through exchange and are forced into being through overabundance. Young men and women are least patient in waiting, but everyone yearns for the event.

Like composers, choreographers first appear in the hot, calm evenings of midsummer. Some songs are borrowed from islands to the east. Ebeye, Naṃdik, Mājro, and Epoon are renowned for their songs of *Kūrijmōj,* but certain songs have march steps or dances to accompany them. The most famous come from Mājeej, where Marshall Islanders claim the first *beet, Kūrijmōj* dance steps, were choreographed in the 1930s. Other Wūjlañ and Āne-wetak songs come from the Caroline Islands, and some of these have marching steps as well. On Wūjlañ and Āne-wetak, however, a choreographer often picks and chooses, selecting from movement sequences of past atoll performances and combining their selections with the refashioned movements from islands and atolls to the east and west. In this respect dances resemble songs, bringing together bits and pieces from historically and spatially distant places to create new, uniquely Wūjlañ and Āne-wetak fragments of identity (Lévi-Strauss 1970: 17–30). Through the nightly practices of *Kūrijmōj* these fragments are embedded in the ethos and body demeanor of Wūjlañ and Āne-wetak performers, becoming part of their hexis as well as their habitus (Bourdieu 1977: 78 et seq.), undeniable elements of their very being.

In the performance these movements simultaneously express each actor's empowerment as a performer of a certain level of accomplishment, as a member of a particular songfest group, and as an Wūjlañ or Āne-wetak person.

From within, this expression means that the person has participated in the best *Kūrijmōj* in the Marshall Islands. Although people from other atolls may have different assessments of the relative ranking of identities, the ability of *Kūrijmōj* to construct the critical categories of identity and give them value is a shared dimension for regional comparison. A few of these relative valuations of *Kūrijmōj,* along with their grounding in an Āne-wetak and Wūjlañ model of significance, are explored in chapter 7.

Other inputs come from the radio, but stations do not begin to play Christmas songs from the Marshall and Caroline Islands until long after the first practices. Tunes obtained in this manner become late additions to a singing group's repertoire. These songs are often heard by younger members of the community (radio aficionados) whenever batteries are available. They then practice the tunes in small, same-sex groups as a labor-easing pastime. Although the tunes are obviously generic and available to wide listening audiences, on Wūjlañ their value is transformed into a representation of the singer's cosmopolitan character. On Āne-wetak, only Kuwajleen radio can be heard consistently with small, battery-powered radios, but from Wūjlañ the station in Pohnpei can be heard as well. Radio Mājro is picked up intermittently on these distant western atolls.[2] As Nancy Pollock notes of Naṃo Christmas (1969: 9), song themes may focus on subjects having a significance in Western religious tradition, but they are wholly Marshallese in conception. Instead of being sung in the dirgelike manner of memorized nineteenth-century mission hymns, they are performed in an animated style with lively counterpoint rhythms to offset standard harmonies. The multiplicity of meanings attributed to the verse adds to the expressive values of the songs.

Each *jepta* learns about a dozen songs each year, so the list of *Kūrijmōj* compositions is lengthy. Rather than deal superficially with a large set of songs, I will in chapter 6 concentrate in depth on the analysis of two or three songs and their potential meanings and then typify the entire set in terms of the distinctive characteristics that separate them from other genres of indigenous musical production.

Dancing was condemned by early missionaries in the Marshalls, much as it had been by their predecessors who first came to Hawai'i (Bingham 1821). Although the Kosraean missionary who brought word of the Western deity to Āne-wetak was less damning, the outcome was similar. In the words of one local raconteur:

> They waited a little longer after that time and then the man Jali, a person of Kosrae, came and revealed the word of God in the year '28 [1928]. Perhaps he remained on Āne-wetak for four or five years. Because of the success of that man Jali, the chief (of Āne-wetak), Pita, welcomed him and watched over him. Others did not want the missionary. They spoke with one another: "Why is it that he [the chief] has allowed this worthless thing to enter? What is it that he is going to do? They say he will teach; what is it to be a teacher?" But in that era, the word of God was very potent [*beran*] in these islands and because of this he (Jali) would never leave the island [Āne-wetak].

One time Pita, the chief, said to his people that all present would make food for Jali. The Āne-wetak people readied all types of food. The men searched out seafoods and returned huge groups of fish and turtles, and the women prepared some breadfruit and sweet pandanus loaves and breadfruit and pandanus pemmican [*jāānkun*]. And then the men butchered the largest of their pigs and baked them in earth ovens as the chiefs had requested. And then, when finished, they took all of these foods and more over to the chief Pita.

And that evening they gave the foods to the missionary. The women danced and gave edible foods to Jali, and they danced the sitting chants and the fast hula and raised their skirts to him. This thing is proper, for at that time if a person danced and raised the skirt, this action showed the affection one had for that other person. Such is true of the customs of the past. Nonetheless, that guy Jali was not upset, and there was nothing he said [to offend], for he knew that all of the dirty customs would disappear. At that time everyone also smoked, but they had already finished baptism. Only recently have people come to know the movements that are bad and the actions that are good.

At that very time the man Pita spoke to the women and said they should not dance because Jali had said the movements were unacceptable and bad. Subsequently the women gave the foods and they said, "Look at these remnants of food we [exclusive] readied as edible things for you," but they no longer danced nor raised their skirts. (Wūjlañ Field Notes 1976–1978)

In spite of missionary tabus, today's *Kūrijmōj* dances emerged after World War II, when the initial religious fervor described above is said to have moderated. By the 1950s, Wūjlañ people had to reconcile their early perceptions of a Christianity with the practices of "Christian" American soldiers who exhibited few inhibitions. A new generation of young *Kūrijmōj* participants matured who had not personally experienced the emotional potency of the coming of the Word to Āne-wetak, and they are said to have introduced the dances into *Kūrijmōj*.

Nevertheless, the newly fashioned *Kūrijmōj* dances are far more subdued than were the early hulas. People do not refer to them as dances at all. Instead, they are referred to as the *beet* (beat) and the *m̧aaj* (march), to separate them from *kwōjkwōj* (hula-style dances with rapid hip movements). Ironically, the word *kwōjkwōj,* once used to refer to intense, communal dance performances, was appropriated by the mission to designate communion. Therefore, *ikkure* (play) became the generic designata for "dance." The hula-type dances, condemned by Protestant missionaries in Hawai'i and then in Micronesia, are said by today's mission converts to have "bad motions." Although the "beat" and "march" of *Kūrijmōj* re-create some hula motions in caricature, they owe as much to Japanese *bon* dances as to the hula. The *m̧aaj,* steps used by a performing group to enter or leave the area of celebration, and the *beet,* linear steps conducted in the central arena, are as embarrassing to the performers as they are uproariously entertaining to the onlookers. Yet only the trickster, who dances alongside the performers, has any real reason to be embarrassed. He or she freely embellishes the hula caricatures of the *beet,* seductively tempts in the ancient style, and brings to the surface the subliminal cause for embarrassment in the younger dancers' minds (see chapter 6; Carucci 1983: 139–51).

Before practice begins, each person chooses to "combine with" a particular performance group for that year. On Wūjlañ there were three *jepta* "chapters" in the 1970s, though in the 1950s and 1960s, when the population was smaller, there were two. The groups are also known informally as *kumi* (group), a term of Japanese derivation. On Wūjlañ, Jittōki (the windward half), Jittoi (the leeward half), and Io̧lap (the center) compete against one another. With the return to Āne-wetak in 1980, the Meden group inherited the Jittoi status, as many of its former members came from that *jepta*. Āne-wetak islet was then divided into windward and leeward, with Jittōki maintaining continuity with Wūjlañ's Io̧lap in its new location, still interstitial between Meden and Jittoi. In 1987 and 1988 two new *jepta* were added, and an entirely new church, Assembly of God, forced the community to rethink what participation in *Kūrijmōj* actually entailed.

The historical derivation of the *jepta* and the interpersonal sociology of affiliation will receive more attention in chapter 2. There are many reasons for joining a group, yet "it is possible to join any *jepta* one wishes; after all, this is *Kūrijmōj,* a time of love and happiness." One critical feature is participation, and all community members who can walk are included. In addition to the three adult *jepta,* therefore, a children's group is included in the celebration, as is a women's group, Rādikdoon, for the church "mothers"—all female church members and members-in-waiting.

I will analyze each of the phases of the celebration in the chapters that follow. Here I present a synopsis to orient vicarious participants to the major sequences of a Wūjlañ *Kūrijmōj. Kaatak* (singing practice) begins early in October, as each group attempts to organize itself, develop a sense of cohesion and motivation, select and learn songs, and learn to work together to gather foods and prepare feasts (see chapters 3 and 4). Once each *jepta* establishes a small repertoire of songs, after three or four weeks of practice, group competitions begin. These gatherings, known as *kaṃō̧lo* (to engage in singing), are times to display a group's skills, make jokes, outdo other groups with food, and overwhelm other groups with eloquent, highly rhetorical speeches. Although quantities of high-ranked food are difficult to overlook and although polished, extemporaneous speakers are persuasive, a group's performance comes into focus in the performance of its songs, because pieces that are well composed and "down pat"—*kilōk* (closed)—can "grasp the throats" (the locus of the emotions as well as of musical production) of the listeners, much as performers in the United States "touch the hearts" of their audience. These performative persuasions, when well executed, capture a group's affect in a manner reminiscent of Kaluli or Ilongot performances (Schieffelin 1976; M. Z. Rosaldo 1980: chap. 2; R. Rosaldo 1989: introduction). I shall consider closely the modes of verbal enamorment in chapter 6.

American-trained island missionaries who reached Āne-wetak in the latter half of the 1920s brought with them *kaṃō̧lo*. Marshall Islanders claim that

Mājeej residents added dance steps to *Kūrijmōj* performances in the 1930s, but the songs and celebration did not approximate their current Wūjlañ and Āne-wetak forms until late in the 1950s. *Kaṃọ̄ḷo* is now described as a time for play (a game) and a time to do battle. The former metaphor reflects the overall *Kūrijmōj* theme of "creating happiness"; the latter discovers its fun in a strategic military exercise that pits the strengths and weaknesses of different songfest groups against each other. Although aspects of *kaṃọ̄ḷo* may be planned well in advance, the decision to gather food is made at a practice the night before the event, and the group to be visited remains a *jepta* secret. As soon as a fishing party leaves the village, all are aware a *kaṃọ̄ḷo* is planned, but with three Wūjlañ groups and five on Āne-wetak today, the recipient of the visit remains a surprise. Other groups must begin their counterpreparations, thus intensifying the level of *kaṃọ̄ḷo* activity. Because a *jepta* can never predict with accuracy when a *kaṃọ̄ḷo* is in order or how much effort it will require, it is critical to keep one's forces in constant readiness *(pojak wōt)*. From precisely such preparedness derives the interface between *kaatak* (practice), *kaṃọ̄ḷo* (songfest), and the games that complicate the songfest encounter on Wūjlañ and Āne-wetak *(karate* and *kalbuuj)*.

Food is critical to any Marshallese social encounter, and it is of particular importance in the competitive *kaṃọ̄ḷo*. Other small gifts may be given along with food—matches, soap, or small sums of money—but, hand-in-hand with evocative songs, a group must present substantial quantities of high-ranked foods. Subterfuge and intrigue are added to *kaṃọ̄ḷo* battles by *karate* and *kalbuuj,* for in these games of Wūjlañ design even the best plans to obtain foods and gifts may be interrupted.

Like *kaṃọ̄ḷo, karate* is used in both a nominal and verbal form. It is simultaneously an event and activity. My first encounter with the activities of *Kūrijmōj* was a form of *karate*. As a liminal event, *karate* allows women to mimic ideal male forms of action, re-creating their images of filmic and historic self-assured Japanese warriors. In their reversed gender roles women adopt the aggressive poses of men engaged in battle. The women of one *jepta* steal the raw materials (usually foods) gathered by the men of an opposite troupe. Rather than leave them destitute, the women compensate their victims with a feast. The battle is highlighted with whoops and cries, and constant jesting transforms the contest into a fragment of a larger sexual war. A variety of sexual relationships is suggested as the women of one *jepta* and the men of another resolve their differentness through promises to be special partners of the other group. The sexual banter is woven into speeches that follow the sharing of cooked foods, and in an act reminiscent of the *hiuwai* of the renowned Hawai'ian Makahiki, the play is continued as men and women of opposite groups throw each other into the water and frolic in the shallows of the lagoon (see Malo 1951; Valeri 1985 on the *hiuwai*).

Not without recourse, Wūjlañ men engage in a counterbalancing game. In *kalbuuj,* the men of one *jepta* re-create reminiscences of "jail" from the Spanish colonial era. Cookhouses and sleeping houses within the town space, the women's domain, become the "cells" for women captured from opposite *jepta*. The "arrests" are made as the women return from pandanus- and coconut frond–collecting trips into the bush, trips that, ultimately, will result in manufactured handicraft items to be given during *Kūrijmōj*. While in jail, visiting women are asked about and reminded of the fine treatment they receive in terms of food and sexual bliss. They are convinced that they have no reason to leave, although, after a few days or a week, they are returned to their home *jepta*—cross-dressed as men, so that the perfect unions established with their jailers are not tarnished.

Karate has continued to the present day, but *kalbuuj* was discontinued after a few attempts on Āne-wetak. The reasons are simultaneously cultural and historical. First, with the return to Āne-wetak, women seldom collected pandanus and coconut fronds for mats and handicrafts because the trees on the major residence islets were far too immature to yield high-quality materials. Second, even on Wūjlañ *karate* had been a more popular game because it was far more humorous. The success of the humor, as I will argue in chapter 4, is rooted in the more perfect role reversals attained in *karate*. Moreover, during *Kūrijmōj,* men fished far more frequently than women collected handicraft materials. *Karate* immediately disrupted planned *kaṃōḷo*. In contrast, *kalbuuj* disrupted another group's ability to amass display items to exchange on December 25.

After six weeks of these activities, resources and energies become substantially depleted, yet during the three weeks prior to December 25, each group continues with *kaṃōḷo, karate,* and *kalbuuj*. In 1977, no fewer than eighteen such episodes took place during the time that church members call *atpen* (advent). By 1990, far more inter-*jepta* confrontations occurred, because the number of *jepta* had increased.

In addition to the standard activities, each group is given an opportunity to present its full array of songs after the Sunday church service. The *jepta* also prepares food enough for all of the residents of the atoll. Saturdays are always dedicated to food collection and preparation, and during *atpen* the collecting activities of the *jepta* responsible for that week's performance are not immune to *karate* and *kalbuuj*. The advent-week presentation is not as significant as are the main competitions that will occur on December 25, but they offer each group an opportunity to prepare for this event.

Often, other events are scheduled during December, and each *jepta* grasps the opportunity to prepare food for the occasion. Council meetings may thus be transformed into other arenas in which the *jepta,* including the women's and children's groups, compete for recognition and honor. Although such collective gatherings notoriously run far behind schedule, the gathering and food-preparation activities of each *jepta* commonly create new opportunities to engage in casual public banter with other community members. These occasions provide time for informal discussions with members of one's own *jepta* and, more important, for public jesting and boasting about one's group and its encounters with the other songfest groups. An adroit orator and humorist can do much to build an inflated symbolic image of a *jepta* with skillfully fashioned recollections of the events of the past weeks.

The weeks immediately before December 25 also provide a time for the young men of a *jepta* to build the *wōjke* (tree): a large, piñatalike money tree reminiscent of a New Year's Day parade float. The exterior of the tree, often in the shape of a ship, airplane, missile, or bomb, will be painted with phrases that reflect a group's theme, and the interior will contain all of the gifts to be given by a *jepta* to the minister. These key condensation symbols are analyzed in greater depth in chapter 6, but part of their potency is thought to come from (or be maintained by) the secrecy surrounding their construction.

During the final weeks, everyone eagerly anticipates the events of December 25. By December 21 or 22, all except a few young men and women have decided that no time remains for *karate* or *kaṃōḷo*. In 1977, two months had passed since the last government-operated supply ship. The small amounts of Western food that remained had to be saved for December 25, leaving little with which to *kaṃōḷo*. In any case, little time remained. Every available moment had to be dedicated to last-minute preparations for *roñoul lalim raan* (The Twenty-Fifth Day). The final *kaṃōḷo* was conducted on Wednesday evening, December 21. There were a few feeble attempts to *karate,* but none organized by an entire *jepta*. The activities of the past weeks were forced into the background by a more labor-intensive and sleep-depriving set of "movements" focused on December 25.

In 1977, as in most years, all of a songfest group's songs had to be perfected so that the entire series could be performed at a single time. The repertoire of fifteen or twenty songs had to unfold smoothly on December 25. The entry march and other dances were brought into final form, and the *wōjke* was tested at a final practice. The minister's family had to be fed, and families, homes, yards, and cookhouses were thoroughly cleaned and polished in preparation for the highlight of the celebration.

Food was prepared for the final practice and testing of the tree. The young men of the *jepta* revealed the accompanying skit to other members of the songfest group during this dress rehearsal, and once in place in the center of the group, the *wōjke* was exploded. After prayers of praise, distinguished *jepta* speakers honored their group and the tree's designers. The distribution and collective consumption of the food then cemented the solidarity of each group prior to the display of its members' prowess in the public performances of December 25.

Each year during the week preceding December 25, a time to sing for the minister is also set aside by each *jepta*. This event takes place at the minister's house, which shares a land parcel with the church. The event takes the form of a mellow *kaṃōḷo*. Special foods and gifts are gathered, and after some warm-up at a practice session, the group marches to the minister's house. Following several speeches and songs by members of the *jepta,* the gifts are presented, accompanied by a song of giving. The minister responds with a speech and, on occasion, with a countergift of tea or coffee. After a

Figure 5. Family members ready pandanus fronds for rethatching the cookhouse and making mats in preparation for *Kūrijmōj*. Wūjlañ, 1976. (Photograph by L. M. Carucci)

second round of songs and speeches the group retires to its practice house to discuss remaining preparations for December 25.

Along with all other preparations, new clothes must be stitched and older ones thoroughly cleaned, all inhabited parts of the island have to be cleared of brush and refuse, and living spaces must be resurfaced with *ļā* (small, white, polished coral paving gravel). Homes must be in good repair and handicrafts, bags of copra, and bottles of coconut oil readied for the gift exchanges that accompany a group's performance. Most important, the money to fill the *wōjke* must be collected from the members of a *jepta,* and the food must be gathered or measured out from the remaining meager supplies and distributed to each food preparer.

In most cases, food gathering and preparation takes place entirely within each *jepta,* perpetuating the competitive spirit among the groups that has prevailed during the past months. Nevertheless, in 1977, each actual church member's homestead became a preparation area for food, and the *jepta* members were split apart and recombined into the novel homestead groups for purposes of food gathering and preparation. This reinforced the fact that, even though competitive elements persisted through New Year's Day, at this juncture the critical effort focused on the community as a whole and its exchanges with the deities and their intermediaries (the ministers and the chiefs). All prepared food must be shared equally among the members of the community, but the method for best accomplishing this end varies from year to year.

Much of December 23 and all of December 24 are spent in gathering and preparing food. As I will demonstrate in chapter 3, the baskets of food must be extremely elaborate and must include a wide diversity of foods and a plethora of edibles that are highly ranked. Each resident must be overwhelmed with food because giving in excess, with much wastage, is the aim. A good deal of food sharing among *jepta* mates or kin ensures that each of the food baskets, ultimately twenty-five to forty pounds of food, will be impressive. Nonetheless, a subtle competition underlies the food preparations, and the most desirable baskets come from three or four households that are typically the most prepared. Occasional rumors suggest that other food baskets will be equally highly ranked on account of a successful fishing voyage or other fortuitous circumstance. Nevertheless, the pervasive exchange networks ensure that the most skilled and favored cookhouse groups will produce the most highly ranked baskets of food.

Early dawn of December 23 brings the sounds of the church bell as each *jepta* gathers to clean the church grounds. Often the "time to broom" lasts only an hour or two, to be followed by softball or volleyball games that serve to anticipate the inter-*jepta* contests of New Year's Day. On Wūjlañ it was always the young and adult men who played softball, but as a marker of the new way of life on Āne-wetak, volleyball contests between the women of each group have become equally popular. Although these matches are not as serious as those to follow, the competitors play hard, cheered on by the onlookers from their *jepta*.

Even as the games are being played, food preparation must begin for December 25. Knowledgeable women prepare their steam ovens to receive the bread they will cook later that night. Men begin to search for the pigs they intend to butcher on the morning of December 24. If imported foods are in short supply, children are sent to the homes of relatives or other *jepta* members to search for some uncooked rice or flour. A final practice is scheduled to add polish to the songs and dances to be performed on December 25, but, even though the practices are scheduled early to allow for a timely return to other tasks, many group members are too busy to find time to attend. Women often work the entire night at last-minute sewing or cooking tasks, and men are in the bush long after dark readying sprouted coconuts, preparing bags of copra, gathering firewood, or attending to some other task that the *jepta* has decided will enhance its presentations on December 25.

December 24 rivals supply ship arrivals as the busiest day of the year. From dawn until midnight each community member is engaged in some sort of preparatory activity. The success of the following day depends in large part on the dedicated preparations of each participant. Very late at night the youngest children are sprawled across the floors, exhausted from an exciting day. Most adults continue to work and spend a good part of the night—often all of it—completing tasks for the coming day.

Men are responsible for capturing, butchering, and cooking the pigs. Ocean fish and school fish, when available in large quantity, are divided by men into equal sections for sashimi (to be eaten raw) or cooked in large earthen ovens. Men are also responsible for preparing the ovens to cook sprouted coconuts. In addition to capturing pigs, the young men gather drinking coconuts. On Wūjlañ, two or three thousand coconuts are thrown from trees already ravaged by the *kaṃōḷo, karate,* and Sunday feasts of the past weeks. The young men also cut palm fronds to be used to weave food baskets. Groups of men always set sail on December 24 in hope of bringing home fish. Often, they will stop on outer islets to find additional coconuts to supplement the meager supply remaining on the main residence islets.

The women prepare rice, bake bread in steam ovens, fry doughnuts, and ready any other special foods they are able to secure. A few off-season breadfruit are often combined with the remaining stores of *bwiro* as an accompaniment to pig. The *bwiro* must be unearthed, thoroughly kneaded in salt water, and then rinsed in drinking water, prior to being cooked. There is no time to process arrowroot, but if a twenty-count cloth container of prepared arrowroot has been saved from the songfests, the women fashion it into an unleavened arrowroot cake or mix it with pandanus to make the more highly valued unleavened cake, *peru.*

The youth of the community, especially the young boys who are of little assistance in the cookhouse, are responsible for final cleaning of residence sites. If the path requires further care or if the *ḷā* have not been spread around the cookhouse and outdoor living space, the older boys must complete these tasks. All refuse should have been burned on the ocean beach during the past week, but last-minute additions of palm fronds, grass, and trash will be set ablaze on December 24. The village must be immaculate on December 25. Young girls help in the cookhouse, do the last-minute laundry, and serve as baby-sitters. They also pull grass in the village and help the young women weave baskets to hold the food.

The senior women in the village rush to complete sleeping mats or handicrafts that will be used as gifts the following day. The most skilled seamstresses are relieved of some cooking tasks so that they can finish the uniforms that will be worn on December 25. Less-skilled couturieres rush in with unfinished projects and with promises to prepare food to compensate for the rapid construction of a critical chemise.

Even on Āne-wetak, where the favored local foods of Wūjlañ are not available, the day is never long enough. Work continues far into the night, and many women never go to sleep. Most men complete their labors by 1:00 or 2:00 A.M., only to be reawakened by 3:00 or 4:00 A.M. to begin dividing the food. This is a time-consuming task. Each type of food must be divided as evenly as possible among the waiting palm-leaf baskets. Inevitably, an extra basket of food is required, or a shortage of some specific item is discovered. To compensate, trees are climbed, baskets constructed, or food exchanged with relatives in order to augment the foods that were prepared.

Tea and coffee are made in the early morning hours. These items will accompany the baskets, but the first rounds are always exhausted by the workers. Those families who have reserved some cola or ship's biscuit (a thick, unsalted cracker) include these treats in the food containers. Although these items have become common on Āne-wetak since weekly flights from Mājro were inaugurated, only rarely are such items available on the field-trip ship, so they are highly prized on Wūjlañ.[3] More commonly, food-preparation groups mix a large container of *malolo* (Hawai'ian punch) to supplement the tea, coffee, and drinking coconuts.

As the first bell sounds, members of the community start to congregate. As always, three bells are rung. The final 6:00 A.M. bell signals the time at which the celebration begins. *Awa in M̧ajeļ* (Marshallese time) prevails, however, and few are assembled at the designated hour. In this instance, tardiness does not reflect a lack of diligence; with all of the preparations required for the largest feast of the year, most people are simply not ready at the designated hour.

ROÑOUL LALIM RAAN

Every few years, as in 1977, the celebrations of December 25 are slightly modified to include the rituals of the Sabbath. In their absence, however, *roñoul lalim raan* begins with a short 6:00 A.M. church service. Following the matins everyone returns home to gather the food prepared during the previous days. After community members have reconvened at the church, a short talk is given by the minister, followed by comments by the magistrate or one of the chiefs. Then comes a prayer of thanksgiving for the day of happiness, for the food, and for the opportunity to gather together to witness this special event. Baskets of food are then divided outside the church, special bits are eaten publicly, and shouts of gratitude fill the air before people take the food home to be stored and consumed at a later time.

The foods must come from another group, not from one's own *bōrwaj* (household) or from the food-preparation group in which one may have labored during the preceding days. Usually the food comes from a member of another *jepta*. The main principle of distribution involves equality of the received prestation—in this case vested in a random match between food giver and food receiver. On Wūjlañ, each member of the community beyond nursing stage receives a basket of food. On Āne-wetak, each pair that prepares food is given a container of edibles in return.

The palm-leaf baskets must be overflowing with food, because overwhelming the recipient is a core part of the message. Those who remember past celebrations contend that in bygone days each person received even larger hampers of food. Nowadays, they say, there are so many children that the baskets have become smaller. Nonetheless, although some complain about wasted food, most realize that overpreparation is an integral part of this feast. In the words of one seasoned *Kūrijmōj* participant, "Sometimes in the midst of battle you lose everything that is yours: food, clothing, everything. Then you really have to try hard. The only thing that remains is your gun; and for *Kūrijmōj,* songs and dances are your weapons of battle." Many others say that *Kūrijmōj* is a time of giving. You must "exhaust your ability in the things that you give."

The community must recongregate in the church building by 10:00 A.M. to allow enough time for each *jepta* to perform before dark. Nowadays, with five *jepta,* it is still impossible to finish in time. The final group often has to perform in a dimly lit sanctuary to the din of generators. The minister commonly introduces each *jepta,* notes its theme, and relates the theme to relevant biblical verses with a moral for the lives of his parishioners.

Naan Aorōk and Rādikdoon are the first to perform. The children's group has all of the elements of a *jepta* performance, lacking only the number and range of vocalic contrasts in its counterpoint harmonies and the tricksterish mimes in its dances, but the women seldom have a *m̧aaj* and commonly perform two- or three-part harmonies. Neither group prepares food to exchange with other *jepta,* but both prepare food for the minister(s) and give gifts as well. Of the two, only Naan Aorōk builds a *wōjke.*

The members of each main *jepta* hope that their group will be the first to perform, for there is a strong belief that the first position carries some advantage. Each *jepta* enters the church with a *m̧aaj,* paired parallel lines of males and females that split and reconvene once inside the central performing area. The *m̧aaj* progresses forward to the beat of a song with hopping steps, small kicks from side to side, or side and back steps as the *jepta* parades into the church. Often a guitar or ukelele accompanist marches next to the lines of singing dancers.

The crowd responds to the first entry *m̧aaj* with shouts and applause. *Roñoul lalim raan* has begun. Most marchers, bedecked in their fine new clothes, are further adorned with head leis of flowers, colored paper, or candy. Necklace-style leis of these same materials or of shells are also worn. Colorful combs offset these decorations for women, young men, and a few older men. All adornments are taken by zealous spectators who rush into the arena, seize the performers, and strip them of their finery. Members of a singing group may feign resistance, but they willingly relinquish their ornaments.

The appropriation of all personal articles is further continued in *tōbtōb* (to tug on repeatedly). In this Wūjlañ and Āne-wetak game, opposite-gender–opposite-*jepta* members seize a piece of clothing and tug lightly on it. Watches, jewelry, and all articles of clothing may be seized by members of the audience. The pieces must be sacrificed in a spirit of generosity, though critical pieces of personal attire are not given during the ceremony. They will be delivered to their new owners later in the evening. Storytellers claim that this custom continues an ancient Āne-wetak practice during the *kiye,* when everything a dancer had on was given to the onlooker who found his or her sacred performance irresistible. *Tōbtōb,* they claim, is the mission-approved equivalent of this time-honored activity.

Those who rush into the arena to *tōbtōb* douse the performers with perfume, sprinkle them with baby powder, and coat them with pomade. As performers are "beautified" by these fragrant ablutions they feign retaliation, with attempts to seize the containers of perfume. When they succeed, they use these scented items to douse the instigators and other members of the audience, making them equally irresistible. Indeed, members of the singing group may also bring perfumes with which they "make [onlookers] fragrant" as they dance and sing their songs.

At the end of the *m̧aaj,* members of the *jepta* congregate in small circles, divided by voice parts but all clustered around their song leader, to sing their songs. The songs are introduced by the most skilled speaker, either the song leader or another respected *jepta* member. With the exception of Rādikdoon members, all of the speakers, like the song leaders, are men. The speeches express the group's theme, often relying on metaphors of arduous travels by sea, land, or air to stress the accomplishments of the *jepta.*[4] Some speakers describe their group's journey as originating at a distant location; others envision the performance on December 25 as a return home after a lengthy voyage. Trials, obstacles, and talk of battles won through concerted communal effort are commonly woven into these stories. The *jepta* theme is also entwined into the story, and it is certainly fashionable to show how the theme was inspired by biblical precedent. Some typical themes have been *l̦otak* (the birth), *naan eo* (the word), *pilān eo* (the plan [of God]). Along with biblical references, perhaps even excerpts from the Scriptures, the best speakers will support the themes with ancient Marshallese stories and with descriptions of daily practices.

The speeches are followed by a series of songs. Each song is introduced with briefer words, including the title of the piece. Minimally, the speaker will say, "OK, the song that opens up now, it says [is entitled] . . ." Mention may also be made of how the tune relates to the theme or how the group's activities support the title. Each song is received with applause, shouts of approval, or jesting remarks. Spectators occasionally rush forward to play pranks on the conductor or on members of the singing group by imitating their motions or singing style. Women may also rush forward and attempt to lift a man and drag him from the premises. These joking ploys constantly disrupt the performance, bringing to the show an element of the unexpected analogous to *karate* and *kalbuuj.* This representational component is critical, for the community must together transcend the unknown as it faces each new year.

Time must also be reserved for the *beet.* Like the *m̧aaj,* the *beet* is a dance performed by lines of males and females. These steps are far more intricate, however, and the linear configurations may be fairly complex. Most groups perform the *beet* near the beginning of their exhibition, and many troupes may dance immediately following their entry into the church.

Males and females begin the *beet* aligned in two separate lines. As the dance unfolds, new combinations of male-female pairs may appear. The initial same-sex lines may thus reconfigure into lines in which males and females alternate. Overall patterns are limited to lines parallel or perpendicular to the entryway, squares, circles, and X or T crossovers. Each of these formations is created while the individual dancers maintain coordinated movements. The dancers perform in time with their own singing and accompany the foot movements with clapping or slapping parts of their bodies. Still, the individual dancers never touch one another, as might be the case in a quadrille.

A *jepta*'s *beet* is a highlight of the presentation, and it is always received well by spectators. Shouts and loud clapping can be heard throughout the performance. The audience responds to each dancer's personal style, but accentuated hip movements inevitably draw the most enthusiastic response. The Ioḷap *beet* in 1982, adapted from a Ratak dance, drew repeated waves of laughter and shouting. It ended with rapid hip movements and the words *Mojen dikdik* (small, repeated motions). Members of the audience yelled out, "Once again [for me] please," or "Once again [do your] little rapid motions for me." And each sequence brought a louder response. This sequence was a perfect condensation symbol: transcending the church walls, it harkened back to the days of *kiye* dances, when the best dancers could "shake the foundations of the universe" as they engaged in provocative hula-style dances *(kwōjkwōj).*

Almost every *jepta* also has a provocateur, one who performs purely for the audience's entertainment (see Carucci 1983). This clown enacts a timely misperformance, purposefully missing cues, mocking the antics of one dancer or another, and stressing the most sexually suggestive maneuvers. Bawdy interpretations are the provocateur's constant theme. At times the personified portrayals intensify motions of the dancers, but they may equally well accomplish their aim with movements antithetical to the actual dance steps. This dancer enacts the work of Etao, the culture hero associated with sly thought, trickery, and transcendence of mundane power by magical, superhuman forces that brought many physiographic and historic features into being in the Marshallese universe (cf. Goodenough 1986). Etao also taught humans about sex. Etao's position is often taken by a mature man, though women are even more skilled at the contrarian's dance. Hers is truly a labor of love, Marshallese style. The suggestive shuffles are irresistible to the audience. They scream and clap wildly. They rush forward and *tōbtōb*. And the provocateur is often the first to lose his clothes.

The culmination of a group's performance is the time when the *wōjke* is revealed *(kowaḷọk).* The young men present the tree as part of a skit at the conclusion of the dances and songs. The 1970s skits focused on military themes, often innovative portrayals of work parties or repair crews. Although these themes have not died out, more recently they have been balanced by greater diversity. In 1982, skits still had a military focus, but work parties were no longer popular. One group enacted an ancient warring party, another concentrated on modern fighters, the third attempted a *Star Wars* imitation. In 1991, airport crews competed with dry-dock repairmen, but one group simply hauled in a Western-style artificial Christmas tree without a skit. Lacking a skit and lacking an explosive tree, the onlookers responded with noticeable ambivalence. Afterward, community members grumbled about the substandard performance of that *jepta*. Many of these shifts reflect the changing contacts of daily life—in the 1970s, the military and civilian personnel working on Āne-wetak during the clean-up era and, since then, the increasing contact with a wide diversity of power-engendering performances as a result of the popularity of video-cassette movie houses on Āne-wetak atoll and the intensification of the Marshall Islands diastema.

Construction of the *wōjke* usually follows a modern wartime motif as well, with images of the most powerful weapons and wartime vehicles. Bombs, rockets with "nuclear" warheads, and spaceships are favorites. Space battles are thought to be real because, as condensed representations of nearly inconceivable power, spacecraft must have a destructive potency equal to that of bombs and missiles. Ronald Reagan's Star Wars fantasies were brought into being by Wūjlañ *wōjke* a decade prior to their launching in the United States.

All *wōjke* are made with an internal wire or string suspension system to which money is attached. Other valuables may be stacked inside the tree or around its base. An outer casing in the form of a bomb, missile, ship, or some similar vessel covers the valuables, and members of the skit crew must have a means of exploding the tree in an apparently magical manner. In local terms, the explosion must be "a thing of amazement." The standard outer-island method is to use batteries connected to wires whose bare ends ignite piles of sulfur scraped from several boxes of matches.

As the crew finishes its preparation, a speaker may begin to narrate for the audience, explaining the significance and meaning of the *wōjke,* or members of the *jepta* may begin to sing their best song. This is a composition that, in the course of all of the *kaṃōḷu,* has brought them the most renown and has come to represent the group. On cue, members of the *jepta* shout, "Explode! Explode! Blow it to shreds," or some similar chant as the circuit is completed, sparks fly, and, with luck, the vessel covering the valuables is blown apart. Although misfirings are not uncommon, successful *wōjke,* those that fracture according to plan, bring shrieks of approval from the audience as well as from *jepta* members. The song is repeated in increased crescendo, and vociferous members of the *jepta* dance wildly about, tossing perfume and baby powder onto the crowd. By 1990 *pānuk,* a Marshall Islands import, was added at this time, with small gifts, mostly candy strung into small head leis and bracelets, tossed to the onlookers.

A successful performance, with great songs, dances, and a successfully exploded tree filled with many gifts, will be so irresistible that the audience is overcome with the emotion of the moment. They run up to the performers in *tōbtōb,* smear them with perfumes and oils, and contribute additional gifts to those that have been publicly revealed in exploding the *wōjke.* These gifts are "for God," and the entire community bears witness to their display. Even though the valuables often go to the minister, people contend that in the past they were distributed among the entire community. Indeed, this is the culminating moment of *Kūrijmōj,* a moment repeated several times during the day as each *jepta* performs.

The presentations must be completed by nightfall, and they are followed by a prayer given by the pastor thanking God for the happiness and good fortune brought to all by the festivities. He may also thank people for their generosity. Ensured of his own happiness, he reminds people that the joy and good fortune will persist in the days to come if they are kind and loving and follow the will of God. If visitors are present, they may be given a special gift at this time. In past times the chiefs also received special recognition and gifts at this, the culmination of December 25.

The gathering closes with community recital of the Lord's Prayer and, perhaps, the Ten Commandments. These verses are followed by a song that is sung by all participants. A favorite song, such as *Anij Iọkwe* (God [Is] Love), written by a former minister for the members of the Wūjlañ community, is selected:

Anij Iōkwe	[God is love
Anij im Jouj	God is consideration
Wānōke kōj	Make us [inclusive] righteous
Kōjparok kōj	Care for us [inclusive]
Komin leļọk	You [plural command] give away
im koṃṃoolol	and give thanks
Elap jān joñin	More than that which is expected
an maroñ ba.	to be possible to say.
. . . . .	. . . . .
Kwar kabooļ iō	You have filled me
kin Am Iōkwe	with your love
im Wānōke iō	and perfected me
jān ao jorāān.	to save me from my destruction.
Ttọļim dāpij iō	Search around in the dark and hold me
ilo lur in pāim	in the calm of your hand
ijo riAenōṃṃan.	(in) that place [indefinite] (where) the people
	of peacefulness (reside).]
	(Wūjlañ Field Notes 1977)

Roñoul lalim raan comes to a close. Everyone goes home to relive the day's events and consume small bits of food distributed during the special celebration. Some discuss the performances, while others listen to tape recordings of the singing and practice the dances revealed that day.

Huge amounts of energy have been expended during the past weeks; many participants are relieved that the event has reached its climax, if not its conclusion. Symbolic transactions involving the exchange of material objects, of people, and of consumables have been carried out at an exhausting rate. With resources depleted and energies expended, residents face the conclusion of the celebrations and the beginning of a new year. For most, the benefits have not been on the material plane. Valuable memories of events are discussed as the community members relax in their houses nibbling on the remains of picked-over baskets of food. The only person to have realized any direct financial benefit from the celebration is the minister, and he has accumulated wealth as a result not of his human status but of his position as an intermediary who represents God.

Celebrating does not end with December 25, but the pace of life does ease. On the following day a softball game is held between two of the *jepta*. The winner plays the remaining group's softball team either the following day or a few days later. These games are much more serious than the practice games of the week preceding December 25, and the winner of each contest is awarded a prize. In 1977 the prizes consisted of rice, at that time so rare that its value was greatly increased. More recently, cash gifts of $50.00 have not been uncommon. But the greatest reward comes in terms of renown for the *jepta* that wins. Therefore, each *jepta* will try to convince its most skilled players to participate. Arguments over the elimination methods to determine a winner and accusations of magic by members of an opposing team are not uncommon, particularly when teams thought to be inferior win. When these inevitable arguments arise, however, people are most concerned that the spirits who witness the trouble will bring misfortune to the community in the coming year.

Ambivalence, apprehension, and foreboding always mark the period between December 25 and *Nuu Iiō* (New Year's Day), and the games in part seem to be aimed at replacing the ambivalence with a potential source of happiness. In 1976 the games were disrupted by arguments, accusations of magic, and concerns about subsequent superhuman sanction. In 1977 a typhoon disrupted the sequence of softball games, and most villagers agreed that it was due to the bad conduct of two drunken community members who had begun a fight just outside the church on December 25. In 1982 and 1990 other worries overwhelmed people. The matriarchs on Wūjlañ and Āne-wetak suffered the most during these times. They consistently voiced some variant of the following platitude: "Perhaps we will never again see another *Kūrijmōj;* all sorts of things around us are becoming worse; we are truly unfortunate."

THE NEW YEAR

The attempt to maintain happiness continues until the first day of January. On Friday and Saturday of the week preceding New Year's Day, preparations begin for another feast. Foods do not have to be as impressive as those readied for December 25. They tend to be similar in amount and composition to the smaller feasts on the Sundays prior to December 25, but, in this case, each *jepta* prepares food for the same day. In 1977 New Year's Day fell on Sunday, but Wūjlañ people postponed the day to allow Io̧lap to present their *Kūrijmōj* songs. Realigning New Year's Day accommodated both church requirements and residents' expectations as to what constituted an adequate New Year's celebration. For the people, such a celebration required softball games, and because these activities were prohibited on the holy day, the decision to postpone New Year's Day seemed to be the best solution.

The New Year's feasts involve all of the elaborate food events of the weeks that culminate on December 25, but the symbolic nature of the exchange shifts. On this occasion, each *jepta* consumes its own food, and, although food is provided for the minister(s), only token amounts are delivered to each of the other groups. Another exchange of gifts takes place among the members of each *jepta* on one of the first days of the New Year. Lengths of cloth, some money, articles of clothing, or small bottles of perfume are typical of this exchange. The exchange reinforces the sense of unity that develops in each *jepta,* but it is not essential to the success of *Kūrijmōj.* In 1978, when Wūjlañ was ravaged by a typhoon and tropical storm in each of the two weeks after Kūrijmōj, these exchanges were overlooked. In 1983 they took place only among those who had worked diligently within each *jepta.*

The activities of New Year's Eve center around the children. The evening is somewhat reminiscent of the celebration of Halloween in the United States but is closely related to *milamala* in the Trobriands (Malinowski 1954, 1965). On Wūjlañ, families remain at their places of residence until midnight, engaged in typical evening activities of storytelling, casual conversation, and joking. Dozing is hardly disruptive, however, for some participants commonly fall asleep in the middle of evening entertainments. Children, in particular, strive to remain awake on New Year's Eve because they do not want to miss the activities. Indeed, all children are to be involved, though a few of the young men and women may also take part. Qualified participants are separated from others in comments like, "You [plural] are not *Naan Aorōk* [the valuable word: children], you [pl.] have entered darkness [lost your chastity]."[5] Only true children, those who are sexually inexperienced, are allowed to participate in the New Year's Eve rounds.

At midnight the children begin to walk from household to household throughout the village. They approach each house in small groups and begin their singing. The songs are joyous and are sung with great verve. After each group has sung one or two songs at the door of each household the children cry out in unison, "Happy New Year!" In response, household members applaud and show their approval. They present the singers with gifts of matches, soap, coconut candy, popcorn, change, and other small, desired items. Some groups are asked in for coffee or tea or a small amount to eat, but other groups, especially the youngest, rush on to the next house to be sure they receive the most gifts possible.

These activities continue through most of the night, though younger participants make a quick round of the village and return home to the welcome of a long-overdue sleeping mat. Older Naan Aorōk members continue their singing visits until 3:00 or 4:00 A.M. In these early morning hours, children are commonly joined by overaged pranksters out to increase the general goodwill and reap some of the youngsters' benefits. This occasion provides a good excuse for the mature group to visit their lovers or search for food or cigarettes (in perennial short supply on Wūjlañ) in exchange for a song. Though often the brunt of jokes, the older group is received with the same spirit of goodwill given members of Naan Aorōk. Banging on buckets or ringing the council-house bell goes on through the night, and the lights and torches accompanying the touring carousers connect the evening light with that of dawn.

The festivities continue on New Year's Day. This time has been long awaited by the young people of the community, for it provides them with an opportunity to display the softball- or volleyball-playing skills of their *jepta*. All of the games played in past weeks have been in preparation for this one event, the atollwide "world series" or volleyball "world cup" of New Year's Day. If the championship requires more than a few matches, some of them are contested in the coming days of New Year's week.

New Year's Day begins with a church service announced by the ringing of a bell at 5:30 A.M. Although most members of the community do not go to sleep until dawn, all gather drowsily for the church ceremonies. It is critical to start the year properly and be neither late nor absent from the initial church service. Attendance is far greater than one would expect at such an hour, and few are late to the initial meeting. Similar services are held every morning through the initial week of the year, and the group of gatherings as a whole is termed *maan iiō* (the front of the year).

Maan iiō represents an entire spectrum of acceptable actions as well as the early services. During the week, any actions conducted in other than an ideal manner are reprimanded with the phrase, "You [command form] shall not *maan iiō*." Proper behavior is imperative during the initial week, but the phrase of warning is heard for the first four to six weeks of the annum. By mid-February, behavior has evidently strayed so far from the ideal that the dictum is no longer recited.

In addition to prompt church attendance, a long series of redeeming activities is part of *maan iiō*. In all public settings it is important to exude an ideal sort of demeanor. It would be an especially bad time to be caught in an illicit relationship or to break any other law. Drunkenness, the most common legal offense on Wūjlañ and Āne-wetak Atolls, is most apt to "ruin the face of the year." Each improper action, whether missing a church service or committing a more serious offense, is reprimanded with the explication, "You [have] very much *maan iiō*," or with the negative equivalent. In either its positive or negative form, the phrase indicates the improper positioning of an action in relation to the year. However we translate this concept—"getting in front of the year," or "offending the face of the year"—the first moments of a newly lived segment of temporal existence must be properly marked with virtous actions in order to determine the texture of the whole. Thus, these purified representations are living icons that represent the ideal forms of everyday action on Wūjlañ Atoll.

The games on New Year's Day follow the same format as the earlier games, but the stakes are much higher. In 1978 the winning softball team received forty dollars in return for its efforts. With increased access to money, the financial rewards increased concomitantly for the winners of the volleyball games on Āne-wetak. The New Year's Day games are so popular that every able-bodied person in the community shows up to witness the exhibition. Each team plays at the height of its ability, and the onlookers become engrossed in the contest. The onlookers add to the fervor with animated cheers and shouts of support. They beat with sticks on biscuit tins, and a few of the less inhibited dance with provocative gyrations of the *kwōjkwōj*. The scene is all-involving and transformative, a dreamlike period when all participants take on the primordial qualities of beings of the past.

Each team selects a theme for the game that parallels, though does not replicate, the *Kūrijmōj* festivities of that year. They fashion players' T-shirts with the theme and numbers signifying relationships with secret lovers indelibly etched into the warp and woof with magic marker. In 1978, one group used the word *rup* (to explode) as a theme in an attempt to capture an element of the power inherent in the explosion of its *wōjke* (tree). Another *jepta,* upset at the minister for having chosen another group as the "best" in that year's celebrations, had two sayings on its shirts: "Born to be a loser" [in English] and *"ejjab jide"* ('it is not yet ascertained,' or, perhaps, 'our potential or fortune has not been realized'). At the conclusion of a game, the shirts of the players from the losing team are ripped from their bodies by the members of the winning *jepta*. In the coming weeks, members of the winning team wear their shirts with pride, while other members of the winning *jepta* wear the T-shirts from the losing groups. Those who have stolen the shirts from the players who lost go out of their way to remind the losers of how they attained the shirts in battles that pitted the groups against each other and in battles that represented the world order for the coming year.

Following the games and the week-long series of early-morning church services, life on the atoll gradually returns to normal. Nearly four months pass with no nightly activities, no song practices, no *kaṃōḷu,* no *karate*. Morning activities, church services, and intergroup contests also cease. The festivities become fond memories over the coming months as participants recall the special occasions, the notorious performances, and the most humorous moments. Members of the community are relieved of the burden of activity brought on by *Kūrijmōj,* but by March or April everyone will be eager for the festive cycle to begin once more. A small celebration takes place on Easter, with groups reconstituting themselves to present a few songs and to prepare food for Easter Sunday. But people are much more excited at the prospect of another *Kūrijmōj*. The eagerness begins as reminiscences of past years. It builds with accounts of relatives' *Kūrijmōj* on other atolls. It begins to coalesce with a combination of ideas to create new songs and dance steps. In the coming months people again begin to make preparations for another *Kūrijmōj*—for the practices and *Kaṃōḷu,* for *Tijemba* and *kijen wiik* (weekly food preparations), and for *roñoul lalim raan* and another *Nuu Iiō*.

CHAPTER TWO

Fundamental Principles

Contexts of Exchange

Kūrijmōj is filled with a series of continual and repetitive exchanges. As communicational events, these exchanges carry a great deal of information about the nature of the transactions as well as about those who engage in them. Recently, Annette Weiner has suggested that the relationship between the giver and the object is more critical than is the symbolic value of objects as they relate to and participate in a system of exchange. Therefore, the principal reason for giving is to be able to retain, and "all exchange is predicated on a universal paradox—how to *keep-while-giving*" (Weiner 1992: 5).

I agree that all exchanges have a perceptually unbalanced element in them that allows each party in the exchange to seek symbolic advantage over the other party. Indeed, this is an important empowering element of the exchange and a significant part of its raison d'être. It seems to me, however, that a realistic theory of value cannot rely on the a priori relationship between a valuable and its "owner." Instead, valuables only become meaningful markers of identity as a result of the valuation of objects in relation to one another. They must first participate (at least in a comparative conceptual sense) in the universe of exchange before they become worthy of representing elements of identity, particularly the most aristocratic. Indeed, from a semiotic perspective, if inalienable relations linked objects of value with certain social persona, the fundamental dyadic inspiration to either initiate or to continue an exchange would never arise. Instead, both parties to an exchange must perceive gain, or they have no reason to continue the exchange.

Such a dual mentality of advantage means that, over the long term, all exchanges must be fundamentally balanced and egalitarian. Rather than being vested in inalienable relations between goods and persons, the entities being valued (objects, knowledge, or sacred force) depend on a relative balance of differential valuations by the exchanging partners.[1] At one level, the exchanges must be satisfactorily equivalent in order for the relationship to continue. Yet, in fact, the differential interpretations of value on behalf of each exchanging partner and the manner in which these alternate valuations are vested in different interpretations of the immediate situation allow each person to feel that he or she is the one to have come out ahead. In *Kūrijmōj* the exchanges are particularly prolific and important. For this reason, I use them as important interpretational devices in which to ground my analysis of the celebration.

Two different contexts for exchange are found within *Kūrijmōj,* and, not surprising, these contextual varieties are fundamental to the worldview of Marshall Islanders in general and of Wūjlañ and Āne-wetak people in particular. The word *contexts* is critical here because, I believe, it is context that differs, not forms of exchange. In other words, the idea that there are two different types of exchange, reciprocity and redistribution, each with its own rules of operation, seems to me fundamentally incorrect. All exchanges seek an advantage from two or more perspectives. To be continued, however, all exchanges must be fundamentally balanced. Interpretations and contexts vary, and this variety is particularly evident in *Kūrijmōj.* The contextual difference is that, for Marshall Islanders (and for many others in the Central Pacific as well), the world is made up of two fundamentally different sorts of beings, ordinary humans and sacred, inherently empowered, beings. The latter category includes God, ancient deities, and ancient (if not always present-day) chiefs. In many senses, all noncorporeal beings share at least some qualities with this latter category of beings. Even though the nature of exchange is, itself, constant, the fact that gods and chiefs have inherent sources of power not possessed by ordinary humans alters the context and dynamic of any exchange. These differences are particularly apparent in *Kūrijmōj,* and, as I will demonstrate in this and subsequent chapters, these differences are critical because *Kūrijmōj* serves both as the instantiational device that local people use to bring the categories of existence into being and as a mechanism to legitimize or justify their taken-for-granted form.

The first set of relationships has to do with the *jepta,* with their formation and intramural activities, and with their interrelationships with other *jepta.* These are all relationships among equals, as evidenced by the mechanisms of exchange, but their dynamic shifts significantly with the move from internal to external exchange.

THE LOGIC OF INCLUSION AND JEPTA *AFFILIATION*

Some of the first activities of *Kūrijmōj* involve the creation of songfest groups, a process that relies heavily on a historically consistent core group of participants and on the use of exchange for purposes of recruitment. Although to a one-time observer the core group seems simply to exist, its members were once recruits. Moreover, at certain liminal moments, core members may switch alliances, though with long-standing members this is rare. I consider one such case in detail in the section on core and fringe members.

Strategies of indebtedness are commonly used during recruitment in order to create in the potential recruit a necessary feeling of cohesion. Because each *jepta* is a small group, these feelings are easily enforced with constant reminders of upcoming events and joking strategies that inform wavering recruits of their unreciprocated debts.

The balance to all of the accolades and gifts bestowed on potential recruits comes in the form of time and work, for to have a *jepta* with any competitive promise requires hours of practice, of food gathering and preparation, and many other forms of labor. These are precisely the mechanisms that operate within *bwij* (bilateral extended families), for which the *jepta* is a precise metonym. Recruits find themselves in the position of children, core members in the position of adults, and aging patrons in their own aged rank, contributing as they can, but reaping the share of a fully active adult, the reward for former years of labor invested in the songfest group.

"You may [celebrate] *Kūrijmōj* with any *jepta,* because at *Kūrijmōj* we [inclusive] work in the manner of kindness [love] and happiness."[2] Although it is true that anyone may *Kūrijmōj* where he or she wishes, a look at *jepta* membership through time shows considerable continuity. Attractiveness—a quality that would allow groups to assemble members in a laissez-faire manner, (and a valued attribute of groups as well as members of groups [for reasons explained in subsequent chapters])—fails to account for group continuity. Each *jepta* is comprised of at least two types of members: a core of persons who remain stable from year to year and a fringe of people who change membership after one to three years of participation. Principles of recruitment and criteria of group choice are outlined below.

Wūjlañ Atoll is divided into two approximately equivalent divisions of available land space. These two halves are discussed by Tobin (1967) and Kiste (1976) as the "political divisions" of riĀne-wetak (the people of Āne-wetak) and riĀnjepe (the people of Ānjepe). Though residents were encouraged to maintain their Āne-wetak and Ānjepe identities when they moved to Wūjlañ, ethnohistoric accounts make it clear that Wūjlañ people think the groups that now exist, riJittōki and riJittoi, are very different from riĀnjepe and riĀne-wetak.

> There are only on Āne-wetak [Atoll] the Āne-wetak people and the people of Ānjepe, but on Wūjlañ we [exclusive] say, "the people of Jitto-eņ [the western half] and the people of Jittōk-eņ [the eastern half]," as appropriate for the group of Ebream [the former chief of the western half] and the group of Ioanej [the chief of the eastern half]. You see, Ānjepe and Āne-wetak exist over there in that place distant from here; they are not existent on this atoll. (Wūjlañ Field Notes 1976)

What anthropologists have classified as political subdivisions have different meanings for local people. Although Ānjepe and Āne-wetak are used for what we might call political discourses, they are also markers of personal identity that must be supported by commitment to land. Thus many riĀnjepe are also riĀne-wetak because they, or their parents and grandparents, have labored on lands in both halves of the atoll. Current residence is also a component of identity because, as with bilateral extended families, one must assist others in one's group and improve one's own land to substantiate claims to an Āne-wetak or Ānjepe identity. Land claims on Wūjlañ derive from an equal division of land among all members of the community who were alive prior to 1950, so the people of Jittōki and the people of Jittoi do not line up precisely with the Āne-wetak/Ānjepe division. As one person told me:

> Before the war I used to live on Ānjepe because, as you see, our [dual inclusive] grandmother had land there. My father, though, a lot of his land was on Āne-wetak, and sometimes I lived on Āne-wetak as well. When we moved to Wūjlañ, I thought I would float with Ioanej [the chief of the "Āne-wetak"/Jittōk-eņ half], and all of my land is in Jittōki, but the woman [his wife], her land is in Jitto-eņ and sometimes we lived there also.
>
> In the times of the past, at the time of *Kūrijmōj*, we used to divide into two *jepta*, riJittōk-eņ and riJitto-eņ. But now, because of many people, we divide into three *jepta*, not two only. [Three *jepta* are constructed rather simply since the two sides of the village are each subdivided into three "towns" *(taun)* or "places" *(jikin)*.] (Wūjlañ Field Notes 1977)

In the village organization, a combination of the dual and triadic frameworks apparent in daily life provides the framework for the resultant divisions into various action groups, including *jepta*. A dyadic organization into opposed sides of the village, Jittōk-eņ (the place facing windward) and Jitto-eņ (the place facing leeward), is permuted by the triadic organization of each half, yielding six towns *(taun)*. The three towns in Jittōk-eņ are Akadik, Ļọpat, and Waikiki; the three in Jitto-eņ are Ṃajọḷ, Nuu Yaak, and Iakjo. These are then recombined into three pairs to yield a new balance of groups that constitute the conceptual framework according to which *jepta* on Wūjlañ were convened.

As "suited for *Kūrijmōj* only," the *jepta* of Jittōk-eņ is made up of Akadik and Ļọ-pat; the *jepta* of Jitto-eņ is composed of Nuu Yaak and Iakjo; and the *jepta* of Ioḷap is comprised of Waikiki and Ṃajọḷ. Ioḷap takes the central town of each half of the village (Waikiki in Jittōk-eņ and Ṃajọḷ in Jitto-eņ), whereas Jittōk-eņ retains the easternmost two towns of that half of the village, and the westernmost two towns of the leeward half of the village constitute Jitto-eņ (see figure 6).

It would be convenient to say that residence determines *jepta* membership,

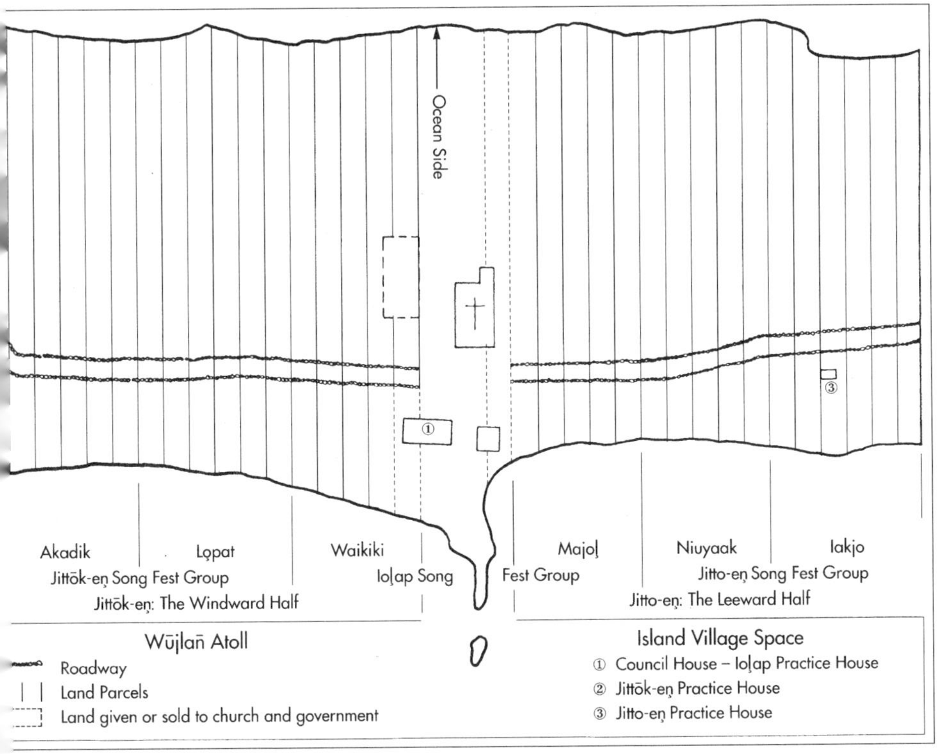

Figure 6. Village space on Wūjlañ Atoll. "Towns," songfest-group lands, and the "halves" of the village are shown, as are the *jepta* practice houses and the lands held by the church and by the community. (Cartography by L. M. Carucci)

that the *jepta* used to be the same as the Jittōk-eṇ/Jitto-eṇ division, and that Jittōk-eṇ/Jitto-eṇ is the same as the former riĀne-wetak and riĀnjepe split. A population-expansion explanation, like that adopted by the informant I quoted above, would account for the switch to three *jepta*. Although residence and population expansion are relevant factors, to accept them as determinants of *jepta* affiliation would drastically oversimplify the processes by which groups develop and would obviate the reasons that community members select a group with which to affiliate. The oversimplification is apparent when one tries to specify who actually participates in which *jepta*. The implications, however, are more far-reaching, for they lead the analyst to overlook a long series of discourses and actions that focus on situating persons and groups in constantly negotiated relations of power. Power is not the directly stated aim of the celebration, but the negotiation of power forms a critical subtext of *Kūrijmōj* (Foucault 1970: chap. 9). This is equally true of mundane actions (like one's selection of a *jepta*) and of highly ritualized actions of a more sacred order.

Thus the historic continuities core members use to legitimize their membership in a *jepta* may reflect a basic prototype that condenses the *jepta* Jittōk-eṇ with the corresponding physical location on Wūjlañ and with the corresponding social group who resides there. These core members may draw additional potency by noting folk continuities between the group living in Jittōk-eṇ and those who lived on the Āne-wetak half of Āne-wetak. This gives them a link to sacred lands that are a part of their being, and the justification of their ritual pleas for ongoing assistance from God during *Kūrijmōj* rests in the ethnohistoric rootedness they have traced to Āne-wetak. Each statement includes among its meanings a statement of legitimacy and a claim to power. This strategy of empowerment works because it makes sense in ethnohistoric terms that rely on a set of ideal relationships among groups. The same strategy, however, fails to work for a member of Ioḷap who resides in Waikiki even though all historic linkages except *jepta* selection are precisely the same as for members of the Jittōk-eṇ songfest group. Thus the model that explains processes of *jepta* recruitment must deal with the way groups and individuals situate themselves vis-à-vis others through the use of empowering communicative strategies. Population expansion can lead to changes in group formation, but it cannot, in and of itself, explain the cultural forms that change adopts in its own process of self-instantiation.

CORE AND FRINGE MEMBERS OF A JEPTA

Jepta recruitment may take place at any time during the year preceding the celebration. A person's decision to support a new *jepta* may be the result of a feeling that his or her participation in a particular *jepta* the previous year created conflict. The decision to affiliate with a new *jepta* expresses one's discontent without creating further conflict. It allows differences of opinion to be forgotten. This pattern precisely parallels the way in which domestic arrangements operate. A youngster has many sets of parents, and residence often shifts as a way of allowing disputes to disappear without public exposure of the details of the conflict. Newly married couples and hangers-on—adults who are separated from their spouses and families—adopt similar strategies.

In the case of *Kūrijmōj,* minor disagreements are usually worked out between established members of a *jepta* before the next year's celebrations begin. Exceptions do exist, however, and these are revealing about situating relations of power. When I traveled to Āne-wetak in 1982, a former core member of Jitto-eṇ had defected to Ioḷap and at that point was one of the central leaders of that group. Indeed, when practice began, he moved in with his sister's son, in a dwelling that was on the fringe of Ioḷap territory. His own house was located far to the leeward, in the land space occupied by many of his former *jepta*-mates. Members of Ioḷap often joked with him about becoming increasingly like a young, unmarried male, and, indeed, his spouse had died within a year of the time people had returned to Āne-wetak. He had sacrificed his membership in the church, allegedly for smoking and adultery, and these signifiers reinforced his identity as a resurgent youthful male. This banter, however, covered a more serious set of disagreements that had long served as a potential source of alienation among members of Jitto-eņ. According to some members of Jitto-eņ, the man in question had married a tabued relative, a woman he once called mother. As long as she was alive, her sons by a former marriage complained privately about the union. Once she had died, however, their complaints became increasingly public, expanding the shame that the widower had to face. His move to Ioļap—as we shall see, a *jepta* formerly associated with young, unmarried, men and women—not only went along with his newly acquired position as a single person, it represented a way of avoiding a potentially disruptive source of disempowerment.

More commonly, young couples and single men and women, those who comprise the group's fringe, are the ones to shift their membership from year to year. This same age group is likely to be the most residentially mobile. To gain the alliance of these tangentially attached persons, each *jepta* employs techniques of enticement that parallel those utilized by the senior members of an extended family to encourage the commitment of its members.

SOURCES OF UNITY AMONG CORE MEMBERS

The members of a *jepta*'s core are related not only in large part by residence but also by at least one common path of relationship. Stated another way, residence codes one of many possible ties of relatedness. These common paths are most apparent on Āne-wetak Atoll, where landed groups are the residues of the long-standing efforts of humans to bring residence and subsistence lands into being. On Wūjlañ and Āne-wetak, people "process and remain" on land, and land parcels only "appear" as a result of oriented human action. Because land is so critical to life, the groups that share commitment to, and labor on, land are conceived of as being bound together by solidarity. Land is part of one's soul *(an),* and its possession is classed precisely as such (*bwidej eo an Jojeb,* the land belonging to Joseph or, more closely, the land that is an integral part of Joseph's soul).

Shared souls, linked through labor in land but only grounded in shallow generational terms, also link the townsfolk on Wūjlañ Atoll. When people were relocated on there in 1947, land was divided in an attempt to re-create the idealized primordial equalities of land division on Āne-wetak Atoll. Each living person received an approximately equal parcel of land in the same way that, in oral historical accounts, each sibling received equal shares in the first division of Āne-wetak lands. Because families rapidly became unequal in size, however, Wūjlañ residents never equate current landholding on Wūjlañ with the initial equalities of Āne-wetak land division. Indeed, since their return to Āne-wetak, people have been unable to agree on boundaries or even, in some cases, on who has legitimate claims to specific land parcels, even though the initial divisions among a few ancient inhabitants are well known. The inequalities in access to land that developed during thirty years on Wūjlañ and, even more so, those that have been recognized since the community's repatriation on Āne-wetak, are threatening to the ideology of equality that continues to be valued in people's current images of their community and in the recollections of pastoral serenity in terms in which ancient Āne-wetak times are described.

The Wūjlañ inequalities at this later moment reflect the inevitable inability of residents to account for the differential development of families through time.[3] Even if the developmental position of each family had been taken into account in the 1949 land division (Goodenough 1955: 73–83; Fortes 1958: 1–14), the reproductive success of each family could not have been predicted in advance. Adoption provides one way of alleviating some of these inequalities. Nonetheless, many large, expanding families presently have inadequate amounts of land, and other families with few members—families that were developmentally diversified prior to 1949—are land rich.[4]

The bickering created by these cyclical inequalities serves as a reminder that, for pragmatic purposes, land is divided among members of a *bwij* on Wūjlañ and that the *bwij* is united by an ideology of sharing and equality. People with more land consider themselves fortunate. Yet when they must support the legitimacy of their claims to larger land segments, they necessarily base their arguments on differential ties of interpersonal relationship and hierarchy, principles that contradict the symbolic properties that unite them to others within their *bwij*. Such wealthy landowners, however, realize the contradictions they face on Wūjlañ. Other community members argue that they are haughty, like Americans (who refuse to share) and like Marshall Islands chiefs (who, in Wūjlañ constructions, claim actual rights of ownership to land). Land held by a *bwij* should be shared, because each member of the bilateral extended family has an equal right to land as long as that person works to maintain and improve the land.

Thus, when I say that the ideology of *bwij* is made manifest through land, I do not mean that those who can make other claims to more or better land as a way of increasing personal power will not attempt to make them. Many claims will be made, but on Wūjlañ each defendant must be prepared to argue against an ideal situation in which loving, caring for, and sharing—the qualities that typify interactions within the *bwij*—are recognized not only in bringing land into being but, equally, in the processes that determine the proper settlement of past claims as well as the transmission of land to one's descendants.

Whenever possible, the *jepta* use residence and landholding, along with the bilateral extended family, as symbols of unity. This is critical, for the aims of *Kūrijmōj* are intimately linked with the symbolic processes in terms of which both land and landholders are given existential form. Bringing humans into being through reproduction, bringing land parcels into being through labor, and bringing *jepta* into being in order to compete with one another and, thereby, entice the gods to make both land and humans fertile are integrally related tasks.

Not surprising, then, ties within a *bwij* unite all residents of Iakjo. A much larger (more extended) *bwij* includes all of the residents of Iakjo and of Nuu Yaak, the towns that comprise the core of the *jepta* of Jitto-eņ. There are several different ways to trace these ties of relationship. Similar bonds are found in Jittōk-eņ (which includes the towns of Akadik and Lọpat). Io̧lap, however, a *jepta* comprised of one town from each half of the village, is united by extended family ties, but those links are less direct than they are for the other two *jepta*. The conglomerate nature of Io̧lap (fashioned from a section of Jittōk-eņ and a section of Jitto-eņ) means that this group must establish a solidarity in spite of the polarities that split the traditionally opposed halves of the village. At one point, these halves were *jepta,* and as mentioned, each group's members could claim continuities with sacred primordial spaces on Āne-wetak and Ānjepe.

ALTERNATIVE SOURCES OF UNITY

Io̧lap in many ways utilizes ideas of unity developed on Wūjlañ to transform the conventional order of the festivities. Paths within various *bwij* extend beyond the boundaries reflected in residence to create new cohesive units. This same ploy has been used with facility by Wūjlañ people to claim that all atoll residents are "really one" or "all one family." A diagram of extended family links for Io̧lap is much more complex than is a *bwij* diagram for Jittōk-eņ or Jitto-eņ. Io̧lap's logistical problems are also more complex because its territory is always surrounded by opposing groups. The lands of its members are split between Jittōk-eņ and Jitto-eņ, and to reach those lands the residence parcels of one of the other groups must be crossed. These contradictions, realized spatially and socially, place the *jepta* of Io̧lap in a unique position for *Kūrijmōj*. The way these contradictions affect the celebration are discussed in chapter 5, but they are grounded in structural indeterminacies of a historical and cultural order. Such uncertainties are manifest in the different ways Io̧lap and the other groups manipulate the symbols of *bwij*.

Jittōk-eņ and Jitto-eņ are able to rely on close ties within *bwij,* generationally truncated extended families, and established residence patterns to solidify their respective *jepta*. This multiple-coded set of signifiers is deeply rooted and easy to follow. The lines of unity are well traveled. For Io̧lap, on the other hand, ties of relationship through a *bwij* are more distant, and the paths are traveled less frequently. Thus it is said, half jokingly, that "all Wūjlañ people remain slightly [participate a bit] in Io̧lap." The group's ecumenical nature derives from the necessity to use symbols of *bwij* in a fashion comparable to the way they are employed when describing all Wūjlañ people as members of one family.

Nevertheless, for Io̧lap the symbols must engender a much tighter solidarity than when they are applied to the entire population of the atoll. They must serve a stronger unifying purpose than they do for the other *jepta,* precisely because there are fewer symbolic layers of sharing. Thus Io̧lap finds itself in a paradoxical position. Everyone can identify with Io̧lap, for the dictum, "You may *Kūrijmōj* with anyone," indicates that at one level, "all islanders are one, just the same, in God's eyes." In this newly created songfest group, anyone can belong, everyone can trace a distant link to the group, and there are no long-standing, entrenched leaders. At the same time, Io̦lap's members have a paranoia that is not present in the other groups. They sense they are not the equal of the other *jepta,* and these latent fears manifest themselves in competitions. They voice fears of injustice and inherent weaknesses. When the minister (as "judge" of the competition) fails to properly recognize their skill in singing or dancing, Io̦lap people say it is because he (the minister) does not like them. They deny that such judgments might be a just appraisal of ability.

Io̦lap's innovative use of the symbols of *bwij* makes it the most successful group when seeking commitment by fringe members—young couples and unmarried men and women. Similarly, on Āne-wetak Meden, the most unusual and least entrenched *jepta,* attracted a large group of fringe members.[5]

What is it about recruitment and the choice of a *jepta* that makes Io̦lap (and Meden) attractive to fringe members? Both groups have large concentrations of young men residing in common dwellings (not unlike the ancient "men's houses" for unmarried young men), and this proves inviting to other singles. Concomitantly, having built reputations as the youngest, most innovative, and most permissive groups, these *jepta* continue to interest younger members of the community.[6] Finally, being a member of Io̦lap or Meden allows young couples to avoid making a permanent commitment to one of the other *jepta.* This may be useful when the parents of the newlyweds are from opposite parts of the community.

METAPHORS OF IRRESISTIBILITY

Recall that all children begin their participation in *Kūrijmōj* as members of Naan Aorōk. By mission logic they are free of sin, so they may come in contact with the deities without defaming them. A young person who leaves the ranks of Naan Aorōk always does so by "falling from grace" (*e buñ*: becomes dark or enters darkness). The proper method of falling from grace is by being wed in the church, but more commonly one has simply gotten married (*koba:* "to combine"),[7] has engaged in "illicit" sexual relations (that is, the acts have been admitted or discovered), or has been caught smoking cigarettes or drinking. These latter activities "damage God's laws," whereas being wed in the church or married separates one from the purity of childhood (a purity that keeps one close to God) without breaking earthly laws. (The minister and a handful of committed church members think that *koba* marriages also break God's laws. Others consider public marriage—a proclamation of one's married status accompanied by cohabitation [without being church wed]—an acceptable way to fall from grace.)

Entering the darkness marks a beginning point of adulthood, and the concomitant loss of purity excludes one as a messenger of God (cf. Carucci 1983, 1987a, 1987b). Indeed, the purity necessary to be called Naan Aorōk (one who knows no worldly sin) is precisely what qualifies one to maintain contact with God and to carry out God's work. All others are mature. And all adults except those who are incapacitated participate in one of the three *jepta* that compete in order to gain God's favor.

Newly married couples will likely *Kūrijmōj* with the wife's or husband's parents. A couple commonly begins by celebrating for a year or two with the husband's parents and then participates in the *jepta* of the wife's parents (or vice versa). The participation pattern may, but need not, correspond with the young couple's selected pattern of residence. Following the first years, however, the couple will usually stabilize its *jepta* affiliation with one of the parents' groups. In most instances their choice will line up with the location of their household.

Single persons who fall from grace are one source of new *jepta* members. If one claims to have entered the darkness unintentionally,[8] and if one is willing to repent, that person will likely participate in the same *jepta* as his or her parents. Most of the few who seek such reconciliation are young women who have been coaxed into a sexual liaison. For the majority of young men and women, the place where their parents decide to *Kūrijmōj* need not have anything to do with the decision as to where they themselves decide to *Kūrijmōj.* Young men, whose culturally proscribed character causes them to travel around more than women, commonly deviate from the selected *jepta* affiliation of their parents. When they do select another *jepta,* the decision may be affected by where age-mates have chosen to *Kūrijmōj,* where joking relatives (such as the mother's younger brother or a favorite grandparent) may *Kūrijmōj,* and, especially, where one's "real female friend" has chosen to *Kūrijmōj.* Young men or women will try to *Kūrijmōj* where their same-sex friends decide to celebrate, but definite consideration will be given to one's "real friend's" choice. Either the same *jepta* will be joined, or a person will select the *jepta* expected to compete most aggressively with one's real friend's selected group.[9] A few young men said it was desirable to be in the same group with one's female friend, but others thought it best to be in a competitive group. In contrast, most of the young women I questioned thought it was best to be in a group with one's young lover. These attitudes may be significant, in that actions with others in one's own *jepta* are modeled on extended family lines, whereas those among *jepta,* as we shall see, use the oppositional prototype of warfare and marriage between clans.

Other reasons given for joining a particular *jepta* include notions that "the people are better," that "the singing ability [of a group] is better," or that "the happiness of that *jepta* is greater." Among the reasons for not joining a particular *jepta* that Wūjlañ adults mentioned are "Some people in the *jepta* are disagreeable," "They have much bad luck," or, "They are worthless; it is not even worth their trying." Some of these latter statements are ways of competitively inspiring members of opposite *jepta.*

These statements not only reflect historically grounded interpersonal conflicts with others but also provide comparative contexts in which one's own *jepta* projects a sense of renown. Such confidence in one's own insurmountableness is a critical recruitment strategy employed by core members of a songfest group. Each person is of great value to the *jepta,* and boasting about internal strength must be backed up in singing and dancing presentations. Every additional member also increases the workforce that provides a *jepta* with its "weapons." War objects include bulk goods and cooked foods. Persons of renown have greater supplies of these items and maintain superior channels of acquisition. It is thus very advantageous for a *jepta* to recruit powerful persons—those with established networks who can accumulate goods quickly—but these people are also those most likely included in a group's core. Valuable recruits will be found among the younger "unattached" members of families of rank and among outsiders who may also prove to be fluid sources of material items. I was recruited into Io̧lap with this latter hope in the minds of some well-established members.

The dynamics of recruitment were placed in sharp relief during my second year on Wūjlañ Atoll. In the midst of that year's festivities a boat arrived from Mājro with a number of council members and other potentially valuable people of the community. Although all of the new arrivals were Wūjlañ people, most of them had been away for some months and had not been involved in the early practice sessions of the various *jepta.* Many of the newcomers also brought much-needed supplies from the government center. Competition for the patronage of the new arrivals was intense, and any *jepta* that convinced a new member to join its group scored a major tactical coup. Ultimately, the passengers were divided in a relatively equal manner among the competing *jepta.* Once the first newcomers committed themselves to a group, members of other *jepta* argued privately that remaining travelers should join opposing groups to maintain a balance that would not damage the intensity of competition. The egalitarian ethic on Wūjlañ is thought to be especially important for *Kūrijmōj* because the celebration relies on an extended competition between closely matched groups for its success.

Even though overall balance is important to the celebration, those seeking new members for their *jepta* do not have equality in mind. Core members of a group talk to potential recruits using phrases that stress group confidence and superiority. They typify their *jepta* as "extremely good" or "the very best." Reference to previous performances are made if the group has won recent competitions, but the conversation also stresses plans for the present year. Because many young men are uncommitted to a particular *jepta,* older men (grandfathers and mothers' younger brothers) often point out that certain young women, permitted sexual partners of the potential recruit, belong to their group. The same technique is applied to young women recruits, but with a twist. For the men, talk of same-aged cross-cousins is interspersed with seductive quips about women with reputations as adept sexual partners. For women, discussions of potential male cross-cousin mates are counterbalanced with jokes about relations with a series of older men who like to think of themselves as desirable but who are, in fact, thought of as clowns. Many of these hypothetical arrangements are posed humorously, but each has a serious intent of constructing a view of the group as irresistible.

All of this jesting impresses potential recruits by conveying images of a group's power in a highly valued, sly, discursive style. One's curiosity is piqued with images of intrigue that condense tales of personal seduction with the irresistibility of the *jepta*. Joking serves as the medium through which such messages are conveyed, a particularly appropriate communicative genre that allows a recruiter to accomplish two simultaneous tasks. The joke exudes the proper ethos of *Kūrijmōj*, an ethos of happiness. At the same time, it is a form of congenial banter that need not be taken seriously. If the potential recruit goes elsewhere, the recruiter need only say that he had joked with the person about the possibility of becoming a member but had not actually asked the person to join (and been rejected).

When recruits voice an interest, a core member will invite them to attend practice. Core members make special trips to a valued recruit's house, remind them that practice is about to begin, and wait until the new member accompanies them to the event. These actions are important, for otherwise the recruit who has voiced a serious interest may decide to go elsewhere. The presence of a core member forces the recruit to attend or to make a public display out of negatively valued "two-headedness."

The activities of each *jepta* do not vary much, but this is irrelevant to the discursive claims of recruiters. Once a person has shown up for practice, the public nature of his or her attendance itself represents a tentative commitment. It is only necessary to lend permanence to the decision. Symbols of *bwij* solidarity used to unite the *jepta* become the primary tools that change an unattached person into a *jepta* member. Going to practice and remaining or participating is the initial indication of commitment. People then make comments such as "Yes, he or she went over with that *jepta*, sat down and remained *(bed)*." Such simple actions—sitting with and remaining—substantiate rudimentary solidarity. The same activities are prototypical indications of interest and caring when a grandmother or grandfather enters very old age and, to some degree, apply to most encounters. Strangers who frequently refuse to involve themselves in these basic activities in terms of which acceptance is coded are said to be *kabbil* (haughty or stuck-up, often used to describe Americans) or downright bad.

Those who attend one group's practice sessions and then decide to change groups do not attend any *jepta* for a period of time. Such people will tell members of the first *jepta* that they are not feeling well or perhaps will just say that they have not yet decided where to *Kūrijmōj*. Those who move between groups too readily are said to be lost or not fully conscious.

Those who remain with the group they initially decided to attend—the vast majority—are incorporated into the *jepta* through the use of symbols of solidarity. These signifiers are most explicitly expressed in the prototypical unit of solidarity, the *bwij*. One's position in the *jepta* as core or peripheral comes from longevity and from the intensity of "working with" and "helping," as well as enacting context-specific signifiers like "practicing with" the group. Significantly, newcomers are not asked to do anything other than help with activities. Only after an extended period of participation will a person be asked to give material items to the *jepta*. By that point, it would be offensive for a member to shift affiliation, so core members can legitimately ask the recruit for food, money, and other objects of value. Such objects are requested with an appeal to symbols of *jepta* solidarity; references to helping, to the assistance provided by other members, to kindness, and to love unite a *jepta* through enactments of the ethic of *Kūrijmōj*.

Whenever requests are made for objects used to *Kūrijmōj*, they are legitimized with an appeal to the sanctified aims of a songfest group. All items, whether money placed on the altar or food consumed by others, are considered God's goods *(an Anij)*. Even the items consumed by the villagers are made sacred by a deacon's or minister's prayer. Most prestations go directly to the minister. Whatever the final destination of the objects, their sacred character is confirmed: "The final location of these goods, it is the same; the minister, he reveals God's words, and other people, during *Kūrijmōj*, work in truth and kindness" (Wūjlañ Field Notes 1982–1983).

RECIPROCITY AND THE LOGIC OF OPPOSED BUT EQUAL GROUPS

Many of the activities of *Kūrijmōj* take place between *jepta*, groups that speak of themselves in metaphoric terms as competing warriors on a battlefield and as groups that directly compete on the softball field, volleyball court, or, most centrally, in the song-and-dance performances of December 25. It is in this specific context of exchange that the relationship of giving with the intent of maximization (or self-advantage) described by Weiner finds itself most commonly actualized.

A great number of the events of *Kūrijmōj* utilize the competitive-exchange scenario, including *kaṃō̧lo*, the songfest competitions on December 25, and the activities on New Year's Day. In this context the *jepta* are established action units. Yet the units have largely hollow identities. Members lay claim to fragments of identity based on refashioned histories of past performances, but a group's primary identity will, ultimately, be grounded in the activities of the current round of competitive feasts. With context and intent far different from those in recruitment, the *jepta* use exchange as a primary dimension through which they fashion their groups' identity. This is a scenario of representational advantage among competing, yet theoretically equal, groups, and in this context the *jepta* become ritually fashioned metonyms for *jowi* (matriclans).

Although all Wūjlañ and Āne-wetak people are simultaneously members of a *bwij* and a *jowi* in daily life, in many senses the two units operate in exactly opposite ways. The bilateral extended family excludes no one, whereas, particularly in its idealized descriptive form, the clan is an exclusive group with clear-cut boundaries. The distinction was largely obscured by earlier anthropological writings on the Marshall Islands and not fully explored in previous writings on Wūjlañ or Āne-wetak, but it is critical to daily life. It is equally important to the understanding of *Kūrijmōj,* because the celebration attempts to inculcate and explore the ambivalence between these core activity groups in ritual form.

Bwij and *Jowi*

Some of the ways in which the core symbols of *bwij* are fashioned during *Kūrijmōj* have been noted above, but readers who are familiar with Marshall Islands ethnography will question why I have chosen to gloss the term as bilateral extended family, whereas other ethnographers call the unit a lineage or clan segment (Mason and Nagler 1943; Mason 1954; Kiste 1967; Tobin 1967; Kiste and Rynkiewich 1976). These distinctions are critical, I suggest, because the representations of inclusion that Wūjlañ and Āne-wetak use to talk about the *bwij* are antithetical to anthropologists' Africa-rooted understandings of lineage segment. In addition to the talk about *bwij,* the practices that instantiate it are of a bilateral order.[10] Therefore, both males and females not only claim to be members of the *bwij* of any or all of their grandparents, by birth and adoption, they physically stay with, work with, and care for members of these groups. Although levels of optation are evident in each case, because one cannot spend equal time with all groups, no absolutes apply. One does not, primarily, support patrikin over matrikin over adoptive kin. Indeed, the most empowered community members activate all of these paths, whereas the least empowered are fortunate to activate one or two. Precisely these differences serve as primary markers of relative empowerment within the community. Residence and inheritance largely follow the circuitous paths of *bwij* on Wūjlañ and Āne-wetak.

The expansive and inclusive logic of *bwij,* at the levels of both discussion and practice, are antithetical to those of *jowi*. In the ideal, one is a member of a single matriclan, not many, and although the *bwij* and the *jowi* overlap, the most extended *bwij* include all members of a *jowi* (along with others), whereas the most extended *jowi* is limited to those who share clan identity, which can be fully transmitted through females only. On Wūjlañ and Āne-wetak, unlike the Marshall Islands, all members of a *bwij* form part of a *jowi* only if one includes the "blood of the *jowi*." By definition, blood marks unity along the male line, whereas the *jowi* travels along the female line. When a clan dies, Wūjlañ and Āne-wetak people simply allow it to fade out of corporeal existence. In the Rālik and Ratak, however, clans have been resurrected out of the "blood of the clan." Even though Āne-wetak *jowi* are said to have been important corporate groups in the past, currently they only govern marriage. The conceptual boundaries that delimit *jowi* seem to have remained very rigid on Āne-wetak and Wūjlañ, threatening the category with obsolescence. At the same time, the Wūjlañ and Āne-wetak construction of *bwij* provides the flexible category of social interaction. In contrast, *jowi* in the Marshall Islands appears to have remained resilient, altering its conceptual peripheries to ensure that the category can adapt to the changing conditions of life.

For the above reasons, I choose to translate *bwij* as bilateral extended family. Although it is clear that the conceptualization of *bwij* on Wūjlañ and Āne-wetak in the 1970s, 1980s, and 1990s is somewhat different from its conceptualization elsewhere in the Republic of the Marshall Islands, I do not believe that local people in any of these places understand the *bwij* to be a lineage segment in the sense that anthropologists have used it to describe African social structures.[11] In contrast, Āne-wetak and Wūjlañ people see *jowi* as a core determinant of a person's internal being, something like core personality, except that it is shared with all others along a pathway that travels through women. The living members of this group of persons who share core identity material are only epiphenomena of the identity material that they share along the female pathway. They can legitimately be called a matriclan, though the possibility of resurrecting a dead clan through "the blood of the clan" among Marshall Islanders causes me to question the analytical applicability of matrilineal clan. In opposition to clan is blood, a pathway that travels through men that must be followed in order to discover a marriageable mate, a person called by the term applied (if one is a male) to a mother's brother's daughter or a father's sister's daughter, or by the term applied (if one is a female) to a father's sister's son or mother's brother's son.

Metaphoric Battles with Other *Jepta*

With these general outlines of *bwij* and *jowi* in mind, it is now possible to see how and why the *jepta* manipulates symbols of bilateral extended family to recruit unattached persons by using unreciprocated investment to create feelings of indebtedness. The same types of investments are employed by adult members of a *bwij* to entice offspring of the group to become core members rather than to exercise their option to affiliate with a different extended family. Other core symbols of the bilateral extended family are also used to construct solidarity within the *jepta* (through group activities and in the very act of being together). In contrast, once the *jepta* begin to interact with one another, they rely on symbols of *jowi* to structure their transactions with other groups. The shift in contexts, from inside to outside the songfest group, correlates fully with the differential use of signifiers of extended family and clan and, concomitantly, with alternate uses of the exchange scenario. Each set of relations is important, but they are employed for entirely different ends. Every clan puts signifiers of *bwij* to good use in contexts where its solidarity must be publicly announced. Yet established *jepta,* like clans, develop into bounded groups with well-defined identities. Except for the period of *jepta* recruitment, symbols of solidarity are used to reinforce ties between established members of the same *jepta;* they are not applied at increasingly abstract levels of inclusion, as is the case with *bwij* (that is, *bwij* in Hertej, a subset of *bwij* in Eliji, a subset of *bwij* in LiAngebel, to the level in which all people of Wūjlañ are one family). Thus, in opposition to different groups and in activities vis-à-vis those others, the *jepta* uses prototypical symbols of *jowi*.

Toward a Local View of Clan Identity

In the recent past, four clans were represented on Āne-wetak Atoll, but now three clans are still alive (see Tobin 1967: chap. 4). Each of the four clans is said to have been numerically strong at different times in the past, but all have been subject to the rapid population variations that are typical of small atolls (Goodenough 1955). Currently the *Ejoa* clan is numerically dominant on the atoll. *Ijjidik* is second in numerical strength, comprising about 30 percent of the population of Wūjlañ, and *riPako,* the final clan, will die out when the last of the two male respected elders who resided on Wūjlañ "take their rest." Like *riPako,* the fourth clan was one of the most powerful on Āne-wetak. That clan, *Jiduul,* became extinct two generations ago. The decline of the two clans has made contracting a proper marriage on the atoll difficult.

Clan affiliation is a major means used to determine whether a marriage is proper. Though other possible lines of relationship may rule a marriage out, searches for potential marriage mates typically begin in reference to opposite clan identity. The long history of intra-atoll marriage means that many other crosscutting ties traced through a common extended family may rule out potential marriage partners who are permitted in terms of clan identity. The presence of a large number of "marginal marriages" (those that pair permissible mates according to one path but that also have prohibited paths of relationship) reflects the long history of intra-atoll unions under conditions of population reduction.

Āne-wetak Atoll is one of the most geographically isolated atolls in the Pacific Ocean, and, until quite recently, contact with other atolls has been infrequent. Prior to the establishment of a trading station on the atoll by the Japanese in the 1920s, such contacts were largely limited to the occasional warring ventures of Āne-wetak people and of Marshallese or to infrequent landings of those lost at sea. These few notable encounters are recorded in the atoll's oral histories. Therefore, until the mid-1930s, the possibilities for marriage were almost entirely among indigenous residents. But other ethnohistoric details indicate that, in spite of Marshall Islanders' typifications of Āne-wetak and Wūjlañ marriages as incestuous, local practices currently reflect the exigencies of postcontact, pre–World War II population decline. Local people claim that the atoll used to be divided in several different ways into intermarrying chiefdoms, the most recent of which was the split into the Āne-wetak and Ānjepe halves. At an earlier point, however, people made note of three divisions—Āne-wetak, Ānjepe, and Wurrin—and chiefs and ordinary people alike selected marriage mates preferentially from another section of the atoll.

For Pikinni, a similar atoll, Kiste (1974: chap. 3) shows that population imbalance inevitably leaves a number of people unmarried, or those persons are forced to marry persons prohibited to them by the rules of marriage. On

Āne-wetak Atoll this quandary is even greater because larger imbalances in clan membership have developed. When the intermeshing array of paths of relationship are considered, most permissible marriage partners disappear. The recent response to this involution has been to marry outside the atoll, a rare possibility prior to about 1935.

In Kiste's account (1974; see also Kiste and Rynkiewich 1976: 216), only one path of relationship is considered critical between any conjugal pair. In all Wūjlañ unions (and elsewhere in the Marshalls where I have inquired), several paths of relationship are considered when contracting a marriage. On Wūjlañ there are twelve major extended families, and knowledgeable persons can recite ten or more paths through which partners to a union (both born on the atoll) might trace a relationship. For Wūjlañ people, "none [of the paths] is better, but some are closer." All are paths of value, though they are put to various uses. One of these uses is as a cross-check to an otherwise viable cross-cousin marriage. In the years following World War II, with the population hovering around 150, cross-cousin pairs (people of opposite clan identity, of course) were inevitably related through other ties that could prohibit marriage. One male informant astutely suggested that "In these days, there are no ways of marrying which are good. Only a few. Now they search for a permissible path, they are not cautions about prohibition."

Local histories, however, suggest a far different scenario for past times when Āne-wetak Atoll populations were higher. In one man's view:

> It seems as though, in those times, plenty of children were being born. And so, when it was time to marry, you could select from a range of women. That is why the young men would always be sailing to the other islets [in the opposite section(s) of the atoll]. Yes, there were plenty of women in the other clans. (Wūjlañ Field Notes 1977)

All of these factors reveal that people on small, isolated, atolls such as Āne-wetak or Pikinni married in accord with cultural rules that were as elaborate as the population of the times would allow. In ancient times, a multi-clan, three-section system may have been viable. Certainly, it is conceptually salient in people's recollections of the past. More recently, only two sections have been viable, and during Japanese times and in the first years on Wūjlañ after World War II, just contracting a viable cross-cousin marriage became a struggle. Beginning in the 1930s, and once again in the 1960s, as transportation and contact with other atoll groups increased, new forms of out-marriage became the norm. Although these marriages produced new sources of marriage mates for the coming generation, unlike many neighboring atolls, Āne-wetak and Wūjlañ people did not recognize the identities of new clans that women who came to reside locally brought with them. Instead, the marriageability of offspring of such women (just like those of in-married males) is judged according to pathways of relationship through the local parent. The failure to recognize these new clan identities, I believe, is related to the strength of solidarity on Āne-wetak and Wūjlañ and, concomitantly, to a certain paranoia about losing control over that identity to outsiders, particularly Marshall Islanders.

Clan Identity and the Metaphoric Battles of *Kūrijmōj*

A clan's oppositional nature is evident in the characterizing signifiers it uses to construct relationships between permissible marriage partners. Comparable structural characteristics are found in the celebration of *Kūrijmōj,* where interaction between groups is often described as warfare or marriage. The games and jokes of the celebrations are complex tropes that explore the dynamic relationship between symbolic opposition and reunification, domains Claude Lévi-Strauss often saw as complementary and necessary to cultural productivity (1969: esp. chaps. 5, 29). These themes are elaborated in actual wars and marriages of Āne-wetak and Wūjlañ history and in many contexts of current life.[12] Warfare may result in expansions of power rooted in land or influence, and influence is commonly characterized in local historical accounts as a way of spreading the identity of a clan or a chiefly domain through reproductive success. Not only do warfare and marriage use the same logic of opposed groups, Marshallese commonly use warfare as a preferred metalanguage to discuss cross-sex relationships between the members of opposite clans.

These themes are particularly important at *Kūrijmōj* precisely because they become a means of achieving the symbolic aims of the celebration. The competing *jepta* are represented as prototypical clans opposed in warfare and marriage. The exchange scenario used to create and maintain empowered identities by *jepta,* just like those of opposed clans, are reciprocal gift-giving schemes oriented toward outdoing the other side, and they are certainly represented as such. The aim is cultural production, most particularly at *Kūrijmōj,* the reproduction of humans and the regeneration of nature that are recurrent semiotic concerns.

The analogies between clans and *jepta* are most manifest in the way that exchange is used to overwhelm the opposite group. People say that ancient wars took place between people of different clans and different atolls. In warfare, a relationship "among men," the aim is to outdo the opposition with demonstrations of strength and valor. Primordial descriptions portray warriors with superhuman characteristics who could withstand the onslaughts of small regiments of enemy soldiers. The prototypical warriors of this sort on Āne-wetak were Jurāān and N̄iinjurāān, who conquered a large segment of the Rālik Chain before being defeated by hoards of warriors on Aelōn̄ļapļap.

A related set of characteristics governs interclan marriages. In marriage, which involves the double opposition, cross-clan and cross-sex, relationships begin by small exchanges of gifts, often male-provided goods exchanged against female-provided intimacies. The aim is to make oneself irresistible, and the method is to overwhelm the other with the irresistibility of one's gifts. Among married pairs, the two clans that are brought together in the persons of wife and husband still compete, with elaborate displays of food at first-birthday celebrations or celebrations of death. At the same time, strategies of disparagement are used to point out how inferior the contributions of the other clan were on any particular occasion. In both cases, the symbolic aim is to point to the net superiority of one's own clan in the exchange.

In *Kūrijmōj, kaṃọ̄lo* provides the first context in which the *jepta* exchange, and the aim of the prestations, as with the encounters between *jowi,* is to overwhelm. In this instance, the entire identity of a songfest group is vested in the outcomes of the exchanges, and the overall aim is to win the entire year's competition between groups. Elements of the *kaṃọ̄lo* encounters intensify as the celebration progresses, with more songs, longer speeches, and, most important, greater quantities of and more highly ranked foods displayed at each songfest event. Whereas the investments in the recruits are soon followed by remuneration, in the form of the recruits' return labor and time, the expenditures of each *jepta* in *kaṃọ̄lo* are directed largely toward unlimited gift giving, winning over the other *jepta* by increasing the renown of one's own group. Although at its core this means winning the performative battles of December 25 and New Year's Day, each incremental win during *kaṃọ̄lo* serves as a representation of the group's developing image of itself. Of course, these wins may be distributed among *jepta,* but the emerging contour of each group's identity is evident to everyone within the community. *Jepta* that are stingy during *kaṃọ̄lo* will never win the overall competition. Unless a group really tries, other *jepta* are not apt to pursue interactions with them during *kaṃọ̄lo, karate,* and *kalbuuj.*

Even though goals such as creating happiness are also important in *kaṃọ̄lo,* pleasing God and building an internally cohesive identity through continuous success in comparative performances are central. In terms of exchange, each of these goals requires giving in perpetual excess. For the *jepta* competition, excess is required to transform the balanced opposition between groups into a recurring set of ranked interactions. Overinvestment occurs because a group never really knows how much will be required to outdo the others, particularly in the case of foods. For the deities, perpetual excess meets the requirement of maximum expenditure, maximum reward. The participants come to this interaction differently ranked, however, which also changes the implementation of the exchange.

EXCHANGES OF HIGH AND LOW

The main raison d'être for the entire celebration lies in a set of exchanges between common human beings and others who are inherently empowered. The most critical form of this exchange is between earthly beings and God, because the central aim of *Kūrijmōj* is to obtain the renewal of nature and regeneration of humankind for the coming year. But even though the prestations or valuables in this exchange differ from those in other domains, the form of the exchange relies on the identical principles of perceived advantage and relative balance. Indeed, the small sense of assurance held by local people in their arrangements with God comes from their belief that, having engaged the deity in a debtor's position in a relationship of exchange, ordinary people's requirements for the coming year must be met. In the words of one consultant, "If we exhaust our abilities during *Kūrijmōj* and do not do things wrongly, then God must watch over us in the subsequent months."

Given these reciprocal requirements, what separates these ranked exchanges from those between earthly beings? I am arguing that nothing at all separates the reciprocal principles but that the inherent, transcendental, and often magical empowerment of otherworldly beings separates them from common humans who must labor to bring things into being. These characteristics, then, become the metonymic prototypes for the relationships between ordinary humans and chiefs, or ordinary humans and the minister, not because these latter beings are not to reciprocate but because they need not or, more properly, must not work in order to reciprocate. Chiefs and ministers, like deities, have their own mythological prototypes of inherent empowerment. Nevertheless, in these days the characteristics of the exchange relationships between ministers or chiefs and commoners both create and legitimize the conditions of their being. As Bradd Shore notes for Samoa (1977), persons of rank should sit still and be cared for by others, not engage in labor. The primordial rationale for such treatment rests in the inherent and magical empowerment of deities and chiefs. Simply through their blessing, goods appear, crops grow, and moving creatures multiply. But for today's commoners to honor living chiefs and ministers, their productive potential must be matched by generosity. *Kūrijmōj* provides an elaborate ritual mechanism to bring these pragmatic necessities, along with many more abstract ones, to ordinary humans through the use of exchange. But if the exchange requires reasonable balance, the interaction of those who engage in magical labor and those who labor manually provides a new context for implementing the exchange.

Human Gods and Godly Humans

A. M. Hocart's richly ethnographic analysis of rank and hierarchy in the Lau Islands and Vanua Levu (1927, 1952) provides an insightful perspective that helps clarify the analysis of rank in historically related regions of the Pacific. In *Kingship* (1927), *Kings and Councillors* (1936), and "The Divinity of the Guest" (in *The Life-Giving Myth and Other Essays,* 1970), Hocart brings to light the critical importance of the continuity between divine beings, kings, and the larger set of interpersonal relationships among humans. More recently, Gananath Obeyesekere has caused European readers to requestion the sources of the man-god trope (1992); yet, interestingly, Hocart developed his theory about the Fijian theocratic polity with specific attention to the dangers implicit in the use of Western analogues and naive translations. In response to Obeyesekere, Marshall Sahlins also pays close attention to issues of authorship and agency for the man-god trope in Hawai'i (Sahlins 1995). Indeed, from the time that missionaries such as Edward T. Doane began to codify the language they called Marshallese in the 1850s, concepts of rank have been translated naively, with insensitive categories and metaphors. These classifications have, to some degree, reshaped local practices (cf. Carucci 1987b). Early missionary accounts aligned what was, in their view, a radical separation between the sacred and the profane with another taken-for-granted division between the world of the living and that of the dead (the real and the ephemeral). Even today, however, Marshall Islanders' categorical boundaries and alignments bring these assumptions into question. Almost certainly today's categories reflect something of the ancient indigenous forms, for they are unlike missionary interpretations of the world at the same time that they are closely related to the distinctions Hocart posited for Lau Islanders. Therefore, whereas Hocart necessarily relied on European categories to paint his Pacific portrait, the recognition in his writings of the divine source of Fijian political legitimacy allowed him to overcome some of the shortcomings of a view of kingship rooted in the world of the mundane.

The set of metaphors Hocart selected to portray Lau Islanders' beliefs are applicable in the Marshall Islands and elsewhere in the Pacific (for example, Gill 1876; Williamson 1933; Beaglehole 1938). The Marshallese view of the past in which ancient chiefs are portrayed as earthly gods is widespread. Although this view was not questioned by German or Japanese ethnographers, American missionaries in the nineteenth century—and American administrators after World War II—found Marshallese views of chiefs disturbing. For Doane and other early translators of the Bible, the divine nature of chiefs should have been obvious. In spite of their biases, they selected the term *irooj* (chief or king) (Abo, Bender, et al. 1976: 78), particularly in contexts of address, as a gloss for God. In other locations, the notion of God is glossed with the term *anij* (cf. ABS 1971; UBS 1979), which, likewise, is tied back to the actions of earthly chiefs. *Kaanijnij* (to foretell the future [literally, *ka* (causative prefix, to make happen) plus *anij* (chiefly or godly action plus reduplication: repetitively]) is an activity associated with high chiefs.

Nowadays, *anij* commonly refers to the missionaries' God, but the term also takes the form *anij ro* (the gods [plural, human]). *Anij ko* (the gods [plural, nonhuman]) is an unacceptable Marshallese statement. So, like the deities of Greek or Roman mythohistory, *anij* simultaneously represents human and potentially plural entities. It was not fashioned with either the Judaic monotheistic model or the Durkheimian sacred–profane opposition in mind.

In addition to the use contexts of *irooj* and *anij,* a large series of stories describes the actions of god-chiefs. Indeed, the mythological materials that account for the yearly cycle and for the ancient celebrations of renewal are represented in the tale of the god-chiefess, Lōktañūr, and her offspring. Other well-known god-chiefs include Etao and Jemāliwūt. The stories of Lōktañūr and her offspring not only clarify the relationship between earthly and noncorporeal entities, they are critical to an understanding of the central themes of *Kūrijmōj*. The following is one Wūjlañ version given to me in 1977:

The beginning of the story. A very long time ago eleven (male) siblings were born to the woman Lōktañūr.[13] Of the chiefly line, all took their sacred blood from the woman, their mother, the highest female chiefess [primal matriarch] in the Marshall Islands. The chiefs resided on an islet known as Buoj,[14] a sacred spot on Aelōñļapļap, the ranking atoll in the Marshall Islands. One time, Lōktañūr called all of the young men born to her together, and then she proclaimed that the son who would be ruling chief of the islands was to be decided by a canoe race across the atoll's lagoon, a very, very large lagoon.

Each son began to prepare for the race far in advance; they worked on their canoes day after day; Lōktañūr watched the progress each of her sons made. When the day of the race had almost arrived, Lōktañūr went to the canoe shed of her oldest son, Tūmur. She watched her offspring working on the canoe. She told him that on the day of the race she needed to go to the windward tip of Aelōñļapļap, the finishing point of the race. She asked if she could ride with him, her oldest son, on that day.[15] Tūmur responded and said, "It is unfortunate, you could board my canoe but you have too many possessions; there is no spot for them on my outrigger." He told her to ask his next youngest sibling for permission to board his canoe. So, after that, Lōktañūr went to her offspring, he who was second born, and after watching him work on his canoe she again asked if she could board his boat and ride with him to the main island. He responded as had his older male sibling, "You see, ma'am, mother, you are welcome to board my craft, but there is no space for you and all of your things. Be kind and ask the one who is a bit younger than me." And so it went on this way, and he who was third oldest excused himself and told her to ask his younger sibling, and the fourth oldest asked her pardon and suggested she ask his younger sibling. But she proceeded, and she asked each of the young men born to her if she could board their craft, but each refused, saying he did not have enough room for her and all her belongings. Lastly, she went to Jebrọ, the smallest [youngest] of her offspring. She watched Jebrọ as he chopped on his canoe, and then she asked Jebrọ if she could board his craft and ride with him to the windward tip of the atoll. Jebrọ eyed her closely and saw the great number of possessions she had, and he was overcome with sadness. His sorrow came forth because he knew that with the added weight of his mother and her things he could not win the race. But he who was the smallest could not say no to his mother. He hid his sadness and told his mother, "I am happy to assist you. Bring your bundles to our boat early on the day of the race. The two of us will store them so we will not be late."

On the day of the race everyone was excited; each of the brothers wanted to win the race, each wished to be the ruling chief. So when the race was started each brother launched his canoe and paddled rapidly toward the windward islet. The wind was stiff and the canoes moved slowly. Tūmur, he who was the very oldest, was much faster than the rest. But the smallest of them, Jebrọ, was very slow. It was not only that he was small, but also that his mother and her heavy bundles made him slower. They paddled onward, but Jebrọ was left farther and farther behind. And then his mother, Lōktañūr, began

> to unpack her belongings. First she took out a *jāki* [sleeping mat], but it was different from the ordinary kind, with rows, combined and elongated above. And then she took out some *ekkwaļ* [coir or coconut sennit; locally made rope]. She told Jebrọ to free the three long spars that she had made him tie to the hull of the canoe. At this point Jebrọ could see that he would never win the race, and he began to become upset; but his mother told him not to be troubled but to do as she instructed him. In defeat, Jebrọ lashed together the ends of two of the pieces of wood; as his mother attached the mat to the two staves, she instructed Jebrọ to use more sennit to raise the third piece of wood in the middle of the canoe, to center it on the *petak* [windward platform], where she sat. She taught him how to secure the mast by lashing it fast with moorings at the bow [and] stern ends of the canoe and to the outrigger. After they had lashed the mat with three corners to the front of the canoe, they hoisted sail. The canoe flew. It was very fast, and soon Jebrọ and his mother began to overtake the others, his older siblings, who had almost disappeared ahead of them. And then, as they began to see people standing on the shore of the windward islet, Jā, they passed Tūṃur, he who was the oldest. So much faster than the rest, he was certain he would be the ruling chief.
>
> When Jebrọ and Lōktañūr landed and beached the canoe, all were happy; people danced and prepared a big feast. A huge gust of wind descended, a typhoon, and [according to one version] caught the canoes of Tūṃur and the other siblings and cast them out into the open sea. There was much damage, and the older siblings drifted and were cast about in the ocean, to leeward and to windward, with movements of the wild sea. After they feasted, Jebrọ, the ruling chief, and his mother sent men out to retrieve his older siblings, and the ocean was calm, for the storm had subsided. Reunited, Jebrọ and Tūṃur agreed that the youngest would rule the earth for one half of the year and that Tūṃur would rule when Jebrọ was away. This was straight, for Tūṃur was the oldest, but Jebrọ had been proper in his treatment of their mother. This is as it is, for as Jebrọ [Pleiades] sets, Tūṃur [Antares] rises in the east. The siblings cannot be seen at the same time, and this is as it was agreed on and as it should be. Lōktañūr [Orion] appears with Jebrọ, because it was Jebrọ who cared for his mother, and the sail of their canoe is in between and ties them together. This completes the account. (Wūjlañ Field Notes 1976–1978)

The importance of this story for Marshall Islanders in general is evidenced by its widely spread and perduring character. In addition to the account by Augustin Kramer and Hans Nevermann in note 15 of this chapter, it forms the first entry in two recent compilations of Marshall Islands stories (Knight 1980; Downing, Spennemann, and Bennett 1992). Michael Rynkiewich (1972) also notes the relevance of the tale to an understanding of social organization on Arṇo Atoll.

What does the Lōktañūr tale tell us about god-chiefs, about *Kūrijmōj,* and about the exchanges that accompany its celebration? Most important, the story delineates the causal relationships that underlie the important differences between summer and winter (or the rainy season and the dry, windy season), between the times of marginality and the times of plenty. These differences are accounted for by the caring and generosity of Jebrọ and the self-interest and stinginess of Tūṃur. The actions of the youngest and eldest toward their mother first provide evidence of those characteristics, which are then extrapolated to the social and cosmological planes. Ample evidence of these connections exists in all versions, but they are most apparent in the version of La Bedbedin (Knight 1980). In his story, Tūṃur is taken aboard Jebrọ's canoe because, as the younger brother passes him, he has pity on him. But Tūṃur becomes angry at his mother and throws her overboard. At her request, Jebrọ cuts loose one *dipāākāk* (boom mooring) and swims to her. They reach Jā first, swimming because, without the sail mooring, Tūṃur cannot *riak* (come about, by switching the sail to the opposite end of the canoe):[16]

Tūṃur drifts back to Wōja and carves out another dipāākāk. He sails again, this time he picks up Mājlep. He finally reaches Jā the next day—still before all other brothers. He thinks Jebrọ has drowned. He beaches his canoe and stands up on the outrigger. He lets off his chant:

"Up rises Tūṃur and drifts west
force of Mājlep will fall
he churns east up
he churns east up
he churns east up, beats up!"

Then Jebrọ steps out and chants:

"When Jebrọ rises at sunrise
he calms down upon water
he loves everybody."

Tūṃur is ashamed and turns away and sails back westward. And he has never looked back at his brother since.

Whenever you look up and see Jebrọ, you know Tūṃur is not in the sky. He waits until Jebrọ sets before he rises. Then when he rises it is just as he says. He churns up east wind. Falls like a storm everyday, every day except no rain, only very strong wind that tears palm leaves and beats the ocean up into froth. Sky becomes hazy with salt and leaves turn brown. Most days water is too rough to sail and currents are so strong across the reef it makes it bad for fishing. When Tūṃur rises, it is beginning of a bad time for us. Strong wind every day. And every morning we find him a little higher in the eastern sky and then sunrise.

And then after the moon passes one time, winds die down and we know Mājdikdik (little death)[17] is rising. Then after two or three days, winds whip up again strong as before. And every morning we find them, Tūṃur and Mājdikdik, a little higher in the sky and then the sun rises.

After one more moon pass over comes Mājlep. Mājlep rises a little to the south of east, but Tūṃur and younger brother take a path directly across the sky. With Mājlep, life gets worse 'cause there is no food and it doesn't rain. We say:

"Star of bad time because
dry sun comes.
Hide food because
drought coming
to kill!"

There is no breadfruit and no pandanus, and they'll be one long time coming and one long time before rain. This is when we tell our sons to take their spears and forge [sic.] food for themselves. So every day they go off to the ocean to spear fish chanting:

"We eat at ocean
till eyes pop because
won't get our fill with
mother and them
they'll piece us apart!"

Ancestors say Mājlep is a demon who strings us like fish and drags us upon coral and shorehead. If you tear loose you die. This is time of sickness and death. It is the time of jellyfish. They sting us when we try to fish.

Mājlep tosses us down upon the shoreline, then builds his fire. Now comes the wave called No in Eererak. Several days of huge swells that crash upon the reef and spill into the lagoon at high tide and wash his stringer of fish upon the sand to bake in the hot sun. Now is when he lies before his fire and buns up his long hair, and a tiny cloud comes to sprinkle a little bit of rain across the horizon. We say those clouds are drops from the bun of Mājlep. This is the time we call sun—fire of Mājlep. When he turns his back to us and eats up the last of the pandanus. You know in Marshallese custom it is very bad to eat and not offer to others. So that is the measure of how bad are those days of Mājlep. They last till two moons pass over and the star Mājdikdik will rise.[18] And then comes another wave called No in M̧wijm̧wij that will break up our stringer and set us free again—those who live.

Last rising star is called Jape and you know *an̄ōnean̄* is passing. We have two seasons here in the Marshalls. An̄onean̄ is when the sun rises and sets to the south—wind is strong and comes from the northeast. An̄ōnean̄ means force of the north. Because wind is strong and wants to come from the north. Rak is when the sun rises and sets toward the north—winds lighten and come from the south. Now is time for Kapilōk. We say:

"Don't sail too far away
from the island—because!
Tomorrow Kapilōk'll fall!"

That storm we call Kapilōk is very quick to come and you must be careful because wind and wave will break your canoe and put you in bad luck.

Now is when Jebrọ disappears from the sky. You look for him one evening in the western sky and he is gone. Then, after a while, Tūm̧ur rises. By sunrise, he'll reach the western horizon and you know that Jebrọ is about to take control of the East. Winds come as light breezes that we call the "breeze of the resting

King." Jebrǫ goes to rest in darkness. And when he rises from his pool in the East, he is a young man again. His strength has returned and he is in control once more. He rises one morning just in time to catch the bun of Tūṃur setting in the western sky—and then sunrise. Before, our ancestors made one big celebration on his rising. They would watch for two stars that appear above the cloud line called the "Post of Jebrǫ." When they find these they know he has reached the East. Jebrǫ brings days of rain and windless sky. And all of the reef smells. They say "perfumed oil of the King" spread out upon the ocean to make the water calm and shine like a shell. Good for fishing. Breadfruit ripen and pandanus. There is a lot of food and this is one big time to share with one another. One good time for us. So we say:

> "When Jebrǫ rises at sunrise
> he brings calm down upon the water
> he loves everybody."

Next to Jebrǫ you see the sail of Lōktañūr. That bright star there they call Ḷoujlaplap—one tuna who is hungry for those two little stars together there that make up a part of her sail. They say those are the daughters of Jebrǫ. And there over to the south is Jāljel and Kouj and down a bit—Lāātbwiinbar and, lower still, Lōkañebar. You see that little star between them? We call that Bar, or basket of food. The reason why Lōkañebar [literally "he who eats the head"] is so bright is because he keeps stealing food and eating it as they carry it along after Jebrǫ.

Then in the middle of rak season rises LaKublele. We say, wind of LaKublele, meaning from many directions, comes from south, comes from north, comes from west—changes every day.

Then when Jitata rises you know the season we call rak is coming to an end. We say Jitata sweeps the sky clean because he rises in a cloudless sky for many days. At sunset Jāpe is directly overhead. And then after a few weeks, when Jāpe passes into the western sky at sunset, it pours thick rain for several days and you know that will be the last water of rak and best save it because that dry time is ready to come.

And then at the end of rak rises Kumko. Two stars, they say, "Kumko north and Kumko south—waves fall north and waves fall south." Waves we call "Fall from the East" swell up on the reef and you know those winds of winter are on their way. First winds fall with the rising of the star Daam-Ad. But not really at rising—but later when the star rises above the cloudline.

All these stars after Jebrǫ bring days of light wind when they reach the East called jo. We say jo of Kumko, then jo of Daam-Ad, then jo of Ad as these stars reach East. But when they rise over the cloudline, winds blow under each star. We call these winds aññat and these churn up the East until Tūṃur rises and bad times again begin. (Knight 1980: 1–7)

In this telling, the actions of these ancient deities are clearly encapsulated in conditions of the cosmos that are then brought to bear on ordinary people's lives. Common people celebrate the coming of Jebrǫ, who is born again as a young man at the beginning of each summer season. He delivers plentiful food and brings an easy life during the days of *rak* (summer) because these are the characteristics of a caring and beneficent chief.

The ancient celebration of the coming of Jebrǫ is recalled by Wūjlañ people as a type of *kiye* (cyclical dance ritual), but larger and more extended. Although many types of religious rites are remembered as private or extended-family affairs, placing food offerings at the base of a sacred coconut or pandanus, the *kiye* was a public ritual. The best dancers, accompanied by drummers and tonal chants, performed for the chief. The songs are now remembered as being horrendous, but much of their negative portrayal today serves to separate the times of darkness, before the arrival of the mission, from the subsequent times of light. Not only were the best dance troupes honored at the *kiye,* these were also occasions when food was shared among members of the community.

With the coming of the missionaries, these ancient forms were discarded. Nevertheless, their rethinking "represents not the revolutionary, but the conservative" (Marx 1963: 125). A series of logical condensations leads local people to associate Jebrǫ with Christ, both beneficent younger siblings and deities of love (Christ is described as Adam's younger sibling)(cf. Niditch 1985). I will explore these matters further in later chapters.

More enigmatic was the shift from a springtime welcoming celebration for Jebrǫ to a winter-solstice feast for Christ. This alteration proved not to be particularly smooth, for the midwinter event greatly taxes people's ability to sustain themselves during the final months of the dry season. But whereas La Bedbedin portrays Jebrǫ (rising at dawn) as a god-chief who rules the summer skies and brings the wealth of produce during that time of year, Wūjlañ people now speak of Jebrǫ as a god-chief who rules the winter skies (visible after sunset beginning in late September). Nevertheless, Jebrǫ brings the wealth of summer resources. In their view, when Jebrǫ dives under the sea (during the summer months when he is not visible) he brings renewal of life to earth through direct contact with the bottom side of the earth.

How explicitly do local people voice these connections between Christ and Jebrǫ? It depends on the consultant. For many, especially the core church members, indigenous beliefs, particularly those that appear to conflict with Christian teachings, are relegated to constructions of the ancient past. Nevertheless, it was a knowledgeable Wūjlañ man who first connected the stories of Jebrǫ and Christ for me. When I asked him to elaborate on the significance of *Kūrijmōj,* he made some short remarks about the *jepta* competitions and about the interactions among males and females of different songfest groups. He also indicated he would return that evening to tell me more. The delay was not to seek greater privacy, nor to survey his relatives in the interim. Instead, he returned that evening, led me outside my house along the lagoon shore, and began to point out the visible Marshallese constellations, Jebrǫ, Lōktañūr, the sail that connected the two, Lāātbwiinbar, and others of those outlined in the story of La Bedbedin. He recited a version of the story of Jebrǫ, and when I asked what this had to do with *Kūrijmōj* and the *jepta* and all of the food, he said, "Everything. All of this 'remains under' [can be understood as part of] Jebrǫ. Kindness [consideration] and love, these are the important things."

Figure 7. Young boys look on as a large turtle is butchered on Jitto-eṇ lands, Āne-wetak Atoll, in 1982. The several types of meat are separated into stacks (foreground), and special portions are set aside for the chief and the minister. Added to other foods for *kaṃōḷo,* such high-ranked complements increase the chances for a *jepta* to win the evening's songfest competition. (Photograph by L. M. Carucci)

How do the exchanging relationships with deity-chiefs and with God differ from the interactions within the *jepta* during times of recruitment or from the interactions among *jepta* during the celebration? In one sense, exchanges with deities follow the *bwij* metaphor, in that there is an exchange, with delay, and an expectation (if only hopeful prayers) for return. Unlike the *jowi* metaphor of balanced and opposing groups and the possibility of winning over others, in this case there can be no thought of outdoing the other. With God as one's exchanging partner, a simple guarantee of reciprocity is enough to secure well-being for the coming year. Once again, the difference here is not in the format of exchange but in its semiotic intent and the context of its implementation. The determinant rules that give the exchange a certain texture derive from the fact that deities are inherently more powerful than people are because they have a magical source of productivity that can only be made available to ordinary humans through exchange. The most likely pathway to pursue this exchange is through the loving deities, Christ and Jebrọ, who are considerate of the needs of others. It is this empowerment that local people seek, the hope that the beneficent deity will at least reciprocate their exchange, if not return manyfold the ritual investments of deserving humans.

AMBIVALENT RELATIONSHIPS

Two other relationships are core to the activities of *Kūrijmōj,* but, in each case, there are ambivalent characteristics to their codings. The first is the male-female relationship; the second, that of young and old. In day-to-day life, each of these relationships has an opposite overt and covert ranking, and given the constitutive positioning of *Kūrijmōj,* it is hardly surprising that both relationships engender ambivalences of ritual instantiation.

Like all humans, Marshall Islanders take for granted the legitimacy and logic of their categories of daily use. The metaphor that equates age and rank is already manifest in the chiefly commoner opposition, and its ambivalence in the performances of *Kūrijmōj* is largely correlative with accounts of the ancient deities. Not only are adults ranked more highly than children, older siblings are ranked more highly than younger ones. Indeed, there are a plethora of recognitions of this order in daily life. Not surprising, then, inasmuch as *Kūrijmōj* serves to bring into being the taken-for-granted character of daily categories, the activities of *Kūrijmōj* also recognize this ranking. The main focus of attention, for example, is on adult groups and activities. But also note that the children's group always wins the competition among *jepta,* and although people's actions may only point out the hollowness of such claims, even to mention such a thing means that it has symbolic value.

Indeed, I believe the children's win reflects the fact that children are, in their very beings, evidence of the regeneration that the celebration aims to accomplish. Not only are they logical "others" in relation to adults, they are living icons that point out the success of *Kūrijmōj* and are the reason for dedicating so much time and energy to its proper celebration. Jebrọ, the younger-sibling deity, becomes the ruling chief through kindness, in direct contradistinction to his inherent ranking as the youngest and least empowered. And each year as Jebrọ returns to earth, he reappears in a new, youthful form. Thus newness and youthfulness have a particular representational value that are at the core of this particular renewal celebration. The liminal becomes the mode, not so much to create the values of the mundane through opposition to them but, in this case, to carry core fragments of semiotic value that relate directly to the meaning of *Kūrijmōj*.

The male–female relationship is also multivalent, and its potentials for alternate ranking are fully explored in the games of inversion, *karate* and *kalbuuj,* described in chapter 4. As with age, a gendered element is necessarily inherent in the description of *jowi,* not only because shared identity of *jowi* can only be transmitted along a path that passes through women but also, and perhaps more important, because clans on Wūjlañ provide the channels for marital exchange. Because these marriages are among bilateral cross-cousins, they reflect relationships among groups with equal rank. But because female and male representatives of clans bring different materials to any marriage, the moment such a marriage is constituted, it always involves struggles toward alternate rankings. Given the subsequent potentials for inequality, as well as the initial conditions of equality, the *jowi,* I believe, provides the ideal metaphor for competing *Kūrijmōj jepta*.

Issues of sexual politics as well as gender are critical to the way in which *Kūrijmōj* is conducted. Sexual relations are imperative for local people because the celebration focuses on the reproductivity of humans as well as on a plentitude of produce. I present the material on sexuality as part of this section on gender because Wūjlañ and Āne-wetak people themselves commonly conflate the two, though in slightly different ways from the manner in which the conflation takes place in the United States. Nevertheless, issues of sex and gender are analytically separated to increase the clarity of the text for the reader, not because the division reflects important elements of Marshallese cosmology.

For Wūjlañ and Āne-wetak people, gendered relationships are governed by a typical dynamic of operation. This dynamic is rooted in two cultural dicta: "the man travels about while the woman stays put"; and in public ceremonial events, "the (oldest) sister's brother speaks on behalf of the clan." In geophysical terms the first dictum means, quite literally, that women are more spatially centered around the domestic space, the land parcel on which that domicile is situated, and, with the recent colonial era of centralized villages or urban areas, in town. Men, in contrast, are spatial meanderers, spending much of each day sailing from place to place, foraging in the bush, diving in the ocean, or climbing coconut trees. For most Marshall Islanders, though not for present-day Wūjlañ and Āne-wetak people, moving around also means that typically, at marriage, a man moves to his wife's land, whereas the woman stays put. On Wūjlañ and Āne-wetak, residence is ambilocal. Nevertheless, the distinction between mobile males and spatially centered females is fully reified and naturalized by most Marshall Islanders. It often becomes a rationalization for the frequent (or frequently discussed) illicit sexual relationships of men, whereas the equally frequent sexual relationships of women derive only indirect explanatory value: "What does she think she is doing, working in the style of a man?"

The second dictum is rationalized in terms of, and intertwined with, the first: the man is a public persona, while the female is a private persona. The man thus not only represents his own small, bilateral extended family during discussions in the council house, he also voices opinions on behalf of a clan if he is its oldest living representative. The males, who move about, are therefore doubly vociferous, because they also speak while women remain silent.

To jump to the conclusion that males are somehow ranked higher, however, thoroughly misrepresents my understanding of the situation, either in the Marshall Islands or on Wūjlañ and Āne-wetak.[19] Instead, the universe of gendered relations is reminiscent of Thomas Gregor's depictions of the Mehinaku (1977). This is a society typified by gendered balance through complementary imbalance. One could say that there is an overt–covert opposition, a relation of center and periphery, or a public–private contextual distinction to be made, but no definitive rankings. At the overt, public level, the *a̧lap* (family head) speaks on behalf of his *bwij* or *jowi,* but particularly in the case of decisions that reflect on clans, his word must reflect the underlying decisions of the women who truly head the clan and transmit clan substance. In several cases on Wūjlañ and Āne-wetak, I have seen council meetings reconvened after the women tell their public speakers they would have to reconvene the community, tell them (in shame) that what they had said the previous day was wrong, and relate the correct version that the women have emphatically revealed to the *a̧lap.* Stated differently, the private arena within the clan or extended family provides the context in which both humans and ideas are generated. The community provides a context in which they are exchanged and shared. Within the center–periphery model, which is the one in which women and chiefs share valuations, women remain in fixed positions in the center while men provide for them. In the Marshall Islands this is manifest in an opposition between *ri jerbal,* the male descendants of a clan who bring clan lands into being through their labor, and the women who transmit clan substance across generational lines through reproduction. On Wūjlañ, it is equally manifest in the conceptual balance between men, who provide for a domestic unit through fishing and foraging out in the bush, and women, who stay put and transform those foods into consumable meals for the family. Women, like chiefs, sit and are cared for through the expended labor of men. At the same time, in the domain of food, women must labor within the house and village space to counterbalance the men's work in the bush, the sea, and the sky. Only in the reproductive arena are women more fully like gods and chiefs—living souls who magically bring things into being.

I shall return to these themes in coming chapters to show how the details of these cosmological ideas are manipulated during the celebration of *Kūrijmōj.* First, however, the sexual politics of male–female relationships require some attention. Sex is extremely central to day-to-day life on Wūjlañ Atoll. People find it a highly enjoyable activity, but, even more than that, it is an extremely enjoyable topic of daily discussion. Both men and women invest a great deal of discursive energy in talk about sex and sexual relationships. Nevertheless, because one can neither engage in nor talk about sexual matters when prohibited relatives are within view or hearing distance, such activities and talk require sophisticated management of social situations.

When missionary teachers first introduced Christianity to the Āne-wetak people in the 1920s, it was a religious form that contained many of the same overt behavioral restrictions that were present when the Word was brought to Hawai'i more than one hundred years earlier: drinking, smoking, dancing, and so much as a thought of sexual activity before marriage were prohibited and governed by strict sanction. Although the actions of American soldiers after World War II caused local people to rethink the relationship between the prohibitions and "being a Christian," at the most overt level the prohibitions remain fully intact in the 1990s. This is not to say that the prohibitions are not commonly broken. Indeed, backsliders abound when a field-trip ship anchors off the lagoon shore, bringing tobacco and sources of alcohol, both foreign preparations and materials for local production. And equally numerous are those who fall from grace in accord with Church-defined forms of illicit sexual relationships.

During *Kūrijmōj,* metaphors of sexual activity are brought out into the open for a number of reasons. First, people note that the metaphorically explicit games of *Kūrijmōj* should create happiness and believe the best way of doing so is through the pursuit of sexual activities. But these Machiavellian views are counterbalanced with bows to Durkheim and van Gennep: the liminal creates the conditions for an inversion of daily activity, and if such liminality does not result in the physical and sexual consumption of the totem animal, it certainly displays for the deities the objects of its own desire. These objects are most fully represented in the form of food and of metaphoric sexual relationships that take place between opposite-sex members of opposite *jepta*. I explore each of these activities in depth in the chapters that follow.

How explicit are these metaphors of sexuality? As with the Jebrọ theme, it depends on the consultant. Recall that *Kūrijmōj* is a communitywide event on Wūjlañ. It involves everyone, even though fewer than half of the mature community members are members of the church. For young, unmarried males and females, the sexual themes are central. They are what make *Kūrijmōj* worth dreaming about, and they are discussed daily. But even among long-standing church members, mention of the sexual themes draws smiles or snickers. Like Hawai'i, this is a society that undoubtedly thrived on "discourses of love" (Sahlins 1985: chap. 1) prior to the missionaries' appearance. Now, at its very heart and soul a Christian nation, it bears the scars of an incomplete reconciliation between puritan Christianity and Pacific belief and practice. As young men and women watch the tricksterish antics of the Etao figures parodying *jepta* performers when they dance on December 25, some race from the scene in embarrassment. As young women have their clothing tugged in public by their special paramours, they hide their faces in their hands with equal embarrassment. These are not the deep-seated repressions of puritan men and women in nineteenth-century New England, but they bear some encumbrance of a knowledge of those values juxtaposed closely with an ideology that smoothly transforms human sexual labor into entertainment.

Wūjlañ people describe sex as work. As already discussed, humans are fundamentally different from deities in that the latter can bring things into being magically. Humans, however, must work. This is equally true of human reproduction. Yet, although sexual work is required for reproduction, it does not, in and of itself, guarantee it. It is here that *Kūrijmōj* comes into play. When a man and a woman cannot have children, they will seek a local medical specialist who provides medicine to "clear the pathway" so that a child can be born. But these are not genetic interventions. A woman can birth a child by a lover of years past by simply dreaming about him. Similarly, by praying and "thinking clean thoughts" a woman can seek to have God bless her with a child. *Kūrijmōj* operates at this level of exchange, but in behalf of the entire community. Sex is required to have children, but it is not causal. The celebration of *Kūrijmōj* is replete with metaphors of sexual activity to remind God that human reproductivity is necessary if Āne-wetak clans are to be able to perpetuate themselves. The ritual process purposefully places God in a subordinate position in an imbalanced exchange in order to guarantee that God must respond by keeping open the reproductive pathways that bring clan substance into being on the face of this earth. In this way, *Kūrijmōj* provides a mechanism of empowerment for ordinary humans who use ritual labor to reproduce sexual labor to create the preconditions of corporeal existence.

CHAPTER THREE

Eating the Food of My Enemies

Production, Consumption, and the Work of the Gods

Along with song and dance, food is the major item that is exchanged during *Kūrijmōj*. The festivities are in many respects designed here, for hours of each day are spent gathering and preparing food, all oriented toward exchanges that communicate something of the central intent of the celebrations. Other important gifts are involved, but food is one of the most concise containers for renewal and regeneration. Even though I have discussed the semiotic value of food in detail elsewhere (Carucci 1980b, 1984), the potlatch-like nature of food exchanges during *Kūrijmōj* demands particularly close scrutiny.

On Āne-wetak today, the vast majority of foods for *Kūrijmōj* are purchased from the U.S. Department of Agriculture or imported from the governmental center. Indeed, even on Wūjlañ in the 1970s many critical staples came from outside sources. A complete celebration thus depends on the arrival of a supply boat in November or early December. In spite of Naṃo's close proximity to Kuwajleen, as Nancy Pollock (1969: 12) notes, the success of the festive event is contingent on a boat's arrival prior to December 25. The extended duration of the Wūjlañ celebrations, their intensity, and the added distance from the source of supplies serve to intensify problems with food. In 1976 and 1977 the community depended on staples purchased in early November and late October, respectively, to make the festivities a success. Though ships also touched the atoll in late November 1976 and early December 1977, they carried few supplies and were of little help in supplementing local goods.

With the benefit of nuclear compensation funds, Āne-wetak residents (quite like Northwest coastal Native Americans postcontact) have been able to intensify their investment in goods with productive potential. Each year, with little reference to the market conditions that govern their nuclear compensation trust funds, Āne-wetak people request large sums of cash to be spent on *Kūrijmōj*. Observers who measure value in terms of dollars see this as economic waste. Analysts with a substantivist economic frame of reference may view expended trust-fund dollars as reinvestment—a view somewhat closer to the Āne-wetak interpretation. From this perspective, the money must be spent to ensure that renewal and regeneration—the central aims of *Kūrijmōj*—are achieved. Yet conscious rationalizations of this sort are not voiced by local residents. Their choice to spend compensatory cash in this pursuit is more of a collective compulsion, agreed on by all but seldom rationalized in economically logical terms.

In essence, the expenditures contain several communicative scripts. At the intra-atoll level, the goods obtained are integrated into battle plans on behalf of each *jepta*. It is here that the *jepta* energize themselves, and each group must become as strong as possible in order to create a group identity infused with generosity and caring, core symbols of *Kūrijmōj*. At the atoll level, the same theme of largesse and display allows *Kūrijmōj* investments to serve as semiotic forms of empowerment vis-à-vis other atolls. Most critically, however, the displays of food send messages of gratitude, appeals for attention, and requests for future well-being to superhuman entities. I discuss these messages in detail in subsequent chapters, but no other sets of objects can communicate messages about renewal of sources of raw food in a more appropriate manner than the display and distribution of cooked foods.

During *Kūrijmōj* mundane labors are suspended in favor of four months of ritual activity (as I discussed in chapter 1). Yet some ritual movements are so commonplace that a casual observer might easily confuse them with day-to-day actions. Local residents labor to ensure that life goes on, yet the continuity of life is precisely the focus of *Kūrijmōj*. Therefore, as people busily gather and prepare foods and, with great pleasure, consume them, they bring to a conscious level the critical value of food for the continuity of life on this small, isolated atoll. Recitation of these desires occurs in the form of prayers of thanks given to God for the necessities of life, prayers not unlike those offered each day at mealtimes or those that accompany community feasts. There are differences, however, that radically separate *Kūrijmōj* activities from everyday labors. It is these ritual peculiarities that code more specific information about the nature of the celebration.

Most obviously, the intensity of food gathering and preparation far exceeds that of day-to-day life. Although food consumption increases slightly, what is eaten is less critical than what is prepared. The display value of the foods far exceeds their caloric content. Nonetheless, the composition of a meal and the combinations of foods that are consumed also tell us about communicated meaning. Much larger quantities of highly ranked foods are prepared and consumed during *Kūrijmōj* than at other times of the year (Tobin 1952; Maifeld and Carucci 1982). Because highly ranked foods include those that are particularly fatty or greasy, cultural ecologists may argue that *Kūrijmōj* is an adaptive strategy to increase the consumption of high-satiety foods during times when fishing is difficult. But *Kūrijmōj* does not rely on a logic of rational economizing or adaptation. Instead, the communicative value of overproduction and consumption is stressed, even though this course of action results in a strain on resources and times of hardship in the late-winter months (January-March). In the islanders' view, the nearly certain shortages of late winter are worth enduring because *Kūrijmōj* aims for a more important end. It seeks the sacred empowerment to ensure that the sun will return on a northward path, that plants will be plentiful, that the fish will run and become properly greasy, and that local people will continue to exist and their families will expand on Wūjlañ and Āne-wetak Atolls (cf. Beckwith 1951).

To communicate the plea for renewal, food production and consumption are modified in a manner that shifts their semiotic value. Although, in general, community members produce food in ways reminiscent of day-to-day life, during *Kūrijmōj* one's own food is given away, and people consume the food of others. The circularity of this process stresses interdependence. It produces the reunion of opposites necessary to ensure the regeneration of nature and reproduction of humankind. At one level, this reunion occurs with metaphoric spouses, members of other *jepta* with whom one interacts as if they were members of opposite clans. More important, the reunion occurs with God and the ancient deities, the loci of sacred force on whom earthly beings depend for their existence.

As *jepta* interact, the productive strategies that typify the domestic unit are ritually brought into being. In that context, men produce foods from the male domain: high-ranked (and uncooked) seafoods that community members desire. At the same time, women collect land-grown staples from the female domain. Each food is then readied for consumption: pig, fish, drinking coconuts, and baked sprouted coconuts are prepared by men, with whom these foods are associated. The raw staples, which include not only breadfruit and arrowroot but, nowadays, rice and flour in various cooked forms, are made by women. The foods are then combined into elaborate, festive meals, and the members of each *jepta* give them to other *jepta* who, in return, provide the first group with different foods to be consumed at that time or taken home and eaten later. Women and men prepare foods that are representative of their respective domains.[1] But only after the foods have been transformed into meals and exchanged do people consume these meals. In the process, human thanksgiving for a completed cycle of yearly production is demonstrated, and the ritual attempt to engage the deities in an exchange to guarantee a subsequent cycle of regeneration is set in motion. If God reciprocates with the renewal of the raw materials of nature, these new foods will be transformed into edibles through the labor of fishermen, gatherers, and cooks. This is not simply an idle appropriation of taken-for-granted products of nature but rather a complex series of cultural acts that manipulate social relationships and productive human labor to create the continuity of human life.

During *Kūrijmōj,* one *jepta* not only consumes foods that other groups have prepared and gives its own edibles away, each meal comprises edibles that promote the growth and sustenance of living humans with a gendered balance of internal, strength-building land foods and external, beauty-fashioning seafoods. This gender-based balance is critical not only for human reproduction but for the production of culturalized foods that, when consumed, "grow" strong, healthy men and women. The interactions among *jepta* provide the interactive framework in which these productive circumstances are operationalized. As we shall see in chapter 4, the games of *karate* and *kalbuuj* add yet another sly maneuver, another surreptitious layer of communication and humor, to this complex scenario in which seafoods and land foods are obtained from metaphoric spouses, not simply consumed within one's own group.

In this schema one "eats the foods of others" or "consumes the windfalls of battle." These rations must be gathered and prepared by one's battle partners and metaphoric spouses from other *jepta.* As in daily life, clans that are opposed in disputes are reconciled as spouses within a single unit. This is how domestic groups, relying on symbols of sharing associated with the bilateral extended family, are formed out of representatives of opposite clans. As we have seen, this is also how all members of the community are knit together into an interdependent entity out of *jepta* opposed in battles with food and promises of sexual companionship.

The community unity that results from eating the food of others leads to a higher-order exchange. Foods, along with display wealth, are given to God in the hope that the same reciprocal requirements that encumbered one *jepta* to balance returns or to return with greater largess will encumber heavenly beings with a concern for the needs of their earthly exchanging partners. The exchanges with God take place throughout the celebration, but they intensify during December, as each *jepta* gives foods to the minister following their Sunday performance. The largest of these gifts is given on December 25, with another sizable gift on New Year's Sunday. On each of these occasions, the minister (and on Naṃo, the paramount chief) receives gifts of food and money. Additional types of display wealth are presented on December 25 and when each *jepta* visits the minister's home to sing.

There is some guarantee of success in these calculated pleas, for one who receives gifts and fails to reciprocate faces public humiliation and loss of rank. Furthermore, all people of high rank must reciprocate received favors with a generosity suited to their rank or sacrifice their renown. What is more, the symbolic attributes of Jebrọ and of Christ, the ancient and present-day deities of love and generosity, virtually guarantee that gifts given will be remunerated manyfold. Therefore, the ritual appeals for assistance and the reasonable expectations of their fulfillment are important ways of rationalizing the significant amount of energy spent on *Kūrijmōj* pursuits.

Wūjlañ people most commonly hone games of *Kūrijmōj* into stories with biblical relevance. Here the stress is on kindness, happiness, and giving, whereas expectations of a balanced exchange are expressed as pleas for support from a more distant deity. Such requests occur in prayers that accompany food gifts. They commonly take the form of overt questions filled with pleas of solidarity that typify interactions within the *bwij*. It is in precisely this context that the role of the father as a provider for the family takes on relevance for Wūjlañ people. In the summary language of one *Kūrijmōj* prayer, "Demonstrate your kindness and watch us, care for us, and assist us in each of our movements during these times."

The most overt signifier of kindness *(jouj)* on Wūjlañ Atoll is giving. As on Ifaluk (Lutz 1988: 88 et seq.), on Wūjlañ social relationships are primary, and the enactment of values like kindness speaks most loudly about the relative value of goods and social relationships. Indeed, in their own view, Wūjlañ kindness separates local islanders from outsiders, even from other Marshall Islanders, but particularly from Americans. Wūjlañ people thus use deeply ingrained irony when they employ what they consider a biblical message about kindness to construct an empowered view of themselves vis-à-vis Americans—those who originally introduced biblical teachings. Wūjlañ people are kind because they are giving. In contrast to Wūjlañ people, Americans are said to be presumptuous and stuck-up *(kabbil)*. The judgment is most often based on the failure of an American to give up a personal possession. For Wūjlañ residents, possessions take on their most significant value as gifts, that is, as they require humans to come in contact with one another in relationships of mutual involvement, of caring, and exchange (Durkheim and Mauss 1963).

Americans, on the other hand, are invested in goods as a direct expression of their personal accomplishments. They develop elaborate constructions of themselves for others to interpret based on a set of accoutrements and adornments collected around them. Although these symbols are shared—in large part they are mass-produced goods—unique combinations of ranked valuables result in a somewhat satisfying, if unstable, mechanism through which the images one has of oneself are conveyed to others.

Food, the prototypical signifier of nurturance on Wūjlañ Atoll, is a special type of valuable. It should never be hoarded (cf. Pollock 1970 for Naṃo). It is given freely, even in times of starvation. As one consultant noted:

> In those times [of famine] we were embarrassed to call out to people to come to eat, for there was no food in the least. We hid in the cookhouses where arriving persons would not see us. But for those who came inside, we gave them food. It was food of the disinherited *[ri jerata]*, but even if there was only a morsel, we gave [them] their food-class objects *[lelok kijeer]*. (Wūjlañ Field Notes 1977–1978)

The use of food during *Kūrijmōj* as an item of war becomes a source of entertainment and humor for Wūjlañ people. It helps create happiness *(m̧ōn̄ōn̄ō)*. The first layer of humor derives from the ironic manner in which war is conducted with the ultimate symbol of peace. At the same time, it harkens back to the final war on Āne-wetak, when warriors were implored by a Marshallese woman on board one of the arriving Marshallese war canoes to love one another and evokes the symbols of love and kindness found in biblical texts. The end of warfare and the coming of the missionaries are events that separate the "age of darkness" from today, "the appearance of the light." In the accounts of many younger residents, the stories are collapsed into a single event. The battles with food that take place at *Kūrijmōj* evoke these stories, for in their yearly enactment they seek to obtain a cyclical pattern of parallel movements from darkness to light.

I have discussed Wūjlañ and Āne-wetak food procurement, preparation, and consumption in detail elsewhere (Carucci 1980b). Therefore, in the remainder of this chapter I will explore a restricted set of ritual applications of food in the celebration of *Kūrijmōj*. This will provide a framework for understanding how foods of differential value are used to communicate ritual information, to specify how these messages are manipulated by each *jepta* to create a winning position during *Kūrijmōj,* and to discuss the way power is generated through the exchange of food.

THE RANKING OF FOODS

Indigenous edibles and imported items are divided into foods and drinks, and food items are subdivided into categories commonly translated as staples and complements. Meals are fashioned according to set patterns that balance items from each category and that, when consumed in proper balance, literally construct viable living humans (Carucci 1985). At *Kūrijmōj,* the most important of ritual occasions, foods from each category are presented for each major event. These events include *kam̧ōļo, karate, kalbuuj,* Sunday presentations during the weeks before *Kūrijmōj,* December 25, and *Nuu Iiō.* As the celebration proceeds, intensity increases, and food provides the most critical way of communicating the intentionality of this increased fervor.

Quantity, quality, and type of food each have a semiotic effect. As *Kūrijmōj* progresses, the quantities of food increase. Food-exchanging events occur more frequently and, as Marcel Mauss (1967) notes, each gift necessitates a return. Although the gift's own spirit is not responsible for the return, the competitive nature of the exchanges in a network of reciprocity in which the rank of one group is elevated by each unreciprocated element ensures that ever-larger gifts will be given. It is precisely this principle of increase, realized first in inter-*jepta* interactions, then later in interactions with God, that serves as a condensed symbol of the overall aim of the celebration.

Like the representation of sexual relationships, making food *(kam̧ōn̄ā* or *tattāāpāp)* is a key symbol in making life, and this is the ritual aim of the cele-

Figure 8. A young woman scrapes arrowroot along the lagoon shore of Wūjlañ Atoll in 1978. A staple of the ancestors and an important food during famines, the small tubers form an important part of the array of foods exchanged during *Kūrijmōj*. (Photograph by L. M. Carucci)

bration. Drinks and foods, and seafoods and land foods must be properly balanced to create viable humans. Land foods, staples, are the unmarked and taken-for-granted category of food that balances drinks and, in the local view, provides for the sustenance and growth of the core of the person. This core is derived from one's matriclan and is nurtured by female-gathered and female-prepared staple foods. The staples are balanced first by drinks, prototypical male foods like drinking coconuts. A meal, even a famine meal, requires these minimum female and male components, a staple and a drink. *Raij bāto,* rice with tea, and *aojek,* arrowroot mixed with drinking-coconut liquid, are acceptable meals when one is starving, precisely because each critical component of a meal is represented. Within the food side of the food-versus-drink opposition, however, land foods are then complemented by seafoods and birds. These foods are provided by males and, on ceremonial occasions, are often cooked by men. They lend balance and strength to the staples and contribute to external beauty (just as males, in sexual intercourse, shape the external features of the fetus). But, unlike drinks and staples, they are not required for human sustenance on Wūjlañ. They contribute to beautiful hair and smooth, reflective skin—qualities of attractiveness, of external beauty, but not characteristics that are a requisite part of human existence.

Thus the minimal meal consists of a male drink and a female staple food, the white coconut milk and cream being analogous in its qualities to male sperm, and the female staples, prototypically breadfruit and pandanus singly or mixed with arrowroot starch, being associated by their reddish or orangish color with female body parts and substances. During *Kūrijmōj* the stress on a plethora of foods provides the suitable elaboration that changes a simple meal into a feast, but the overrepresentation of the complement category among the feast foods is not accidental. Complements create external attractiveness, exactly the characteristic required to ensure the fulfillment of the aims of the celebration. Thus, both in its general ability to bring humans into being through a balance of gendered food items and in its overemphasis on externalized beauty created through greasy complements, food provides one of the primary channels in terms of which *Kūrijmōj* constructs its own conditions of fulfillment as an important part of its processual form.

Food quality is critical at any feast where only the best of foods, those suited to deities, should be given. Best may refer to size, and claims are always made privately that the largest catch of the year or the largest pig on the island forms the core of a group's food gifts. Best also refers to quality, purity, the first representatives of a harvest, and richness or sweetness. For staples, purity of preparation is critical. Only the whitest of rice, only fermented breadfruit washed free of any scent, only arrowroot sieved to free it of all bitterness are of chiefly value. As elsewhere in the Pacific, first fruits were reserved for chiefs in the past, and they carry specially marked significance today. For complements, the richest or greasiest items are most highly valued. Thus, when *jepta* weigh the relative merits of fish in an exchange, rabbit fish outrank parrot fish, but these reef fish are both outranked by yellowfin tuna, the greasiest of pelagic fish. Sweet items are also highly valued, and it is the sweetest pandanus cakes, the sweetest drinking coconuts, the most heavily sugared of beverages that capture the Marshallese imagination. As Sidney Mintz (1986) notes, sweetness is an integral part of how Americans define demeanor. Such is also the case for Marshall Islanders, who criti-

Sea Foods		Air Borne	Land Foods	
turtle ocean fish yellow and blue fin, albacore, wahoo rabbit fish goat fish squirrel fish unicorn fish flying fish chub tang	whale/porpoise lagoon trolling	large birds frigates, boobies brown noddy capped noddy small birds terns	pig dog chicken	sweet pandanus sugar edwaan low grade pandanus breadfruit (sweet varieties)
	↑ complements "sweet" and "greasy"	staples ↓	sprouted coconut muwaan (seeded breadfruit) core of coconut core of pandanus	rice flour arrowroot liok pandanus runner root

Figure 9. A simplified ranking of common Wūjlañ foods. Meals combine drinks with foods and staples with complements.

cize those who might embitter otherwise enjoyable occasions *(kameọeọ)*. Sugar is even thought to have curative properties, so plain water is sweetened not only to add to its exchange value but simultaneously to eliminate the intestinal parasites that might damage a person's stomach.

The ways in which food type can affect the communicative value of an exchange can be seen in the way greasiness applies to fish. Figure 9 captures a few of these simple rankings for each category of food or drink. But the rankings of food are no more predetermined than is the value of any other category. Proper combinations of food are as critical to a successful food event as are highly ranked foods of any particular category. It is thus thought that pig is the perfect complement to a certain variety of baked breadfruit, whereas fish are better complemented by rice. Rice balls provide a proper balance for bland fish if rolled in scraped coconut, whereas rich fish might best be accompanied by plain spheroids of rice.

A *jepta* always comes to *Kūrijmōj* events armed with food, but to win an encounter requires skill, dedication, and good fortune. Large quantities of food, edibles of the highest quality, and highly ranked components from each domain of edibles are critical determinants of value. As the festivities intensify, greater numbers of staples, complements, and drinks must be presented to win a *kaṃōḷo*. Groups dedicate greater effort to obtaining multiple complements—pig, chicken, and birds or turtle—as well as different types of fish. Each of these needs to be balanced by a staple, and staples increase in number as well as quality. By December 25 each group presents as many products from each category as possible, and each product should be highly ranked within its own category. In the domain of food, intensification helps accomplish the transformation from a competition among groups within the community to an exchange between the community as a whole and the deities. Huge gifts of food are displayed and then exchanged among community members. Though they need not be, these foods are commonly prepared by each *jepta*. (Recall that in 1977, food-preparation groups were headed by respected elders in the church and included members of different *jepta*.) Each songfest group also gives large quantities of food and display wealth to the minister, the representative of God. These gifts are accompanied by prayers of thanks to God and by pleas for the future. The pleas are for plentitude in nature, continued food supplies for the coming year, and, equally, for the health and goodwill of the community.

Whereas the food exchanged among community members is of the most highly ranked variety, that given to the minister has a more varied character. Certainly, high-ranked complements and well-prepared staples abound, but groups also dedicate special effort to including indigenous foods. Of particular note is arrowroot, not only in a prepared form but also raw. This is a subsistence food, now prepared and eaten only in times of starvation, and its presence in the minister's basket reinforces pleas for the future. The meaning of this gift is perhaps best captured by the words of a respected, middle-aged woman: "Sometimes we have bad fortune, and the assistance of God is most needed in those times."

A core part of the celebration's intent is encapsulated in the balanced foods the minister receives. It is equally well represented in the good fortune required for a group to win any of the competitions. Certainty always seems to remain contingent for Wūjlañ people, and such contingencies color each food event of *Kūrijmōj*. Even the most organized songfest group cannot be sure that its meal will be complemented by the proper type of fish or birds, for fisherman's luck, or bird-catcher's fortune, always plays a part. Nonetheless, staples are prepared, substitutions are made, and a *jepta* goes forward with a *kaṃōḷo* or Sunday presentation. Indeed, the overall aim of *Kūrijmōj,* to secure well-being in the coming year, necessitates indeterminacy. In the most marginal of atoll environments, and in the midst of the years of greatest deprivation, Wūjlañ people created *karate* and *kaṃōḷo,* games that increased the levels of unpredictability. Just as Wūjlañ people represent themselves as dedicated supplicants, survivors of deprivation who deserve to receive supernatural support for another year, so the members of a successful songfest group combine their labor and good fortune to overwhelm their competitors with food.

JEBRỌ AND THE RENEWAL OF LIFE

The story of Lōktañūr and her youngest son, Jebrọ, provides a critical Marshallese context in terms of which this focus on food and sexuality makes sense. In terms of celestial arrangements, Jebrọ (Pleiades) is the figure who "reveals" or "tows the path of stars across the sky." Jebrọ is conceived of as the end of the empty sky and the beginning of the full sky of stars that appear in the first half of a new year. The "path of stars" refers to the Milky Way, which sweeps across the sky as Jebrọ sets. The same sort of intangible force that gives force to the wind that powers the sails of Jebrọ's canoe and, with his mother's assistance, allows him to win the chiefly canoe race allows Jebrọ and Lōktañūr to drag the stars across the sky. One informant described these celestial forces as "wind." "Wind, is that what moves the stars across the sky?" I asked. "No," responded the elderly man, "not wind; but almost the same. The two have the same shape." Not surprising, then, exceptionally large winds are called *lañ,* meaning "heaven" or "sky," a sacred, heavenly force come to earth. When destructive, these winds are seen as a corrective to human actions gone awry. Jebrọ thus forms the crucial bridge in a cyclical temporal order. Appeals must be made to Jebrọ to realign the heavens. With the assistance of Lōktañūr, Jebrọ compels the sun to return on a northward course and also bridges the gap between darkness and light in the night sky.

These geophysical accomplishments have their social components. The path of stars includes the entire chiefly line, flanked on its two edges by Jebrọ, the youngest sibling, and Tūm̧ur, the oldest. The feats of renewal are performed by the youngest, not on the basis of any cult of youth but by providing a bridge between commoner and chief and between the youngest brother line and the senior lines. Like Lono in Hawai'i, Jebrọ is the considerate soul on whom common people can depend in times of need. In the Jebrọ tale, the youngest son allows his mother aboard his craft in spite of certain defeat in the canoe race. Just as Jebrọ pulls the path of chiefly stars across the heavens, in his representation as the rainbow *(ial),* he conjoins the domains of earth and sky, thereby providing humans on earth with access to the regenerative powers controlled by primordial chiefs—those who originally empowered earthly beings and who continue to revitalize the mundane world. Jebrọ links the old year and the new, short days and long, the dark sky and light, the disempowered with the highly ranked, the generationally old with the young. He provides a way to regenerate lived existence on earth that, if left to its own natural (or cultural) tendencies, would follow the degenerationist course of time. As an avenue of empowerment, Jebrọ provides humans with a potential pathway that allows them to reconnect gradual death and diminishing rank with the rejuvenative sources of their original empowerment.

Food plays a critical role in this tale about aging, interpersonal relationships (kinship and rank), and the yearly cycle. Jebrǫ not only rules the heavens when these conjoining transformations must take place, he is responsible for their accomplishment. By the summer months, Jebrǫ has charted his path across the sky and pulled his older siblings into visible positions in the heavens. During summer, Jebrǫ shares the rule with Tūṃur, who occupies the central night sky. At the same moment Jebrǫ travels under the sea, his back in contact with the bottom of the ocean. His excrement provides food for marine life. As a result, fish that have degenerated and become watery during winter become greasy again; those that have become dried out, flaky; those without flavor, once more delicious. Having directly ingested sacred substance, they are considered tastier, more highly ranked, and more filling.

Later in the year, the albatross may appear. He flies along the outer edge of an atoll, on the boundary between the calm spaces inside the outer reef and the raging sea. His flight pattern is irregular, diving and climbing, knitting earth and sky into a unit. When this unusual creature appears, it is a sign of good fortune. This is "one of the works of Jebrǫ" that indicates that "life is fitted." "All living things, and plants, are still all right," and "life will continue into the future until the coming year" (literally "the lower year" *[iiō in laḷ]*). In Marshallese cosmogony, life itself, reflected here in the semantics of temporal order, must be properly elevated. This process requires the power of Jebrǫ to reattach the passing moments to their sacred empowering source. Christ, Jebrǫ's Christian equivalent, performs a parallel task, linking humans on earth with God, the primordial source of all life.

Land foods go through a cycle that parallels fish, but the details are less well defined by exemplary tales. Perhaps this reflects the fact that Āne-wetak people are primarily oriented toward fishing. They call the residents of Wōjjā, Arṇo, and other lush Central and Southern Marshall Island atolls planters, in order to contrast them with their own interest in sailing and the sea. Nonetheless, the growth of land foods is not taken for granted by Wūjlañ people. Even though plants are nurtured and cared for, the cycle that leads plants through a series of growth stages from infancy to maturity is controlled by superhuman forces.

A precise parallel is drawn between human sexuality and the productivity of fruiting plants, which Wūjlañ people depend upon for food. Some trees are productive, and others fail. This is the work of the gods. Coconuts with blackened interiors are said to have been attacked by evil spirits, and breadfruit that refuse to ripen are not blessed by God. Elsewhere (Carucci 1987a) I have shown the way in which the development of the coconut and the growth of boys into young men parallel each other. Breadfruit and pandanus, in their color and cycle of ripening, are seen to be analogous to women's development (see Carucci 1980b). Fruit and female sexuality are frequently described as unripe, ripe, and even rotten or damaged. Thus it is evident that the productivity of fruiting trees and human reproductive capacities are not seen to be natural processes. Like the year itself, they must be elevated to maturity. In the process they can rot, be made to go bad by evil spirits, or fail to mature properly, and these factors are determined by God.

Even though humans are not responsible for reproduction and growth, they do not sit by idly. Instead, they intervene with all of their energies during *Kūrijmōj* to fashion total uncertainty into the possibility that life will continue successfully in the coming year.

CHAPTER FOUR

Spheres of Symbolic Action

The Feasting Format, Karate, and Kalbuuj

Each major ritual encounter at *Kūrijmōj* entails an exchange, and, as I have indicated, each volley in the battles of *Kūrijmōj* comprises objects of caring and desire. Most commonly, these items include foods and sexual innuendos. The standard template for each encounter, be it *kaṃōḷu, karate, kalbuuj,* or the major exchanges on December 25 or New Year's Day, derives from a generic feasting format used again and again in daily life. Local people often call this generic format a *keemem.* In its narrow sense *keemem* means first-birthday party, but on Wūjlañ and Āne-wetak it also has the generic meanings of communal feast or party.

THE GENERIC MARSHALL ISLANDS FEAST

It would be a distortion of Wūjlañ logic to see the common birthday party transformed into a celebration of the birth of Christ. Local residents do not see it in this way. In its narrow meaning, the first-birthday party celebrates a moment of renewal: the lending of an identity, of naming, the recognition of the successful traverse of a pathway of lived human existence tenuously inscribed on the face of this earth. The omnipresent possibility of death, not so much of a person but of a group of humans tied together by their collective scratches on a particular segment of the earth's surface, is the overriding fear that supports the celebratory joy of *keemem.* In these respects, Wūjlañ and

Āne-wetak people see the *keemem* format as being generalizable to many celebrations, certainly to *Kūrijmōj*. Thus *keemem* applies to all gatherings in which the constitutive materials of life—food, goodwill, and reproductivity—are held up for communal celebration.

The format for feasting is fairly straightforward. I noted its basic components in the descriptions of *Kūrijmōj* in chapter 1. Nonetheless, the simplicity of the feasting format points to its centrality and universality, not to a marginality manifest in lack of elaboration. Historically, the general category for communal feasts, *kwōjkwōj,* was adopted by the missionaries to designate communion, was dissociated from the "debauchery" of other *kwōjkwōj* gatherings, and lost favor as a generic descriptor for communal feasts. *Keemem,* the most frequent and generalized of the remaining communal feasting categories, came to replace *kwōjkwōj* as the general term for communal feast on Wūjlañ and Āne-wetak.[1]

In the narrow sense, *keemem* are large, communal food exchanges to celebrate the first birthday of a child. They occur only once in a person's life and, in premission days, were the time when a child received its first name. The *keemem* marks the end of infancy and the beginning of existence as a named, gendered, young child. The exchanges are sponsored by a child's *bwij* and the *bōrwaj* (household or, literally, rafter stringer) of which the child is a part. Both groups support the child by preparing the feast, though the *bōrwaj* prepares as much of the food as possible. Most commonly on Wūjlañ, the entire community receives the feast, but as the population has expanded and expensive new goods have come to be viewed as needs, some subgroups instead may receive the feast on Āne-wetak. Rādikdoon, the adult church-women's group, is a common new recipient group.

The feast takes place on the land parcel of one of the sponsors (the child's *bōrwaj* or the land parcel of one of the grandparents) or in the council house. An elaborate array of edibles must be provided because the goods that are given will be understood as a measure of the generosity and rank of the family sponsoring the feast. As in the Trobriands, the feast becomes a public measure of accumulated personal wealth and renown (Malinowski 1984: 97, 168–73). In hard times, feasts may be meager, but a family must exhaust its abilities in its preparation, whatever the conditions.

In addition to foods, the family may give away other valuables: sleeping mats, yard goods, or bags of uncooked rice. The ceremony opens with an elaborate speech by the respected elder of the child's clan or by another man of repute in the extended family. The maternal grandmother (or another grandmother if the child's mother is an outsider), the mother, and the child sit on a mat in the center of the audience, their physical presence marking the event's center. After the speech, other respected elders may speak, and the minister gives a prayer. Food is then distributed, and portions of the food are consumed. The minister, the chiefs, and the guests are often given specially prepared foods when the foods are first distributed. Eating and socializing may last for two or three hours, though, on occasion, a singing or dancing presentation or a raffle-style giveaway may occupy part of the time.

The event concludes with one or more speeches of reciprocation by respected elders who represent the community. These persons are from other major extended families. The speeches will be followed by so-called times of giving. Songs of giving are sung, and members of the group(s) that receive the feast come forward and place gifts at the feet of the mother and the child. Box matches, bar soap, or quarters and dollar bills were standard gifts in the 1970s, but some inflation has struck since the community's return to Āne-wetak. Not only is the public demonstration of generosity valuable in constructing an image of renown, the arena also provides an opportunity for important people to proclaim their commitment to each bilateral family they support through their gifts. At the end of the songs, a short speech of thanks is given by the respected elder who opened the *keemem,* and the minister or a church elder may close the event with another prayer.

A similar pattern of feasting is used for virtually every public exchange in Marshallese life. Marriage and death ceremonies are variants of this theme, though in the feast that ends the period of mourning, gifts are not given to reciprocate the sponsors of the feast. The food given by the family of the deceased is "forever." The food should be physically incorporated into the bodies of community members as a corporeal memento of the deceased. Reciprocation is seen as inappropriate.

THE FESTIVE FORMAT RENEWED

The festivities of *Kūrijmōj* refabricate the generalized format of feasting for each of its varied occasions. Whereas the *keemem* is the most generic feast of the current day, the patterns visible during *Kūrijmōj* range from the generic waves of ritual confrontation seen in *kaṃōḷu* to the specific exchanges that typify the mock battles and sexual games of *karate* and *kalbuuj.* The forms of reciprocation and the arrangement of persons serve as symbolic indexes that code critical elements of each encounter. *Kūrijmōj* feasts do not simply replicate day-to-day forms. Instead, the food events pattern themselves on the generic feast even as they transform it. Like *Kūrijmōj* itself, these feasts verify and validate day-to-day practice. They also create something new on the pattern of the old. With such an accomplishment, the symbolic aims of *Kūrijmōj* are fulfilled.

In *Kūrijmōj,* the generic feasting format is refashioned into related feasts, each with its own symbolic intent. In the songfest competitions *(kaṃōḷu),* for example, two *jepta* are seated in a circular pattern in the practice house, but a line divides the members of each *jepta.* Food giving at this stage is a form of action on the battlefield, and as we might expect, food is not consumed in common. Each group attempts to overwhelm the other, and each group eats foods prepared by the opposite group. In this context there are no chiefly shares, and the minister is not present to witness the event. Rank, in other words, is recognized solely by a group's ability to overwhelm its competitor

Figure 10. The magistrate brings a large basket of food to the church in the center of the village on Wūjlañ on the morning of December 25, 1976. Note the spotlessly clean grounds. (Photograph by L. M. Carucci)

in *kaṃōḷu*—and the quantity and quality of its foods provide a core representation of achieved identity. The pattern of the feast follows the generic model, with introductory speeches, gifts of food, entertainment, and orations of thanksgiving. Indeed, the group that gives most generously, given its means, is also honored. Here, then, the generic feasting format is transposed into a symbolic device that allows for the simultaneous demonstration of intragroup unity and intergroup competition, in which winning depends on the performative abilities of each *jepta*. One critical measure of that ability is vested in the ability to stage a superior communal feast.

Kalbuuj and *karate* are the preemptive strikes that are coordinated with the time of *kaṃō̧lu*. Because they are uniquely Wūjlañ forms, local people use these games to lay claim to local elements of community identity. In outline, however, both activities are householding games that transform activities within the domestic sphere into the collective domain, providing a core operational template for inter-*jepta* relationships. The generic feasting format assists in this transition from domestic to public because the *keemem* itself, the most common generic feast, exists on this very interface.

As games of warfare and marriage, both *kalbuuj* and *karate* provide the arena in which the women of one *jepta* and the men of another confront one another, interact as metaphoric marriage mates in games of domestic play, and reconfirm the lines of *jepta* opposition. Whereas *kalbuuj* places men in the domestic sphere to cook and care for captured women, *karate* plays the *kalbuuj* householding game in reverse, making women the prime instigators. Both ritual games are made humorous by reversing typical male-female modes of acting through inversion of spatial modalities, the manipulation of gender stereotypes, and the altered presentation of foods. At the same time, the feasting structure still relies on generic patterns of speech giving, food exchange, and songs of thanksgiving. In both cases, domestic alignments are represented in contorted ways that make them particularly humorous.

As with *kaṃō̧lu, karate* and *kalbuuj* shape the generic feast to their own purposes. Whereas participants in *kaṃō̧lu* exchange equivalent items on an equal footing, *karate* and *kalbuuj* adopt the gender stereotypes of the domestic unit, with different practices appropriate for each gender. Mat-making materials are taken from the women by the men in *kalbuuj,* and women consume cooked foods given to them by male members of the other *jepta*. Raw fish are taken from men by women in *karate,* and men consume foods presented to them by female members of the other group. In each instance, the feasts are fashioned not only to empower the winners of the encounter but also to legitimize a certain set of social practices that are suited to a complementary balance rooted in gender difference.

In the games of *karate* and *kalbuuj* the representational values of the *jepta* are greatly clarified. The symbols of incorporation that people associate with bilateral extended families and the oppositional, competitive characteristics of the clans (discussed in chapter 2) are appropriated and used during *Kūrijmōj* precisely because this renewal celebration is the setting par excellence in which reproductive vigor is transferred from gods to humans. The energy and vigor brought into being during *Kūrijmōj* ultimately become the creational forces that permit families and clans to continue to perpetuate themselves as earthly entities. These aims are accomplished with humor, because the metaphoric battles and unions are games. Creating happiness, one important aim of *Kūrijmōj,* is thereby fully aligned with the energy-seeking aims of the performance.

Karate on Wūjlañ must be understood in the contexts of its logical generation—Japanese self-defense and karate hero Bruce Lee (Prujlii). The most popular film genre in the Marshall Islands, karate emphasizes essential elements of ideal male activity (those also attributed to the activities of the successful warriors of old) (Carucci 1987a, 1987b). In spite of Wūjlañ and Āne-wetak people's familiarity with all sorts of war films, westerns, and filmic violence in outer space, a great preference is expressed for karate films. People say that the karate expert—particularly the prototype, Bruce Lee—is "very much a man." His abilities approach the superhuman as, singlehandedly, he challenges and defeats the entire world with only his own hands. In other violent films, fighters rely on guns and other weapons. The methods of violent activity, therefore, reflect directly on the culturally ideal persona, particularly because, in the 1970s, all films were thought to depict reality.

Other activities are considered appropriate to "real men," but no single form of expression so ideally encompasses ideal male activities as does karate (cf. Chuukese characterizations of "real men" in Marshall 1979). Karate conjures up the exploits of ancient warriors, for it was within the ability of men like Juraan and N̄iinjuraan to "jump as high as coconut trees," "grasp [catch] spears," and "take three or four men and throw them into the ocean." Perhaps the most notable difference between warriors of old and Bruce Lee is that the ancients are said to have been of gigantic proportion, with "legs as large as breadfruit trees and arms as big around as coconuts." In comparison, Bruce Lee is a moderately sized folk hero.

Size, however, only reinforces Lee's popularity, for living Marshallese are comparatively diminutive in stature. The superhuman strengths of Bruce Lee allow atoll dwellers to positively assess their own power—a small people from tiny atolls with a World War II– and nuclear-testing–era knowledge of the strength of outsiders (Carucci 1989). Thus Bruce Lee, perhaps more appropriately than Āne-wetak's own ancient heroes, gives credence to their personal potential. As their great historic tradition is effaced and reconceived through encounters with the Western world, a new and uniquely Wūjlañ form emerges. In an isolated island world, Āne-wetak people of the past could easily construct empowered images of themselves. In the context of the expansive outside world that many Āne-wetak people have had the opportunity to see, these positive images have not been abandoned, but they have taken new and innovative forms. The Marshallese identification with the karate expert resituates physical and physiographic selves; it lends the hope of a great island region to a tiny, unarmed state at the moment of its emergence among other large and powerful nations of the world.[2] Moreover, Prujlii condenses the dreams of Wūjlañ people, until 1980 the most disenfranchised of atoll groups.

In the *karate* of *Kūrijmōj,* women control the powers that prototypically characterize men. The liminal character of the ritual cycle rests on these role reversals, and the inversion of expected arrangements of daily life introduces entertaining elements to the game of *karate*. This emotive tenor makes manifest one overall cause of celebration, the creation of happiness. But *karate* is ritual confrontation, itself a dramatic performance: all acts of real aggression are strictly tabued during the celebration. The different reactions to ritual and real aggression are particularly apparent in people's responses to real violence on December 25. People feared a fight in 1977 because it broke the prohibition on aggression, it contradicted the aims of the celebration, and retrospectively, it was believed to be a primary cause of the typhoon that followed (see chapter 1). In contrast to real confrontation, the ritualized battles of *Kūrijmōj* depict the deeds of ancient conquerors, the overthrow of the pagan era, and the breaking of old habits grown sour in the past year and concentrate on renewal and an improved existence in the future.[3] Indeed, these activities are the core of the celebration on Wūjlañ Atoll.

During the celebration of *Kūrijmōj* segments of time and objects normally of a mundane character are made sacred. The accepted rules of daily action are inverted in this liminal time, but objects and persons are transformed more subtly. At times, special clothing or gift wrapping with a sprig of palm may transform an entity, but objects and persons often appear mundane. In their very existence as part of the celebration, however, the mundane may become sanctified. This sanctity is clarified in statements about valuables being "the objects of God" or, equally correct, "the essence of God" *(an irooj* or *an anij).* Participants in the celebrations are also said to be "doing the work of God," "working in truth and kindness," and "creating happiness and well-being." Thus objects and persons are subtly set apart as elements of the sacred segment of time termed *Kūrijmōj.* The sacred character of the celebration is reinforced by special sentiments that surround its enactment, attitudes not expressed toward everyday life. *Kūrijmōj* is the most important event of the Marshallese yearly cycle. Once in full swing, nothing supersedes activities in support of *Kūrijmōj.* All other labors are secondary and should be suspended if they conflict with *Kūrijmōj.* Persons who go about their daily affairs when ritual activities should be pursued are said to be very stuck-up or self-seeking. Such persons will bring about their own destruction, and death is a possible result.

The interactions of the songfest groups also index their liminal and sacred character. One reason people say the *jepta* are specific to *Kūrijmōj* is to separate the groups from the everyday world. The aim is to capture the primordial past and contact the sacred sources of power, and the *jepta* organization replicates, at an important indexical level, recollections of ancient times when the halves of Āne-wetak are said to have been related as marriage partners. Jittōk-eņ and Jitto-eņ, Āne-wetak and Ānjepe, and before that, Āne-wetak and Wurrin are conceived of in these idealized terms. From these roots Āne-wetak people trace their beginnings; their continuation and proliferation are grounded in the potency of these successful primordial affinal arrangements.

In spite of the historic analogies, however, the *jepta* are not survivals of these earlier groups. Rather, the ritual involvements of the *jepta* draw strength from the early unions. The fertility and increase sought in the festive cycle must be traced to their ritually empowered source. Each performance attempts to reproduce the successful inception of Āne-wetak people in order to tap the undiluted potency of those initial creative moments.

To realize the transformation, the *jepta* reorder day-to-day interactions decisively. Each group includes members of different clans, and, as the battles begin, members of the same clan are opposed to one another in the games of warfare and sexual reproduction. The overall festive aim is to unify the sacred and the profane, to allow everyday humans to tap the sacred source of power that allows life to continue. In this pursuit, the games of *Kūrijmōj* collapse the boundaries of the tabu. The liminal activities of the *jepta* bring relatives who are "prohibited" *(mo)* to one another together and involve them in sexual jokes and ritual confrontations that overthrow day-to-day arrangements.

Indeed, the jokes and affectations of *Kūrijmōj* would be highly tabu in day-to-day life. Ritual selves are brought into direct conflict with day-to-day personae. Indeed, many younger men and women are not able to disavow their mundane selves. They flee the scene in great embarrassment when their ceremonial actions prove too discordant with the rules that govern daily life. In response to questions about their embarrassment, a pair of young men responded, "It [what people said] is all the same [does not matter], for it is a type of game," and "Our embarrassment was on account of those women [female age mates], but the action is to create our happiness."

In the course of *karate,* the women enact the role of men. They instigate the encounter, a particularly male prerogative, and all *karate* activities take place in the bush, the peripheral male sphere. Women direct the action during this game, and, at its conclusion, men are clearly under women's control. They help with final food preparations and carry the women's wares back to the village. Men, the normal providers of raw foods, give their catch to the women. The "thieves" may cook and consume parts of the booty with their newfound "spouses" or take it home to feed their own families (or members of their own *jepta*). The men are always provided with cooked foods and, at a joking level, with the sexual favors of their ritual spouses.

The liminal character of *karate* is coded in conversations filled with sexual banter. These innuendoes are reinforced by actions on both sides. (The men willingly hand over the catch and help with preparations, and the women respond with cooked foods.) The activities and discourse both index the symbolic marriage that has taken place. Talk tells of the women's willingness to fulfill the sexual desires of the men as long as the men provide for the needs of the women. Promises of daily provision follow. Raw foods of the men and cooked foods of the women, when exchanged, signify the realities of domestic life. Metaphors of fishing and cooking are used freely to doubly code the domestic responsibilities of men and women and to joke about the reciprocal cross-gender sex play of men and women. In this metaphoric world of sexual engagements, men "fish" for women as they go about their daily tasks, and with luck they hook and catch them. Women, who, as we have seen, cook the highly valued complements to a meal provided by men, use their cookware to "cook" men, in the language of sex play.

The labors of "fishing until exhaustion" seem incompatible with *karate,* when one sacrifices one's catch freely to women from another *jepta* until its parallel meanings (that is, chasing female companions until exhaustion) are taken into account. "Cooking until near death" and "feeding until others can not eat another little piece" seem counterproductive activities for *jepta* women unless their metaphoric meanings about the sexual prerogatives that women control are noted. Production and reproduction are, in the context of *karate,* forced to move through their respective cycles of development and fulfillment. Men fish—for edibles and women—and provide complements for women to cook as they enjoy the sexual favors of their cross-sex companions. Women cook—raw foods and men—and provide cooked foods for men as they enjoy the sexual favors of their opposite-sex mates. Cooking, a critical contribution women make to the domestic group, is seen as parallel to the growth cycle in which foods ripen and are eaten, or else they rot.

The activities of *karate* exploit the power women have to invigorate the growth cycle through the use of cooking metaphors with sexual referents. Men are not irrelevant to these growth processes, because continual shared sexual intercourse shapes the soft, external parts of a fetus, thus lending external form to an infant. Only when properly provided for by their fathers do children continue to develop pleasing physical contours and desirable external personality features. *Karate* provides an applied arena in which these representations of reproduction and growth are used to create states of being. In both form and content *karate* instantiates critical components of the cycles of regeneration and renewal that *Kūrijmōj* seeks to fulfill.

Other components of *karate* support the themes of fertility and increase. In their roles as providers for, and inseminators of, women, men mediate between female reproductive capabilities and the sacred, primordial beings who lend their life's force to the earth. This is indexed by the fact that the raw foods the men give up are the "catch of the deities." The uncooked foods parallel the resources sought from the deities in the celebration of *Kūrijmōj,* and men, as providers of the highly ranked and greasy foods, re-create the hoped-for actions of the ancient deity Jebrọ.

This condensation of the provisioning capacity of men and gods is doubly marked in women's jokes about men from another *jepta.* On one occasion, Ioḷap men, fishing their way along the edge of the lagoon reef, were hailed by Jitto-eņ women: *"Leddik ran ar; eḷae eḷae!"* (Imagine that! Young women on the lagoon side; there is a slick, there is a slick!). Only the men fishing in the lagoon, not birds or flat water, were visible. A combination of referents is indicated. *Leddik ran* refers to a group of birds flying in a windward or leeward direction above lagoon waters, often just off the interior reef. The birds' windward or leeward inclination indicates one of two interpretations: "There is news" (that a ship is arriving, for example) or "Many supernatural beings are around" (that a death or some other, unwanted change will occur). The connection between young, productive women and sacred force is particularly evident in this metaphor. *Eḷaē* (the slick) is a related sign that can indicate that

Figure 11. Jitto-eņ men fish along the lagoon shore of Āne-wetak Atoll in 1978. At risk of *karate,* secret fishing expeditions are frequent during *Kūrijmōj* as competition among *jepta* becomes keen. (Photograph by L. M. Carucci)

a death or another event of superhuman character is imminent. The directionality of the slick reveals the actual meaning (that there is news or that a death will occur), and the end of the slick may point to the potential victim. On Wūjlañ, *eļae* is often termed *iaļ* (path)—a route or trail along which beings are united. As pertaining to the women's joke, the path of the great chiefs Jebrọ drags across the sky (also termed *iaļ*) is intermingled with the fishermen's path. *Iaļ* also means rainbow, a marker of Jebrọ. Jebrọ, the generous provider who cares for his mother, leads the array of divine chiefs across the sky and marks the new year (cf. Makemson 1941).

Represented here in ritual form by the generous men, Jebrǫ is welcomed by the women. The men, encouraged in a humorous way to enact Jebrǫ's youngest-sibling role, do so readily because they receive promises of sexual satiation in return. They give their foods, the catch of deities, to women in order to fulfill their proper roles as providers for the domestic unit. The foods are the "catch of the gods," the highly valued edibles that Jebrǫ makes greasy to sustain people on earth. Like chiefs, deities must remunerate the gifts from earthly beings, and Jebrǫ, who is particularly associated with kindness and who oversees the cosmos during the winter months, provides the gateway for the exchanges of *Kūrijmōj*. In *karate,* in other words, people not only request the kindness and generosity of Jebrǫ but also fashion a game that forces Jebrǫ to participate in an ongoing exchange and provide the reproductive and regenerative powers that humans require. Their metonymic game models the interactions of men and women in the domestic sphere and, through the use of humorous inversions, "trick" providers into giving up their goods to secure the benefits of a more highly valued exchange.

It is interesting to note that the qualities of kindness and generosity associated with Jebrǫ are realigned with Wūjlañ interpretations of Christ. Scenes of Joseph and Mary in Bethlehem, of wise men, and of the manger are barely mentioned during *Kūrijmōj.* Wūjlañ people find other themes more evocative, including the story of a mature Jesus and his disciples who, returning from mourning John the Baptist, fed the crowds of townsfolk with five loaves and two fish (Matthew 14). At first, this often-quoted Yuletide tale struck me as anomalous, but the parallels between Jesus's magically multiplying loaves and fishes and Jebrǫ's magically lending fertility to the regeneration of nature are undeniable. In *karate,* domestic alignments are humorously posited in which sexual favors are promised and raw fish and cooked loaves are exchanged for one another. It is an arena in which each thing being sought during *Kūrijmōj* is caused to come into being.

Another element makes this abstract level of meaning apparent. Again, the interactions among *jepta* instantiate desired qualities to be derived from the ascendant deity Jebrǫ. A comparison with the water-throwing ceremony in Hawai'i helps us interpret the ritual inundations and water splashing that regularly are a part of *karate* (cf. chapter 7). At its most obvious level, inundation and splashing ritually cleanse the participants, an important component of renewal that lines up with cleaning the village, wearing new (or spotlessly cleaned) clothes, and replacing the paving stones on the household grounds. In the Hawai'ian water throwing, however, bathing represents more than ritual cleansing. It is a form of intercourse between chiefs and commoners that results in the "birth" of the god Lono. When the chiefs and commoners emerge from the water after their frolicking, the image of Lono awaits them on the shore. In *karate* the symbolism is not so sequentially iconic, but the inundations definitely contain an element of frolic that ritually overthrows the tabu. In this case, sexual contact is instigated between the men of one *jepta* and the women of another *jepta*. The reproductive power of the women is intermingled with the men's inseminational potency, a fact encoded in the rampant sexual jokes of *karate*. Whether the men and women also represent the interactions of sacred beings and everyday humans is less clear in the Wūjlañ celebration. The complex explanation of the Jitto-eņ women's joke and comparisons with Hawai'i suggest the viability of this additional layer of interpretational possibility, but certainly the parallel between the men's playing provider for an enacted domestic unit and Jebrọ's providing for the entire community remains at the level of analogy. When I asked directly about this interpretation on Āne-wetak, people just laughed. Even for non-Christians, it would be far too presumptuous for any Āne-wetak person to claim to be "playing God."

The central meanings of *karate* are far more clear-cut: the game uses inversion to overthrow the status quo and ritually enacts a new reproductive beginning by re-creating the initial conditions on Āne-wetak Atoll. Domestic arrangements are reenacted, with males and females each contributing the goods required of them, and promises of continued sexual intercourse create the conditions for the continuity and viability of the union. The men's part as providers for families replicates the desired actions of Jebrọ. These games, in their very performance, thus construct the conditions of renewal and increase to ensure the fulfillment of the core aims of *Kūrijmōj*.

If the analysis is correct, the same elements found in the entire celebration are refashioned in abbreviated form for *karate*. Just as significant, though less frequent, is the game of *kalbuuj,* an inverse counterpart to *karate*. Both involve indexical elements portrayed in other parts of the celebration, but each condenses the ritual forms in time and space. Whereas *karate* inverts daily rules by placing females in charge of a game of warfare and sexual encounter, *kalbuuj* places men in positions normally occupied by women. *Karate* takes place in the bush, the male spatial domain, whereas *kalbuuj* transpires in the village, the female spatial domain. *Karate* rearranges the roles of men—those who challenge the dangerous forces of the outside world, provide highly valued complements for the community, and lend external (visible) form to children. *Kalbuuj* rearranges women's roles—those who manage households, make clothing, transform foods into meals, and transmit the core elements of person to their offspring (the elements of clan identity). These are not the sole contrasts, but they are significant metaphoric elements of *Kūrijmōj*.

Like *karate, kalbuuj* constructs the ritual conditions of its own fulfillment and thus indexically codes the message that the game conveys. *Kalbuuj* (literally, prison) is a men's game in which females caught on the village lands of an opposite *jepta* are taken hostage (see p. 25). But the hostages are not treated like prisoners; instead, as guests, they are welcomed and fed like chiefs. While the prisoners are in the territory of the opposing *jepta,* they are the center of attention and the focus of much sexual joking. When they are finally given back to their own group, they are not returned as the person who was kidnapped but, rather, as an opposite-sex member of that *jepta*.

The elements of *kalbuuj* provide further support for the central intentions of *Kūrijmōj*. Like *karate, kalbuuj* contains a condensed glimpse of the total ritual, but enacted in a manner precisely the inverse of *karate*. Females control male spaces and the rules of interaction in the domestic arrangements of *karate,* whereas *kalbuuj* allows men to manipulate female spaces and specify domestic conditions in their interactions with women. Again, the reversal of the rules of daily existence, the breaking of the tabu, not only creates the liminal and sacred conditions through which *kalbuuj* fulfills reproductive and regenerative aims of the celebration but also qualifies as great entertainment. The promotion of happiness is thereby ensured.

For Wūjlañ people, sexual attractiveness is unequally divided between males and females. In the American folk model, sexual attractiveness is rooted in natural, drive-motivated impulses. It thus qualifies as a prototypically emotive arena (see Lutz 1988) in which humans are not entirely able to control their emotions. On Wūjlañ, females have a similar attractiveness, rooted not in nature but in human propensities. The irresistible character of women, from the perspective of Marshallese men, is the flip side of sexual necessity. It is unhealthy for a man to go without sex, and a man who is denied the release provided by sexual activity will certainly become ill. Death may even result. Women are irresistible in that they possess that which is essential to men's livelihood. A certain mystical element also accompanies a woman's reproductive capacities, and capturing the essence of this reproductive force is a critical part of *Kūrijmōj. Kalbuuj* is a ritual that accomplishes this. In daily life, men possess none of this inherent irresistibility, for women do not possess the same sexual needs. This is not to say that men cannot make themselves irresistible. As we shall see, they do so quite successfully through external display. Men, however, are more marginal to the reproductive process than are women, for they do not manage the mystical reproductive force controlled by women.

This theory of sexuality and inherent female irresistibility makes the logic of the game of *kalbuuj* more transparent. In *kalbuuj,* men become manipulators of allure to attract women from an opposite group to the domestic sphere they ritually control.[4] In the ceremonial encounter, the women realize beforehand the dangers that *kalbuuj* poses to their successful gathering activities. Yet, in a manner parallel to men's going for foods that are certain to be taken in *karate,* the potential of being caught does not prevent women from crossing the territory of another *jepta* to collect pandanus fronds for weaving or buried shells for making handicrafts. In words reminiscent of the cavalier attitudes of young, male suitors, one young woman responded, "Who cares if they throw us in jail *(kalbuuj),* they will feed us and watch over us until the time they return us to this place."

Kalbuuj, however, is not carried out to obtain short-term economic reward. Instead, like *karate,* it ritually fashions the domestic unit in distorted ways in order to create happiness. Men control women's spaces while women wander and take on the day-to-day role of men, who should "travel around while women stay in one place." Young women often travel into the bush in small gathering groups, but in daily life they do so with caution, not with the abandon reserved for *Kūrijmōj*. Once captured, the women's bold jesting with their captors is also somewhat uncharacteristic, because men are the ones who should take the initiative in interactions with women. In their travels, men will come into the view of outsiders, people from other towns and other atolls. But in *kalbuuj,* women travel about in the territory of others and bring themselves into public view.

The men remain fixed, entrap the wandering women in their own territory, and take their collected goods. Most often the goods are pandanus fronds, representative of the primordial weaving materials that Wūjlañ women use to manufacture fine mats and that they once used (in certain varieties) to manufacture clothing. Both are prototypical types of female production. Just as the fish that women capture in *karate* contribute to a *jepta*'s ability to *kaṃōḷu,* the fronds that men capture in *kalbuuj* contribute critically to a songfest group's presentations on December 25. But overcoming hardship is an expected part of daily life, and on Wūjlañ and Āne-wetak it is an important component of *Kūrijmōj*.

Once captured, women are brought into the cookhouse, fed, and treated in grand style. Here the game stresses valued aspects of marital relationships, but in inverse fashion. Men bring the women into the part of the domestic sphere controlled by women. They feast the captives, thereby making them feel indebted, make them comfortable, and prepare sleeping places for them. In so doing, the men take on the qualities of protectiveness and loving typical of females within households and bilateral extended families. When a knowledgeable person recommends a potential marriage to a young man, it is said of the woman's family, "They are good, that family, they will watch over you." This is the woman's part, to stay put, to provide stability and protectiveness (the qualities associated with extended families). Women counterbalance men, whose position is to "walk around on this earth." The woman "remains still" or "stays in one place." A man is expected to be transient and have little sense of fiscal responsibility prior to marriage. When he marries he sacrifices these qualities of real men and begins to build new sources of renown and respect within the community (Carucci 1985).

These are the characteristics of men that women enact in *kalbuuj*. Cared for in the extreme, to parody daily life, by the end of their ordeal, captive women agree that the members of their newly established domestic units are better, and certainly more considerate, than those in their own group. The parodied character of the performance is marked by this excessive indulgence, for, in daily existence, total negligence of one's own relatives in favor of those of one's spouse would be detrimental. The family that adopted me, when making suggestions about how to deal with a particular woman they recommended to me as a wife, said, "Watch that they do not make you think crazy thoughts, for you, sir, are the real offspring of Jalij [the head of the *bwij*]. Do not think of throwing away [disowning] your grandmother." The suggestion was meant to ensure that my family of orientation would not be forgotten even if I decided to marry into another family.

Kalbuuj, however, overwhelms captives with foods and hospitality so that they become totally enamored with the opposing group. In everyday unions there is always an initial inundation with favors, but within a few weeks time the spouse will be expected to help out and "take a little of the weight" of family responsibilities. Separations between spouses are not uncommon when the in-married partner to the marriage feels that he or she is doing all of the spouse's family's work. So much attention is paid the captives in *kalbuuj* that the women perform absolutely no labor. They are treated as guests and receive the privileges of chiefs. The women's treatment as strangers, structurally equivalent to the men's position in *karate,* is reinforced by the many jokes that the women "travel around" or have "lost their direction." The jokes point to the role reversals but also to sexual opportunism, for wandering women without direction are easily seduced. In the words of a favorite young men's chant, "Rub it [female] back and forth, for she has lost direction."

The best of each meal is set aside for the captives. If there is not a pig or chicken to be sacrificed by the family that is harboring captives, a special group of fishermen will be sent out to make sure there will be some form of complement for each meal. The food fed to the guests is given on behalf of the *jepta;* fishing parties are comprised of *jepta* members, and the *jepta* will repay foods to the families who have watched captives, when such foods are available.

Overindulging prisoners forces them to admit to feelings of solidarity with their captors. Here the ambivalence of young males caught between the attractions of marriage and the idealized existence of the single young man (see Carucci 1990 for further detail) is decisively shaped to suit the ritual aims of irresistibility so central to *Kūrijmōj.* If such a thing occurred in everyday life, a man's family of orientation would feel slighted and would be upset. It would contend that the family of its offspring's spouse had made the young man think crazy thoughts. In the context of celebration, though, with women acting the part of their day-to-day domestic counterparts, the captive women readily walk the path of irresistibility in *kalbuuj* that leads to marriage (and ultimately to the reproduction of the social order). Their readiness is promoted by the deified treatment they receive. This treatment doubly codes their position as guests and outsiders: first, as mimics of men within a domestic unit controlled by women where men are, nonetheless, said to head the small bilateral extended family (males are the *bōrwaj* or *a̧lap* of the household); and second, as templates for deities who will also be irresistibly attracted into exchanges with earthly beings during the celebration of *Kūrijmōj.*

Even though, in daily life, newlyweds should split their allegiance and support between their families of orientation and of procreation, in *kalbuuj* the members of a woman's home *jepta* do not blame the men for having made their women crazy. The new allegiance of one of their members is not upsetting, for portrayals of successful reproduction within domestic groups is critical to *Kūrijmōj*. Indeed, when the captives are returned (as opposite-sexed characters), their *jepta* will receive gifts from the kidnappers. Using the logic of a strict clan order, the gifts reciprocate the *jepta* for the loss of a captive's labor. Equally, however, they recognize a woman's reproductive success.

The captive's *jepta* does not intend to benefit from these gifts. Indeed, the larger the prestations the captors give when the prisoners are returned, the more their *jepta* will be seen to have won the encounter. The imprisoning *jepta* members flaunt their pride when—or even before—they return the prisoners. They loudly boast about how well the imprisoned person likes her new home, how the prisoner consumes the most preferred foods, and how she is being treated with great privilege. The members of the imprisoning *jepta* claim that the captives are so satisfied that they wish to remain with the group forever. The captives' satisfaction is talked about in terms of the unlimited quantities of highly desired, cooked foods they receive and also in terms of innuendos of their sexual fulfillment.

All of this rhetoric is important to the ritual on two levels, for complementary types of interpretation are involved. Through their actions, the women enact the roles that the community requires of the deities. They are irresistibly attracted and are so happy with their treatment as guests that they readily agree to the domestic arrangements with living beings where they will aid in the propagation of both humans and nature. The other *jepta* is not upset at the loss of its females, for the entire community benefits from their allegiance to the newly constituted domestic group. In this ceremonial position, the women act in a complementary manner to the fishermen captured in *karate*. With *karate*, the men act like a foreign group that provides food for humanity; in *kalbuuj*, the women represent a foreign group that controls the reproductive force humans require. Imbalanced gift-giving supports this communicative level, for the group that engages in either *karate* or *kalbuuj* gives unreciprocated gifts, prestations in huge quantity that allow the captors to boast of their success: success at gaining access to raw foods, in the case of *karate*, and success at gaining access to women's productive capacities as the makers of mats, clothing, and, most important, children of a clan, in *kalbuuj*. Through these games, the ritual conditions that guarantee productive and reproductive success are constructed.

A second communicational level, which takes as its interpretational context the competition among *jepta*, reinforces the first. The group that captures women, lavishes them with care, and returns them as males, along with gifts, also wins the encounter. The men's public jokes insinuate that the women are totally satisfied, sexually as well as emotionally, and, although actual inseminations seldom if ever occur, the discourse recognizes the metaphoric good fortune. The imprisoning *jepta* gains community honor through these mimes of family life in which the sacred reproductive force that will benefit the entire community is ritually captured and used to metaphorically perpetuate earthly life. The *jepta* that has captured the women win a significant encounter in their competition with other songfest groups, and, in complementary fashion, the men's win in *kalbuuj* parallels the women's in *karate*. Necessary first conditions of social life have been replicated: opposed clan groups are reunited across gender lines in ways that humorously stress the complementary oppositions of male and female, insider and outsider.

Those held captive in *kalbuuj* never disagree with proclamations of the privileged care they have received. Indeed, disagreement would be difficult, for their care is exceptional. But when captives are returned, a skilled orator makes his statements in such a way that the captives could not possibly contradict him. One such orator noted, for example, that the captives did not want to return, so superior were the activities of the other *jepta*. Its singing and dancing were superb, and the care was such that the captive women decided to remain with their captors. This speaker then asked the women, in a fashion difficult to deny, "Is it not true that the food you consumed was very delicious? Is it not true that the singing and dancing were extremely good?" The orator then uses the positive responses to his cautiously phrased queries as confirmation of the captives' pleasure with their newfound family. Because they have been treated with privilege as guests, as prototypes for the actions desired of the deities, the captives cannot deny the claims of the orator. Indeed, they are in a position of indebtedness to the *jepta,* precisely the aim the community wishes to impose on the deities.

One of the most significant aspects of *kalbuuj* takes place when the prisoners are returned. The captive's gender is indexically reversed by clothing her in male attire. A good deal of humor derives from the reversal, because the missionary-inspired dress styles of the current era definitively mark distinctions between men and women. Specifically Marshallese interpretations of propriety accompany the introduced styles, differing considerably from what the missionaries had in mind. Nonetheless, dress not only segments males and females, it also separates those whom Marshallese consider "being in the darkness" (that is, unexposed to the "light" of Christianity, like Yapese and certain other Pacific groups) from those who, like Marshall Islanders, live "in the light." Dress is also a marker that separates Marshall Islanders of today from those of their ancient past.

Several parts of the *Kūrijmōj* message are coded in dress, but the reversals during *kalbuuj* are among the most important. Given the sharp gender divisions in dress style,[5] it is not surprising that *jepta* members gain so much entertainment value from the sexual reversals of *kalbuuj*. The jokes that accompany *kalbuuj* deal with the role-specific qualities of the persons the captives become. Once they are dressed as men, captured females are complimented on their handsomeness and doused with cologne to "ready them for chasing women." Even though *kalbuuj* is primarily a game in which women are imprisoned, on rare occasions men are captured. In such cases the men will be dressed as women and complimented on their great beauty.

Although many gender markers could be selected to represent gender reversal, I believe that *kalbuuj* uses clothing as the marker of choice because (like fish or canoes for males) it is the female good par excellence. Not only do females now manufacture clothing from imported cloth, they manufactured local cloth from pandanus fronds and hibiscus fibers in the ancient past (cf. Weiner 1989, 1992). And, although the actual reasons a group of women may travel into the bush vary, in the case of *kalbuuj* they are prototypically depicted as traveling into the bush to retrieve pandanus fibers to be transformed into fine mats that will form a valuable part of a songfest group's gifts to the minister on December 25. In ancient times, pure white mats were forms of women's wealth given to high chiefs on special ceremonial occasions, and the mats that accompany the array of gifts "intended for God" on December 25 draw important elements from such reminiscences of ancient times.

The logic behind returning prisoners to their *jepta* as beings of the opposite sex is located not entirely in its entertainment value but in a wide series of interpretative contexts that relate male to female, *karate* to *kalbuuj,* and *kalbuuj* to the general structure of the festivities. Gender shifts are required by the oppositional nature of *jepta* as they interact as warring and marrying groups. If the above analysis is correct, *kalbuuj* benefits humans by revivifying their reproductive potential; the changed sex of the returned prisoner indicates the ongoing character of the ritually constructed family arrangements. To return a spouse to the clan from which s/he came would be a mark of rejection. It would not only terminate the exchange between the two clans for this occasion but also would jeopardize further marriage arrangements between the two groups. As metaphoric representatives of clans, the *jepta* are able to manipulate the symbolic intent of each signifying relationship, and, in the case of *kalbuuj,* the celebratory aim is to represent successful marriages. The return of opposite-gendered prisoners promotes this symbolic goal because it is not the captured marital partner who is returned but, instead, an alter of the opposite gender who, now portrayed as a fully naturalized citizen of the new *jepta,* serves to reciprocate the captured person and perpetuate the exchange. On Wūjlañ, with its rules of bilateral cross-cousin marriage, the ideal-type patterns of *kalbuuj* maximize their aims of symbolic empowerment by projecting a series of symbolic marriage arrangements into the future and projecting them as a template for the desired actions of the deities.

THE COSMOLOGICAL BALANCE OF KARATE *AND* KALBUUJ

With the games of *karate* and *kalbuuj* the ambivalent potentials of a set of gendered categories is added to the balanced relationship that exists between the *jepta* as they interact more typically elsewhere in the Marshall Islands. The ambivalent ways in which Wūjlañ and Āne-wetak people describe gendered relationships in general give the domain as a whole highly productive symbolic potential. Both the ambivalence and the potential for productivity make the Wūjlañ games of *karate* and *kalbuuj* extremely enjoyable. Wūjlañ and Āne-wetak people recognize their uniqueness and attractiveness and rely on the games, particularly *karate,* the more perduring and popular, to mark the distinctiveness of *Kūrijmōj* as "the best in the Marshall Islands," "the best in this region of the Pacific," or "the best on Earth."

In both *kalbuuj* and *karate,* the participants represent not only their respective *jepta* but also prototypes or primordial icons of the characteristics that define a gendered person on Wūjlañ Atoll. In spite of the gender reversals in *kalbuuj,* with men as the householders, women remain the only source of sacred reproductive power, the very characteristic that is vested in the female clan heads who first brought living humans into being. The continued guarantee of reproductive potency is precisely what *Kūrijmōj* requires in order to ensure the continuity of the social order. With *kalbuuj,* the reproductive power that women control is metaphorically incorporated into each *jepta* as that *jepta* captures and confines members of another group. Similarly, the reversals of *karate* place women in the men's domain; yet, at the same time, the men represent prototypical providers who, like their primordial forebears, are equally imperative to the continuity of life on earth. Not only do women take the food from male members of the other group, through representation, the ongoing ability of men to provide harvest fruits from the atoll is perpetuated. By reenacting the prototypical characteristics of males and females since the beginning of time, the preconditions for fecundity and plenty in the upcoming year are established.

In sum, the unique games of *karate* and *kalbuuj* are core components of *Kūrijmōj* that shape desired, primordial forces to human ends. Important subsistence and reproductive components of regeneration and increase are brought to earth through these games. The two types of play capture their correlative elements (provisioning and insemination; reproductive force and domestic continuity) in inverse ways that correspond with the complementary opposition between females and males. *Kalbuuj* involves women, as metonyms of the reproductive force controlled by primordial clan heads, in a game instigated by men but conducted in a household within the village, the female domain. In contrast, *karate* engages men, metonyms of primordial males like Jebrọ, generous caretaker and provider, in a mock conflict instigated by women but conducted in the bush, the masculine arena. Opposed to normal conditions, the women manipulate an active game *(karate)* typical of the movements of "real men," whereas the men engage women through a passive activity *(kalbuuj)* that signifies the daily stability of women. These liminal encounters condense the overall aims of the celebrations and give humans a way of gaining access to the symbolic attributes of the ascendant deity, Jebrọ, and to those of clan heads like his mother, Lōktañūr. Control of these forces is critical to social and physical well-being throughout the coming year. At the same time, the games remain competitive, giving the songfest groups a way to win by capturing opposite-sexed members of the other *jepta.* Interaction is intensified in order to win, which only increases the chances for the success of *Kūrijmōj*—success that is realized in the reproduction of the social order and the regeneration of nature.

CHAPTER FIVE

Supportive Devices

Spatial and Social Logistics

In the preceding chapters I sketched several ways in which various components of *Kūrijmōj* on Wūjlañ construct empowering ritual messages by confirming the legitimacy of symbols of daily life and then refashioning them into new shapes that accomplish the celebration's ritual labor. A look at how cultural provisions in physical and social space are manipulated in various performative contexts during the ceremonies will allow me to further elaborate on the interpretations of the festivity I have posited. These spheres provide the parameters for celebration activities; though not always the focal point of those activities, they are important cultural components used to both fashion and interpret meaning. In this chapter I describe two spatial features of central concern at *Kūrijmōj,* one abstract, the second entirely pragmatic: prototypical subdivisions of cosmological space and their use during the festivities, and the limitations placed on the movements of the *jepta* by the existing apportionment of land.

THE LANGUAGES OF SPATIAL RELATIONSHIP

Marshall Islanders use extremely fine-graded spatial distinctions, often in combination with an equally fine-graded set of distinctions of small-group relationships to talk about actions in the world. Both sets of categories convey information about what local people consider important, and, not surprisingly, the sets are interrelated. Quite commonly, the cosmology of spatial relationships is used in ritual, as in daily life, to convey important information about interpersonal relationships. Although games like *karate* and *kalbuuj* often define themselves in opposition to such prototypes, the stereotypes of social cosmology allow for a more nuanced appreciation of specific actions in a complex ritual like *Kūrijmōj*.

Lexical Domains of Directionality

Marshallese use three methods of speaking about directionality, each with its own rules of operation. The three not only overlap, they also intersect with other domains, including the temporal. Space and time are interwoven, and words that seem to fit one domain are commonly used to describe relationships in the other. To speak of any of these relations, therefore, reinforces a certain reified use, but it is precisely these sociospatial stereotypes that are used to convey meaning during *Kūrijmōj*. The three codes are analytically separable into a sea code, a land code, and an egocentric code (which describes ever-increasing concentric circles of definable space vis-à-vis the speaker). Obviously, all of the codes index the speaker, but, in the egocentric case, the speaker, as the center, provides the only relevant point of reference.

In terms of their use during *Kūrijmōj,* both the sea code and the egocentric one are used to describe ranked distinctions. The land code has differential typifications of direction but, in its use by Wūjlañ people, no inherent ranking. Through its standard associations with the sea code, however, the definitionally unranked character of the land code is not always apparent. The mechanisms of ranking employed by the egocentric and sea codes also differ, with the sea code incorporating a simple low–high discrimination; the center–periphery dynamics of the egocentric code offer a more diverse set of possibilities for ranking. From another perspective, however, the land and sea codes are viewed as logical opposites with different gender associations, the female land code and the male sea code, whereas the egocentric code has no gendered attributes.

Domains of Directionality: The Sea Code

The male-associated sea code is specific to spatial relationships in the male-coded domains—sea spaces and those of the sky. This male code allows one to divide space relative to a large, vertically oriented plane that rotates, like a wind gauge, around the head of the speaker. I use the metaphor of a wind gauge because wind direction is the determinant of the precise orientation (in "absolute" spatial terms) toward which the plane gravitates. Any location in this vertically oriented plane may be described, like coordinates on a graph, through the use of lexical segments that correlate points or locations vis-à-vis two imaginary lines that intersect at 90J̌ angles in the speaker's head. The positive end of the first line passes vertically through the head of the speaker and proceeds upward. The elevated end of this line is more highly ranked in a cultural sense than is the opposite end of the same line, which continues through the feet of the speaker and into the ground. The other line intersects the first in the speaker's "center," and its positive end points in a windward direction. The upwind end of this line is also more highly ranked in cultural terms than is the other end of the line, which continues from the speaker toward the leeward. The positive ends of each of these intersecting lines are associated. Both are culturally "higher," and, though the two "highs" are contextually separable, in many cases they are used interchangeably.

I refer to the code of sailing as a male code because it applies to orientations in relation to wind direction. It is the mode of orientation on the open sea, the male sphere, and it applies equally to directionality in navigations in the sky (often represented as an extension of the sea into the vertical plane). The male spatial code invokes simply ranked polarities, up and down, windward and leeward, and these often correspond symbolically with clear-cut discrimination between two otherwise similar entities. Like the men with whom it is associated, the sailing code moves about. It has no fixed coordinates but shifts its orientation with the movement of the prevailing winds.

Positive, windward, *-tak* (verb fragment) or *-taken̦* (noun fragment, a location) and ominous, negative, leeward, *-to* (verb) or *-toen̦* (location), illustrate this simple contrast. In terms of daily practices, birds flying windward bring good weather and good news, whereas those gliding downwind are omens of doom; high-ranked persons should be placed to the windward of low-ranked persons; and "pure" medicinal substances commonly must be taken from the windward tip of an islet or atoll. High and low are also representational equivalents. The high ranked should always remain elevated; low is associated with degeneracy, dirt, and doom. The most highly ranked frigate bird flies above all other birds; people claim that ancient chiefs were carried on platforms to elevate them above common people and mundane objects; and the purest medicinal substances must be mixed in the liquid of an unripe coconut taken from the highest part of the most windward cluster of nuts.

Domains of Directionality: The Land Code

In contrast to the sea code is the female land code. These fixed divisions of space are closer to those used by landlubbers in America, though they can be combined with other directional enclitics into a wide variety of spatially expressive lexical forms. The land code divides space on the earth's surface and in heaven into north, south, east, and west. The plane that passes through the speaker is horizontal, and, although the speaker provides the immediate frame of reference in terms of which the code is applied, the absolute points of orientation in this apportionment of space are relatively static. These culturally "absolute" points of orientation are commonly said to be based on the rising and setting sun and on a line that connects the North Star (Lim̧anm̧an) and the Southern Cross (Būbin Epoon, the grandmother of Epoon [the southernmost of the Marshall Islands], or *debwāāl in rak,* Southern Cross). Certainly, Wūjlan̄ and Āne-wetak people, who base their renewal festival cycle on the astronomic cycle, recognize that the rising and setting points of the sun vary considerably at different times of the year. Indeed, the perpetual southward "disappearance" of the sun is one feature that is of concern to people during the winter renewal celebration. Nevertheless, the sun is the rough marker of east and west, even though the best-informed navigators note that the quadrants occupied by certain stars as they appear and set actually specify the east-west line. These orienteers use a system more similar to that described for I Kiribati (Grimble 1931) than to techniques discussed by Thomas Gladwin for the Western Caroline Islands (1970: chap. 5) to establish an east–west orientation.

The male and female directional codes are not defined relative to their functional nature, for just as the feminine code may be used while sailing, the male code is applied to relations on land. The most important aspect of their gendered associations rests in the static nature of the female code and the variable nature of the male code. Winds are constantly moving about, but stars move along highly predictable paths that provide a constant grid for the interpretation of spatial relations on earth. The sky is divided into quadrants in which specific stars rise and set. Just as atolls are described as permanently affixed to the ocean's bottom on "house posts," so the dome of the heavens rests on series of posts that are affixed to earth, either four or six in number. For those who claim there are four posts, the points of contact are one-third north of the south "pole" (150° and 210°) and one-third south of the north "pole" (60° and 300°). The best known of these latter posts is *Liṃanṃan eṇ an N̄iinjib* (the place of Liṃanṃan's tooth hold), marked by a star in the Greek constellation Cepheus. For those who rest their heavens on six posts, the final two posts are aligned with the North Star and the Southern Cross. The analogous relationships among the placement of the house on the house plot (*eooṇlā*, a space heavily imbued with female symbolism), the placement of atolls on the bottom of the sea, and the anchor points of the universe does not escape Wūjlan̄ and Āne-wetak people. These are all residence locations, though the identities of the occupants vary.

Although north–south and east–west have semantic attributes, these attributes are not consistently ranked, as is the case with the windward–leeward, high–low plane. To the degree that some consistency does arise, it is directly associated with windward and leeward. But I believe that *rear* (east) is said by some to be more highly ranked than its opposite, *rālik,* because of its association with the windward. Both east and west contain associated elements of relevance to *Kūrijmōj:* west because it is associated with the point of origin for inhabitants of the Marshall Islands, and east because it is associated with the ongoing process of renewal that, being pushed from west to east, always finds its cutting edge on the easternmost fringe. Similarly, north and south have different significances associated with them, but they are not inherently ranked low and high. From the perspective of *Kūrijmōj,* the sun's incessant movement toward the south during the dry and blustery times of winter gives an ominous tinge to the southward orientation, but, in other contexts, north has equally ambivalent characteristics.

Domains of Directionality: The Egocentric Code

In addition to these two codes of spatial organization—the fixed north–south, east–west code and a mobile windward–leeward, up–down code—yet another code is used to place persons and things in a framework relative to a speaker's actual location or a narrative frame. Again, the code represents the objective realization of a cultural concern with precise placements of persons and things in relation to the speaker. Indeed, Marshallese have a true cultural fascination with spatial categorization as social arrangement. People, like objects, are "here by me" or "there by you" (the interpretant). When one of a series of persons or objects "there by you" is being designated, that specificity is indicated by reduplication (Bender 1969: 76). Placements at a distance from speaker and hearer but within a reasonable distance (the commonly overgeneralized Peace Corps Marshallese gloss for "there") or at a considerable distance from speaker and listener are common, and less specific spatial placements can be added to any of the above with the infix for "in the general area." When people are the specific object, a marker of gender for the person discussed often forms part of the locational lexeme. An expansive set of we and you plural affixes lend further detail to the cautious notation of spatial and social arrangements among listener, speaker, and one being spoken about.

Wūjlañ and Āne-wetak people utilize centric spatial orientation to metaphorize at least two important sorts of relationships, each of which is of significance to *Kūrijmōj*. The first of these relationships is that of surroundedness, *kōṇak*. Surroundedness is a relation of love, caring, and attachment that is reminiscent of Takeo Doi's discussion of Japanese *amae* (1973). Both the relationship of love between a man and a woman and the relationship of a mother to her developing fetus are described in terms of *kōṇak*. The literal implication of the concept is "being surrounded by," or "wearing" (as with a piece of clothing), and the imagery is used to evoke a sense of envelopment and total protection.

The same centric ordering is applied to the spatial organization of the island, where everything within the exterior reef is surrounded and protected. This includes both islets and lagoon. These interior spaces are represented as female spaces, and the metaphor of centrically organized space precisely parallels the surroundedness that women maintain vis-à-vis a fetus or a sexual partner. In the words of one Wūjlañ resident, the islands provide protection for the lagoon "like a mother protects the child in her stomach," so the islets (actually the surrounding reef) provide "calm for the sea within and, also, peacefulness for the people of this atoll." In a favorite church hymn, the "calm within the palm of God" is also described in terms parallel to the peaceful existence within the confines of the outer reef.

The centric model is applied with other metaphoric intentions, however, and some of these align with the ranked attributes that Claude Lévi-Strauss (1963: 128–60) has noted for this sort of structural arrangement. The focus here is not solely on encompassment, an attribute of the periphery, but also on the relationship between center and periphery. Not unlike Edward Shils (1970: 1–14), though at a very different level, Lévi-Strauss lends a teleology to this relationship that favors the center, and Wūjlañ and Āne-wetak people certainly use the model to describe center-focused modes of action. The god-chief–commoner relationship is often referred to in these terms. At the same time, however, the inverse possibility is frequently applied, and the surroundedness metaphor may be only a variant on this theme. In such cases, the combined weight of points along the periphery outweigh the center, and the teleology of the model points outward. Even though the classical description of chief–commoner relations points to the center, the model that revalues periphery over center is manifest in stories about chiefly dependence on commoners: "Without commoners (*kajoor,* strength), the chief has no strength."

In daily practice, the use of these spatial codes is often complicated by the fact that they overlap. For example, the residents of an islet often talk about its front side, because the residences are concentrated on the lagoon, and its back side, the relatively uninhabited side where people go to expose their own back sides on the reef as they defecate. From this perspective, the lagoon side seems more highly ranked, for the front of an atoll, like that of a person, is deserving of greater respect. Yet, antithetically, the ocean is also coded higher than the lagoon is. Men should walk on the ocean side of women; people of high rank, on the ocean side of those of lower rank. Therefore, the centric code may well come by part of its ambivalence through its intersection with the multivocalic, bipolar division between ocean and lagoon.

SPATIAL ORIENTATION IN THE PRACTICE OF KŪRIJMŌJ

All of these spatial relations are central to the performative aspect of *Kūrijmōj*. Indeed, *Kūrijmōj* is the most important festive event on Wūjlañ and Āne-wetak because, at one level, the wide array of ritual enactments that ensure its success require all participants to re-create the basic symbolic arrangements on which life on earth is based. The very reconstruction of the taken-for-grantedness of a culturally fashioned world allows *Kūrijmōj* to provide access to a certain psychosocial security (Douglas 1966: 41 et seq.; Geertz 1966) But *Kūrijmōj,* I believe, provides avenues of group and cultural empowerment far beyond these. The strategic use of the multiple significances of the different directional codes contributes in subtle but systematic ways to this empowerment.

Even within the practice groups, spatial orientations begin to order social practice in systematic ways that are carried through into other public arenas. For the first practices, recruits sit where they wish, but within a few days each "voice" begins to sit together. As a mark of emerging cohesion, altos, sopranos, basses, and tenors increasingly face one another in four small circles arranged around a piece of plywood or a chalkboard where the songs are written by the practice leader. Although the groupings in part offer a certain pragmatic advantage, the circular order is certainly of local inspiration, for it bears little resemblance to the linear groupings I recall from choirs of my youth. The circular order that begins here is carried through *kaṃōḷo,* and the return of *kalbuuj* captives, to the events of December 25 and New Year's Sunday. The fact that this arrangement puts some singers with their backs to the songfest leader and to the audience is of little concern, for each voice performs as a unit, and only one or two of the dominant singers of each voice need to see the director to keep the separate groups synchronized.

Windward and leeward, or ocean and lagoon, also come into play as women's groups voluntarily occupy the unranked position along one or both of these dimensions. Indeed, this particular gendered arrangement is so common in daily life that the pattern enters the practice house on the fringes of consciousness, but it is certainly a noteworthy social practice. On December 25 a third consideration enters into play, the relation of right to left. From the audience's perspective, male performers occupy right stage, while the two circles of women gather on the audience's left. The right side on Wūjlañ was also the location of the pulpit; though, on Āne-wetak, it is centered in front. The right–left pattern is particularly outstanding on Wūjlañ and Āne-wetak because the orientation of the churches places the women more or less upwind of the men. When I asked about the contradiction, one consultant noted that "it does not really matter here in the church because, inside, there is no wind." Therefore, having men buffeted with potential pollutants of women is, for this person, not an issue in this context. Historically, however, the right and left separation of men and women is justifiably recognized within the church because it is an arrangement that reflects missionary practice.

The circular arrangement, with its themes of unity, recurs on December 25, when each group performs its songs, explodes its tree, and dances around the exposed treasures. I describe these themes in detail in the next chapter, but it is important to note here the way in which the entire community is transformed into a communal body of celebrants at this time, as well as the way in which the centric orientation of the singing group surrounds the central object of binding exchange and is itself surrounded by the community as a whole and the walls of the all-encompassing church building. This becomes the repetitive message format of December 25 and a core defining moment of *Kūrijmōj.*

If unity is represented by these circular arrangements, hierarchical opposition between *jepta* is often included in *kaṃōḷo.* As I have indicated, conflicting views of hierarchy may come into play, but the home *jepta,* the group that hosts a *kaṃōḷo,* sits in a semicircle on the windward or ocean side of its practice house as the visitors who instigate the *kaṃōḷo* enter the setting. This arrangement inverts the guest or chiefly arrangements and gives the local group a subtle form of empowerment. As always, when windward and ocean side are not aligned, either a choice is made between the conflicting sources of rank or the logic of both rankings can be added to create new levels of rank. For example, the Jitto-eṇ practice house in 1977 extended from windward to leeward with long walls along the lagoon and ocean sides. When Ioḷap arrived to *kaṃōḷo,* Jitto-eṇ moved to the windward end, opening the leeward half for the guests. Although both Ioḷap and Jitto-eṇ men occupied the high-ranked ocean side of the building, when I asked a Jitto-eṇ man about the Ioḷap men on the ocean side he noted the Jitto-eṇ men's equally high position along with his group's position in the windward half of the dwelling. Only Jitto-eṇ men occupied the doubly high-ranked ocean-side, windward quadrant.[1]

A similar oppositional frame is used during *karate,* but, in this case, the groups represented are not only of opposite *jepta* identity but also of opposite gender. Using the logic above, the women who *karate* the men are the welcoming group. Nevertheless, the gender theme is stressed in a stereotypical way. In spite of the representational position of women as men, active performers out in the bush lands, when the women give food to the men and when the speeches take place, the two groups sit opposite one another in a circular arrangement, with women occupying the downwind half of the circle and the men of the guest *jepta* forming a windward semicircle. These arrangements may be ad hoc, for I did not specifically question people about their significance, but in the dozen or more *karate* in which I have participated the upwind–downwind, male–female arrangement has always appeared.

Why do women intentionally inhabit low-ranked spaces? I believe they do so to honor the men in a stereotypical way that is self-empowering even while it is subservient. The men, accustomed to being so honored in public settings in daily life, are inextricably entangled in the exchange by accepting the position of honor. In their representative position as providers of highly valued seafoods, they, like the deities who must ensure the ultimate production of these seafoods, are drawn into an exchange in which they give up all of their fish for the metaphoric pleasures of a union with the women of an opposite *jepta.*

The circular arrangement on December 25 accomplishes similar ends vis-à-vis the deities, for the gifts within the tree are "for God," and the community as a whole, encircling the tree, gives honor to God by presenting the gifts to God's earthly representatives. Honor demands remuneration, however: in this instance, reciprocation to ensure the continued productivity of nature and continuity of human life.

The interdependence of positions of rank and the encumbering power of the unranked is also manifest in the games of New Year's Day. In both softball and volleyball games, local people perceive that the team that occupies the windward field gains an advantage. Not only do those downwind wallow in their pollutants, but any magical substances they release into the air will move downwind to cover their intended recipients. And the outcome of these games is often claimed to be affected by magic. Each team, then, wishes to occupy the windward field. Nevertheless, simply by losing the toss to determine sequence and position, a group gains a certain advantage in its ability to rationalize the outcome of any match. From the moment of the toss, the playing field is not equal, and the disadvantaged use their vulnerable physical position to rationalize any loss or, when they win, to point out how extraordi-

Figure 12. Children look on as Io̧lap, the author's *jepta*, begins its *ṃaaj* to enter the church on Wūjlañ in 1976. (Photograph by Lōmentijen)

narily superior they, in fact, must have been, for they overcame a disadvantage to post a win.

Because virtually every encounter has its spatial dimension, these spatial codes are manipulated to pragmatic advantage again and again during *Kūrijmōj*. My aim in this section is not to exhaust each of these uses but simply to point out their critical and pervasive character. The above represent only a few of the ways in which the ontology of space is employed to representational advantage in the celebration.

LANDHOLDING AND THE LOGISTICS OF KŪRIJMŌJ

The spatial alignments on which Wūjlañ people fashion their world are used to situate and construct social arrangements at a number of levels. On this highly egalitarian atoll, each competing group should begin with the same footing in the celebration, yet due to the effects of differential landholding by *jepta* members, equity of access to resources is difficult to attain. In particular, Io̧lap believes that it has a disadvantage in the competition among *jepta*. I analyze Io̧lap's position, along with *jepta* members' reflections on it, as an example of the sorts of strategies of group empowerment that each of the songfest groups employs during *Kūrijmōj*.

Fortunately, Jack Tobin's work on Wūjlañ Atoll allows some of the changes that may have occurred in twenty years to be assessed (Tobin 1967: chap. 6). Tobin notes that land tenure on Wūjlañ Atoll differs significantly from that described for other parts of the Marshall Islands (for example, Mason 1947; Tobin 1958). In his analysis, Wūjlañ people maintained a division between the land of their mother *(jineer)* and the land of their father *(jemaer)*. He suggests that, at the time of his residence on the atoll, the land of the father received greater stress. Given that one was most apt to attend to the lands of the father, it seems likely that residence was also preferentially patrilocal. Although Tobin's analysis certainly points to systematic differences with the Marshall Islands, in the 1970s and 1980s, at least, any rule of residence would have to be called (am)bilocal.

In the 1970s, virtually any Wūjlañ person would confirm that one's father's land was much more important on Wūjlañ Atoll than in other parts of the Marshall Islands, but few contended that it was of necessity more important than one's mother's lands. In terms of use rights, persons maintain equal rights to use the lands of father and mother, both genealogical and social (through adoption). Several young adults on Wūjlañ had lands of their own, because all living residents at the time of the land division (circa 1949–1950) received land. These young people commonly used their own lands, whereas their immediate younger siblings had to exploit the lands of their parents. Actual land use, therefore, varies considerably. One generally works lands belonging to one's household of residence, for an important aspect of identity is constructed around residence, and a critical part of the solidarity of the residential unit rests in helpfulness *(jipañ)*. Everyone who works lands associated with that residential site is said to be helping.

These priorities, however, do not prohibit people from using any lands to which they have a right, either through ties of blood (through a male pathway), ties of clan (the path of the mother), or adoption. On occasion, people use all sorts of lands to which some type of right may be claimed. Given a plentiful supply of brown coconuts, sprouted coconuts, or other objects of wide distribution, people will likely collect these items on lands associated with their present place of residence. In hurried times, and when residential lands are at some distance, it is common to hear one say: "Oh, we will take some copra-stage nuts from the place of my grandmother." In the listener's mind, the very use of an appropriate relationship category establishes the speaker's claims of legitimacy. Exploiting one's right to varied lands is particularly common when a person discovers a pandanus fruit *(bōb)* or special sweet-husked coconut *(kanauā)*. These are scarce items, and the range of lands to which a person has some right is expanded to the widest definitional boundaries in order to take advantage of one's lucky find.

Stories of the land division on Wūjlañ are often compared with tales of primordial times on Āne-wetak, when the first land division occurred. When making the comparison, Wūjlañ residents see some differences, because the ancient Āne-wetak division is always viewed as straight or fitting, whereas the division on Wūjlañ is often termed very bad. In fact, since the return to Āne-wetak the inequalities of lands held by different families have come to light, but, in absentia, these inequalities were overlooked in order to produce romanticized accounts about life in the primordial homeland. At the time of division on Wūjlañ each living person was allotted an equal parcel of land. Thirty years later, however, the failure of these plans of designed equality to produce equality have resulted in frustration. The failure is due to the fact that the families were at various stages in their respective cycles of development in 1949 (cf. Fortes 1958). In combination with the small population effects discussed by Goodenough (1955: 71 et seq.), inequalities in practice have been the result.

Āne-wetak principles of land division are not particularly relevant to an understanding of *Kūrijmōj,* but it may be important to note that different systems of division were used on the Ānjepe and Āne-wetak halves of the atoll. The Ānjepe system, which has some matrilocal biases, is said to have been influenced by Marshall Islanders when a group of intended conquerors failed in its mission, intermarried with local Ānjepe people, and established clan links with locations in the Central Rālik Chain. Those with land rights on the Āne-wetak half of the atoll claim that their methods of land division, with the bilateral stress of the current Wūjlañ systems, are older than the Ānjepe pattern and that the pattern on Wurrin, an ancient division that counterbalanced Āne-wetak in a pre-Ānjepe dual-atoll division,[2] was the same as that on the Āne-wetak half of the atoll.

Each of these constructions of the past serves to selectively empower current divisions of Wūjlañ and Āne-wetak lands. Of greatest relevance to an understanding of *Kūrijmōj* is the division on Wūjlañ. Since the return to Āne-wetak, land considerations have had little impact on *Kūrijmōj* because only a minimal amount of land food was produced on the atoll in the 1980s, certainly not enough to contribute substantially to *Kūrijmōj.* In the 1949 division of Wūjlañ lands, Jittōk-eņ residents started at a point bordering on the eastern line of the village and, after much measuring, decided to allocate three lines of coconuts to each living member of that half of the village. Because the eastern tip of the island has old, unproductive trees from German times and is not highly productive due to sandy soil, a larger area was given to the landowner who received that parcel.

The parcels of land outside town do not correspond with the ordering of parcels in town. The apportionment was different, for the village space is, at its core, a domestic space, and only family heads received house parcels within the village (bordered by a line of coconuts on each side). As with bush parcels, however, the family spaces failed to account for newly emerging families. Claims to land, both in town and in the bush, are made along paths of bilateral extended-family relationship. The allotment of land has been altered somewhat by land exchanges in the years since the initial division. Such exchanges have often taken place to allow older residents to gain access to some lines closer to town. The exchanges benefit both parties, because younger people prefer to have at least some part of their land at a distance from town. The islet is wider there, lines of coconuts are longer, and theft of fruits is less likely. Closer to town there is always a temptation to take two or three coconuts for meal preparation rather than make a long trip to one's own parcel. Because each villager traces relationships to a broad range of relatives, these thefts are justified on the basis of some distant tie. Nonetheless, unless the path to that relative is maintained through active work on that land, others will refer to the use of fruits from another person's land parcel as stealing unless permission has been obtained in advance.

In Jitto-eņ (the leeward half), land stretches from the western edge of town to the western tip of the main island. The islet here is much narrower than the eastern half, but the western half is also considerably longer. Actual land area is, therefore, fairly equal. Jitto-eņ people chose to segment the bush land on the main island into three divisions. The section farthest from the village is termed *Ānekōn̄e* (the islet of *kōn̄e, Pemphis acidula*), comprised of rough trees and coconuts of inferior grade. Though now connected to the main island of Wūjlan̄, in German times a small stretch of water is said to have separated Wūjlan̄ and Ānekōn̄e. Closer to the village is an area that has been totally replanted, called by most people *jenete* (*ijen ete,* there where the short [coconuts are]). Closest to town is an area of *ni utiej* (high coconuts, from the German era, when Wūjlan̄ was a coconut plantation). Much of this area also has been replanted. Each living member (with the exception of one, who was overlooked) was allocated an equivalent number of lines in each of the three land areas. This decision segmented a person's lands, but it also equalized them in terms of their utility. In retrospect, the Jitto-eņ division is considered a better way to divide the land than is the method that was used in Jittōk-eņ.

In addition to the lands on the main islet, the outer islets of Wūjlan̄ are divided among the residents. The islets of Āne-ļap and Āne-ṃanōt were allocated to the residents of Jittōk-eņ and were divided in a manner fairly similar to that used on the main island of Wūjlan̄. The islands of Kalo and Kiloķwōn, in addition to half of the islet of Ra-ej, belong to the people of Jitto-eņ, with each member of the community at the time of the apportionment receiving a parcel on one of the islets. The method of dividing these islets was comparable to that used by the members of Jittōk-eņ on the main islet. The islets were not divided into zones with each community member receiving a share in the various zones. Instead, all members received their land in a single parcel, with some consideration given to size of the parcel based on the utility of the peripheral lands.

Finally, two parcels are chiefly, allotted to them by virtue of their high position. Pietto, bordering on the small passageway, belongs to the chief of Jittōk-eņ and his family; half of the islet of Ra-ej (a much larger islet than Pietto) belongs to the family of the Jitto-eņ chief. Unlike other parts of the Marshalls, the two chiefs receive no share of copra profits produced by those who stay on the land. On Wūjlan̄, the special land parcel is the mark of chiefly rank, given "because they are high" (in rank). People may help the chief make copra on these lands, but this privilege replaces others accorded chiefs in other locations in the Marshall Islands. These lands, worked by the chief and his or her commoners, are the real inalienable class objects (or "really the soul") of the chief and his successors.

In addition to these major islets of Wūjlañ Atoll, a number of other small islets are used as stopping places for food gathering and as locations for picnics. They are held jointly among the adult men living at the time of the land division. Up to a point, other adult men were added as they became eligible to be members of a *wa,* or sailing group (Carucci 1995). In the 1950s on Wūjlañ, the *wa* were groups of men who cooperated in building and caring for a boat; the same group cooperated in food-gathering activities that relied on the use of that sailing craft (Tobin 1967). They also held competitions to make visible the skills of the *wa* as a canoe-building and sailing group. The members of the *wa* held use rights to the small islets where many fishing, turtle-catching, and bird-gathering activities took place. Because the islets are too small to have brackish water wells, they are not suitable for long-term residences.

The *wa* are no longer functioning groups, and use rights on the small islets are now in question. Neither the four large sailing canoes on Wūjlañ in the 1970s nor the eight or ten outboard-motor boats (in various states of repair) were constructed or shared by the sailing groups. One of the canoe groups constituted itself around the core members of an earlier *wa,* but the other canoe-building cadres were either family groups or some combination of members from the various old sailing groups. Although the sailing groups have dissolved from the perspective of canoe building and maintenance and of food gathering, the skeletal residues of sailing groups are still apparent in the use rights on small islets.

Issues of trespass have arisen on these outer islets as a result of the decline of canoe groups. In 1977 the council met to clarify the issue of access to the small islets. The common understanding was that use rights were extended to the members of the families headed by former members of *wa.* To prevent further abuses, the council decided that, unless a person was a member of the sailing group holding rights to a particular small islet, permission should always be obtained from a member of that group before landing on the islet or making use of its products.

In many respects, the land divisions on Wūjlañ Atoll represent a socially negotiated framework that is undergoing constant change. Nevertheless, it provides one template local people use to strategize about *Kūrijmōj* because land-use patterns establish the parameters for the most likely spheres of action in *karate* and *kalbuuj* and determine the available resource base for *kaṃōḷo* and for the major feasts leading up to and including December 25 and New Year's Sunday. Indeed, the outer islets of Āne-wetak have similar significance but, because the most plentiful resources on the atoll at this time are seafoods, outer islets serve as sailing bases for crews of fishermen, not as major food-collection grounds. In contrast, on Wūjlañ, many of a songfest group's most valued food sources depend on the lands controlled by its members. In most instances there is general equivalence, but for some highly valued specialty items—large birds, turtles, pandanus, and so forth—differences in access to lands (particularly on outer islets) determine whether a group will be able to accumulate a diverse array of goods.

Land and the Strategies of Competitive Feasting

Ioļap's sense of inferiority in relation to the other *jepta* is based partly on their location, trapped between Jittōk-eņ and Jitto-eņ. Equally important, the lands that Ioļap must exploit are divided between Jittōk-eņ and Jitto-eņ. This must be the case, for Ioļap is the songfest group that comprises one "town of Jittōk-eņ" and one "town of Jitto-eņ." Constituted of the two central towns of these formerly opposed *jepta,* Ioļapļap is totally surrounded by the towns of the other two groups, by the ocean, and by a short stretch of lagoon. This central position is "high" in a culturally marked sense. Moreover, it offers certain advantages: ready access to the minister and visibility of the group's activities to him. In the tactics of these games, however, centrality can be a disadvantage, because the villages of Jittōk-eņ or Jitto-eņ must be crossed in order to transport foods and other necessities into Ioļap territory. Of course, the logic of these games requires generosity, and a group must give freely in order to win at *karate* or *kalbuuj.* At the same time, a group must have its own goods, not those obtained through these games, in order to *kaṃōļo,* to feed the minister, and to prepare for special Sunday celebrations. The possibility of secret trips to obtain such goods is more restricted in Ioļap than it is in Jittōk-eņ or Jitto-eņ. The only unimpeded access is into the lagoon or out to sea. Even these water routes are less protected, for only a small strip of beach borders Ioļap's territory. The reef is common ground, and the women of Jittōk-eņ or Jitto-eņ can easily venture out onto the lagoon reef to intercept an incoming craft. Although they risk being taken captive by the men of Ioļap in *kalbuuj,* the danger is minimal. *Kalbuuj* is not used to retaliate for *karate;* the two separate ceremonial moments each focus on creating unbalanced exchanges of goods with an opposing group. These wins are fashioned from magnanimity, not from fear.

When Jittōk-eņ and Jitto-eņ collect land foods, they bring them directly to their respective towns. If the Ioļap women are planning a *karate,* they must send a sentry out into the bush lands of Jittōk-eņ or Jitto-eņ to notify villagers of the movements of the men from the opposing groups. The members of Jittōk-eņ and Jitto-eņ often protect the items they have gathered or the fish they caught by landing in the bush lands of their respective ends of the islands. Although this does not rule out *karate,* the women of Ioļap must plan their attack far in advance, and they must intercept the men in a relatively large territory before they cross into the safety of their own town. In contrast, the main advantage of Ioļapļap is that it draws members from each half, and land rights are held on each end of the islet. If members hear that the women of Jittōk-eņ or Jitto-eņ are planning a *karate,* they may shift their efforts to the bush lands on the opposite end of the island. This advantage is more than canceled by Io̧lap's surroundedness. They must cross the village space of another *jepta* to get to any usable lands. Their planned activities cannot escape the scrutiny of their neighbors.

This view is somewhat oversimplified: the crosscutting ties of kinship that unite the village and the fact that the members of a residential group have the freedom to associate with any *jepta* mean that all *jepta* have access to some lands in either Jittōk-eņ or Jitto-eņ. The crucial disadvantage of Io̧lapļap is that it cannot escape its surroundedness. Other groups may use lands in the midst of other's territory, but Io̧lap must do so. More important, the images I have constructed tend to convey the idea that the *jepta* somehow try to avoid the encounters with the other *jepta*. Even though there is always talk about keeping the group's plans secret, all plans become public on Wūjlañ. Moreover, no group would avoid *kalbuuj* or *karate* just because its members thought they might lose. On those occasions when a group reaches home with its foods or handicraft items unmolested, the cause is usually the unpreparedness of the other groups. If a group of men fishes quickly and with success, the women from another group may not have finished preparing foods by the time the men return. In such cases, the men are commonly disappointed that their goods were not stolen!

In other words, full participation in all aspects of *Kūrijmōj* is far more critical than losing or winning a particular encounter. The higher intent of the games rests in perpetuating a series of ongoing relationships between the residents of the island and God or the ancestral deities. The encounters among the *jepta* must occur frequently and intensively in order for the deities to take notice of the community, of the labors that honor them, and, subsequently, of the need to remunerate those honors.

Part of Io̧lap's complaint that its *jepta* is at a disadvantage and that other groups consistently take advantage of it depends on its position as a newcomer. Nevertheless, the entire community empathizes to some degree, and people worry that the overall activities of *Kūrijmōj* may be negatively affected. The point is said to be important because the games of *karate* and *kalbuuj* must be pursued with the same intensity as *kaņōļo* or the other original elements of *Kūrijmōj* that were sanctified through their introduction by missionaries and strengthened by their continuing performance. At the same time, the games must not overwhelm the original activities. If Io̧lap becomes so impoverished that it is not able to provide major feasts while competing groups have an advantage in these pursuits, then the most critical aims of the festivities are endangered.

Without *karate* and *kalbuuj,* Wūjlañ people say, the celebration would suffer from lack of activity—it would not create much happiness. Such is the Wūjlañ complaint about *Kūrijmōj* in other parts of the Marshall Islands. To ensure that the level of interaction remains high, some trips are made by Jitto-eņ women and men to Jittōk-eņ lands where they have rights, and Jittōk-eņ always makes similar trips to Jitto-eņ. Talk about such trips is couched in a joking manner: "Why is it they say that there are a great number of pandanus leaves [or whatever] remaining in Jittōk-eṇ?; there are none left in Jitto-eṇ, and those that remain are not good." On this basis a trip will be organized with full knowledge that an attempt to *karate* or *kalbuuj* will be made by the opposing groups. Inactivity would be to the detriment of the celebrations, and a group that remains active will proudly announce its involvement by chanting, "Are we not going to [be active in] Christmas?" These chants are a call to action on behalf of the *jepta,* and they also serve to create envy among members of other groups and entice them to pursue competitive encounters more intently.

Spatial Components of *Kalbuuj* and *Karate*

Important aspects of the symbolism of *karate* and *kalbuuj,* which I discussed in chapter 4, relate to the spatial domains in which the action takes place. Recall that *kalbuuj,* the village game, is initiated by men, whereas *karate,* the bush encounter, is activated by women. The latter locale is the peripheral and socially marginal domain inhabited by potentially dangerous spirits. Spirits are especially abundant and active at night, are highly unpredictable, and thus require women to travel in the bush during the day and only in groups. Pregnant women should never venture into these areas, particularly unaccompanied and as they near term. The village, on the other hand, is the women's domain. Its centrality connotes the same safety and protectiveness as does the atoll in its opposition to the open sea. Not only do women spend most of their time here, the village is termed *ar. Ar* not only signifies town, its most common usage refers to the lagoon side of the island, as opposed to *lik,* the ocean side. The lagoon side is also a safe, protected, female domain.

The specific apportionment of land largely determines action locations for all of the activities of any *jepta.* Thus, if a *karate* is planned by the men of Jittōk-eṇ, the route they take will be selected on the basis of landholding. Jittōk-eṇ, for example, will almost certainly use the surround method of fishing on the eastern tip of the atoll, for it adjoins land parcels that belong to them. Ioḷap also commonly uses that fishing area, but Jitto-eṇ never uses it. There is no restriction against their use of these waters, for all fishing areas on Wūjlañ and Āne-wetak are held in common by atoll residents, but it would be a great tactical disadvantage for Jitto-eṇ to fish in this area.

Land apportionment on the outer islands also shapes the celebration by placing limits on the range of possibilities open to any *jepta* in search of particular foods. In 1977, for example, those people who held rights to the best bird islands were members of Jittōk-eṇ and Ioḷap. A great uproar resulted when Jitto-eṇ included a large number of birds in one of its feasting presentations. "These birds were stolen," members of other groups insisted. Because theft is a moral breach of biblical law and is to be avoided at all cost during *Kūrijmōj,* many feared that the incident would result in harm to the island. The incident was mentioned at an islandwide council gathering, as a warning to the entire community. Permission had to be obtained from an original member of the sailing group that had rights to a particular islet before anyone else used those lands.

In another incident, Jittōk-eņ women planned a *karate* of a group of fishermen from Jitto-eņ who had gone trolling in the ocean. By late afternoon, the women began to worry that the men had tricked them on their return. Constantly scanning the horizon, Jittōk-en women saw no sign of Jitto-eņ men. Little gasoline was available, and none could be wasted on false fears. Dusk had arrived when the women of Jittōk-eņ began screaming for help to place the engine on their boat. A craft had been sighted. Though several boats were still out, the women insisted they had sighted the right boat, for only the people of Jitto-eņ have rights to Kilǫkwōn. Indeed, far away, across the lagoon, a craft could be seen beached on the shores of Kilǫkwōn. The women left with food in hand and trapped the fishermen on their return across the lagoon. Their catch of more than twenty tuna was stolen. Indeed, the men of Jitto-eņ had tried to fool the women of the other groups by risking a dangerous passage across the reef rather than relying on a more conventional route of return. But the constant vigil and the knowledge that only Jitto-eņ people had land rights on Kilǫkwōn allowed the women to outmaneuver the men of Jitto-eņ and to successfully *karate* them.

In precisely such subtle ways, the cosmology of spatial relationships continually influences the manner in which ritual messages are constructed, and the pragmatic application of a knowledge of landholding guides the way in which *Kūrijmōj* is practiced.

CHAPTER SIX

Supportive Devices

The Symbolics of the Senses in Kūrijmōj

Just as spatial arrangements figure prominently in the ritual enactment of *Kūrijmōj,* providing a variety of cultural features that make the celebrations intelligible, several sensual elements contribute to the way in which festive meanings are fashioned and interpreted. These include songs, various visual images, paralinguistic features, types of touching, and significant scents. Each ceremonial element imbues discourses and performances with critical meaning as major ritual acts are built on one another. The components are constructed in accord with, or in contrast to, culturally accepted interpretations of day-to-day use. These paralinguistic and nonlinguistic communicative elements may not always involve the hierarchically structured grammar of spoken language, but they are core features that contribute to cultural assemblage and to ceremonial interpretation. The boundaries and features of these extralinguistic elements are culturally coded in accord with a simple grammar (an indexical code in Peirce's terms [1932: vol. 2]) that combines cultural and paralinguistic signifiers to communicate certain ideas and uses discursive forms in combination with nonlinguistic enactments to construct other parts of the celebration.

The manifest meanings of *Kūrijmōj* are carried in the founding celebratory acts of the ritual. Songfests are said to have been introduced on Āne-wetak and Wūjlañ by island missionaries, and the persistence of this form, relatively unmodified, represents the incredible source of potency with which Christianity was associated soon after its introduction. "When this thing first arrived it was incredibly potent; but today, it is as though we have sieved it and sieved it, and it is not as strong as previously." The manifest content of the songs, focused directly on Wūjlañ and Āne-wetak interpretations of the strength to be derived from word of God, is an attempt to capture the original potency of Christianity for use in securing the communal desire for continued earthly existence. Ongoing life or salvation is seldom mentioned because noncorporeal existence, life after death, is guaranteed in the Marshallese universe. It is life on earth that remains tenuous.

SIGNIFICANCES OF SONG

Rather than attempt to analyze the full array of *Kūrijmōj* songs, I will use the features of two typical songs, along with the notation of other titles and thematic foci, to represent the corpus. The sol-la or fa-sol-la counterpoint style of the early eighteenth-century New England Puritan songs has had an obvious influence on today's *Kūrijmōj* tunes. Nevertheless, these songs always differ in tenor and performative style from church hymns. As mentioned, they are locally composed, though portions are commonly borrowed from the Marshall or Caroline Islands, and they are performed in four counterpoint voices. In contrast, in most church hymns the melody is accompanied by simultaneous four-part harmonic voices.

Figure 13. The children's songfest group prepares to sing on December 25, 1976, on Wūjlañ. The youth group leader introduces the theme and the songs as the minister aligns the performers. Above the children hang coconut-frond streamers. (Photograph by L. M. Carucci)

The following are among a series of *Kūrijmōj* songs performed by Io̧lap in 1982. As is evident, the babe-in-a-manger sequences of Euro-American Protestantism are far from their focus:[1]

M̧oktata jen kaṃoolol (b: jen kaṃoolol) (a: aaet jen kaṃoolol),
Im jen (s: reilok ñan e) reilok ñan e (a/b: reilok wōt ñan e),
Aaet (b: kin iọkwe) kin iọkwe eo aṇ (b: eo aṇ ñan la̧l)
kin an iọkwe la̧l,
ej kaboo̧l kōj raan ñan raan (a: aolep en raan)

chorus
E men in aō kabwilōn̄lōn̄ (t: e men in aō bwilōn̄),
kabwilōn̄lōn̄ je bwilōn̄,
aaet ar telokin ioon (t: lo kūtuon) la̧l (b: telokin wōj),
kin wōt
kin an jouj im tūriam̄o,
Aaet, ej jibōlep wōt iō (a: jān raan ñan raan)

The voiced counterpoints are expressed here, with a male voice "bearing the weight" of the melody throughout the verse and a counterpoised female voice, soprano, adopting this stance throughout the chorus. In classical call and response mode, the other voices either foretell, reiterate, or elaborate on the message in the back channel. In translation:

The very first thing, we give thanks (b: we [incl.] give thanks) (a: yes, we give thanks),
And we (s: look into the distance toward him/her) look into the distance toward him/her (a/b: continue looking into the distance toward him/her)
Yes (b: on account of love) on account of his/her love (b: of his/hers toward the earth)
Because of his/her love for the earth,
He/she fills us [incl.] up day to day (a: all of these days)

chorus
It is a thing of repeated amazement for me (t: a thing of my amazement)
such repeated amazement (that) we are amazed,
Yes he/she spread the word around (with his/her breath) the space below (earth) (b: it is being spread toward you),
Solely on account of his/her kindness and suffering
Yes, he/she has overwhelmed me personally with sentiment (a: from day to day)

The verse in this song recapitulates the demeanor of commoners toward chiefs and foreign guests (as outlined in chapter 3, but in an unelaborated manner). In the composition above, the distance of the foreigner/chief is noted after the moment of giving thanks. At the same time, thanks must be given to reciprocate the love that has been bestowed on the earth, a specifically human love infused in those who now give thanks. Although the referent of the song for Christian converts is Christ, the personage is never noted. Other community members, recognizing the churchgoers' interpretations, note that the representations are equally applicable to Jebrọ.

In the verse, the typically Wūjlañ and Āne-wetak features of *Kūrijmōj* songs that I noted previously are particularly apparent. Most notable is the concept of amazement, an overrepresented feature of Wūjlañ *Kūrijmōj* songs that provides a central semiotic thread linked directly to the *wōjke* (tree) and its mode of deployment. The spatial separation between high and low (see chapters 2 and 5) qualifies the distance to be bridged in the exchanges of *Kūrijmōj* along with a Wūjlañ people's stereotypic attempt to reconstruct the moment when Christianity arrived in Micronesia. They depict the arrival of the mission as a time of spreading the Word around (the Word that replaced warfare with love as the new interactional mode), a trope that is retrospectively employed to separate the times of darkness, the pre-Christian past, from times of light in the current era. The darkness/light theme forms the core of other *Kūrijmōj* compositions (for example, *Rup Meram* [the explosion of the light]).

The remainder of the chorus concentrates on the mode of spreading the Word, the quantification of this sentimental shift, and the ex post facto reason that the sentimental shift requires reciprocation. Spreading the Word depends on the expenditure of life's force (the breath). Again the referent is left to the imagination of the listener. At one level, Āne-wetak people say that it is Christ, but others believe that it must include the incarnate descendants of Christ (the American Board of Commissioners for Foreign Missionaries [ABCFM] missionaries who originally brought the Word to the Marshall Islands and local believers who spread the Word today). Thus, the living and deceased cadre of believers who share substance in the patritransmittable "blood" of Christ are included. Note that kindness and suffering, qualities that are commonly shared by Jebrọ and Christ, are associated with the transformed temporal era thought to have been brought into being with the arrival of Christianity. In the case of Christ, however, these characteristics are not present at birth in the European interpretation; they only become manifest through lived increments of Christ's life and death.

The Wūjlañ and Āne-wetak interpretation is different, pointing first to the fact that *Kūrijmōj* is not a celebration of the birth of Christ per se but a celebration of local understandings of the Christian ethic, a celebration that accomplishes its aims by aligning the transformation from one year to the next with the core representations associated with the transformation from the era of darkness to the era of light. On Āne-wetak and Wūjlañ, the move from darkness to light takes place in the recent, remembered past, but it is foretold by the analogical move into the mode of kindness from the mode of might that is marked in the "ancient" tale of Jebrọ. To allow for these conflations, Christ's life is "lived in advance" in the song, as if the demonstrations of kindness and suffering already occurred at birth. In Āne-wetak terms, this is perfectly understandable, because (as A. R. Radcliffe-Brown would have it) social action reflects the social structure (1965: chap. 10). In this case, the younger-sibling position of Christ recapitulates the younger-sibling position of Jebrọ, with comparable compassion and love as the result. I explore this theme more fully below.

Finally, the welling up of sentiment makes the message of suffering for love irresistible. This theme is doubly important, because irresistible sentimental force is precisely the processual object being created, both by the inter-*jepta* competitions and by the communal acts of *Kūrijmōj* that follow, and, at the more obvious level, because the song is part of one group's performance, which itself hopes to create, through its singing, the sense of irresistibility that will result in an overflowing of sentiment in the audience.

Another song, which became one of Ioḷap's most popular offerings, is both more obscure (because it incorporates ancient language) and more potent than the first:

Ejuurur elimọtak laḷ rainin,
bwe emōj an jejjet kūtien naan en (t/a/b: naan eo rar kōnnaan kake)
Mōttan jet raan jimạ e le je wawa ioon (a: ara)
Ara buj kōkālok tem jeruj jeberujruj

chorus
Jen al im bar al
ken jujuan am al (b/t: kotak ainikien ko reḷap) ilo mejatoto,
bwe emōj an lotak juon di tel di lomour (b: oh)
ejjab etto jān kiiō

In this song the women carry the weight of the melody throughout, though in one instance altos join the men's voices to elaborate on the second phrase of the verse. A counterpoint similar to the first song reveals the song's message, but the obscure, ancient words give the song incredible potency, the sacred force of the unknown and uncertain. In rough translation:

(Our) excitement is welling up and is firmly implanted on the place below (the earth) today,
because the essence of (the breath/wind contained within) the Word has now been made precise (because it is now the proper time for the true word to be revealed) (t/a/b: the word that they were talking about)
In just a few days or so, you see sir, we will float around on (it)(a: *ara*)
Ara, then make things fly, *tem* (and then) we are brought to life. we are brought to life again and again.

chorus
We [inclusive imperative] will sing and sing again
in many multiples of your song (b/t: lift up the loud sounds) in the air
because one who foresees the future (a prophet) has been born, one who leads us through the woods/the unknown (b: oh)
it is not long from now

As the first song ends, so the second begins, with a focus on concentrated sentiment on earth and the substance of the Word being clarified. In this instance, the audience is asked to await the coming of the Word, an apocalyptic moment in the near future. With this request, the audience participates in a temporal condensation of past, present, and future. Onlookers are encouraged to draw on recollections of the moment when the Word was first revealed, then to be consumed by the potencies of the essence of that word, and, finally, to await its (second) coming in the near future. The potent, primordial word *ara,* the meaning of which is no longer known, is then incanted, first by the altos, then by everyone. The very potency of the revelation of the Word lifts humans up, freeing them from earthly bonds, and brings the possibility of salvation in the near future to humans on earth. As noted, however, Wūjlañ salvation refers to the perpetuation of continuous communal corporeal existence on earth, not to life-after-death desires that are a sine qua non of Marshall Islanders' views of postmortem existence. Although the Word is associated with the time when missionaries brought God's word to the Marshall Islands, the manner in which humans are emotionally freed from earthly constraint is also analogous to the way Jebrǫ was able to win the canoe race—by transforming his transport vessel into one that could fly. And this ability was bestowed as a result of the youngest sibling's demonstrated love and caring.

Like the verse, the chorus transports the audience back to the time when all of this first occurred and re-creates the initial moment in current ritual practice, thus allowing the audience to wait for the moment when these moments of renewal will occur. This ultimately transformative moment will come with the explosion of the tree. The preceding lines are a song of praise ostensibly honoring Christ, but is done generically once again, by presenting the unfamiliar in familiar terms—one who foresees the future, one who leads us through the woods. This is entirely typical of the songs of *Kūrijmōj*. They construct a world of Christ-like attributes and demeanors through the use of fully localized understandings of Christianity, contributing to the transformative power of *Kūrijmōj* through the implementation of taken-for-granted categories of Wūjlañ and Āne-wetak experience. This is not a generic, imported Christianity, the knowledge of which is simply diffused from one society to another; nor is it a hybrid, syncretic form. It is a Wūjlañ Christianity, totally transformed and experienced within the world of the already understood.

Performative style is as important to the songs as is semantic content, and the entire aim is to "capture the throats" of the members of the audience. This equates to "tugging at the heartstrings" for Americans, but the particular evocative qualities of song are themselves vested in the way that singing is rooted in the seat of the emotions, the throat. A well-performed song can literally draw its qualities of evocation directly from the physical locus of emotional force. A well-performed *Kūrijmōj* song infuses the emotional potency of its performers directly into the listeners, creating the characteristics of irresistibility that culminate in the intergender and inter-*jepta* attractions of December 25.

REPRESENTATIONAL EMBELLISHMENTS

Other key performative and paralinguistic components of the celebration are present in the ritual activities of December 25. At this time each group's efforts are concentrated on perfect performances, and a plethora of sensory embellishments contributes to a strong presentation. For this main event, all *jepta* members dress in appropriate matching garb, don flower leis and head wreaths made by the young girls and women, and maintain perfect demeanor. The village is thoroughly cleaned (particularly the celebration arena), the central part of town is decorated, *wōjke* are displayed and exploded, and every member of the community comes to the central plaza to witness and add grandeur to the occasion.

Long before December 25, the women of each *jepta* agree on a particular type of material from which to construct their dresses. On Wūjlañ, the decision had to be made while a well-supplied field-trip ship was anchored in the lagoon. Thus, some time in October or November yard goods are selected, for it is impossible to predict when another boat, particularly a well-stocked craft, will arrive. The Airline of the Marshall Islands now schedules weekly flights to Āne-wetak. The airplanes have eased anxieties about materials, even though the flight schedules are undependable. In either case, unduly delayed decisions, hoping for a last-minute ship or airplane before December 25, always involve the risk of having no material to make dresses and other clothing. *Jepta* members purchase as much material of a single color as possible. There will never be total concurrence with the selected dress material, but most women of each group construct dresses from the same material.

Dress materials are chosen with two considerations in mind. The fabric must be distinctive in color or pattern from those selected by the other *jepta,* and it must be brilliant. Given these two constraints and the limited variety available on a particular field-trip ship, most often Wūjlañ women selected brightly colored solid materials. On Āne-wetak, where a trip to Mājuro might supplement supplies, brilliant prints predominate. The preference for solid colors on Wūjlañ, in sharp contrast to the floral designs preferred for most occasions, points to the high priority placed on uniform dress. Color coordination becomes an important means of representing *jepta* solidarity, and solid colors were commonly easier to obtain in quantity than were prints on Wūjlañ. In lieu of brilliant floral prints, bright solids tending toward reds (the Marshallese category includes oranges and some burgundies or violets) or greens (which also includes blues)[2] are preferred. Whites and bright yellows are chosen in times of cloth shortage.

If the shared character of the uniform is critical, the next most important element is color: it must incorporate a sense of brilliance or shimmering radiance. On Wūjlañ, some seamstresses rationalized the use of solid colors as being reminiscent of the attire of the plain-clothed missionaries, but brilliant prints immediately replaced solids after the return to Āne-wetak. The shift from solid colors to prints also correlates with the new generation's lack of concern about missionary intent (by 1990, less than 2 percent of the Āne-wetak population had witnessed the first missionary teacher's arrival on Āne-wetak, and many of them were too young at the time to remember the details). Whites are often incorporated into the uniforms because extreme whites are desirably intense as well as pure or clean. Intensity and purity are elements of brilliance that are well grounded in people's talk about ancient deities and persons of rank. Only items of the greatest whiteness, for example, were given to the chief. Solid colors, often combined in sharp contrast with white, were used in the manufacture of Wūjlañ attire to accent intensity and purity and to accommodate pragmatic necessity. Although these clothes were rationalized in positive terms at the time, once on Āne-wetak, the expanded array of available goods allowed the manifest preference for brilliant prints to surface. Seamstresses then revalued the solid-colored uniforms of former years, fashioning them into representations of the materially impoverished past life on Wūjlañ.

Men's dress is no less important than women's, but it is less innovative, inasmuch as all men's clothes, except shirts, are purchased "tailored," that is, ready made. Generally, men have only one set of dress clothes, and they are apt to conform to the accepted standard: dark trousers and a white shirt. A tie, shoes, and, on occasion, a dress coat are desirable additions to this attire. Even during privileged moments when Wūjlañ and Āne-wetak men have

Figure 14. Alternating lines of Jitto-eŋ men and women perform their *beet* on Āne-wetak in 1990. Men's shirts and women's dresses, cut from matching bolts of a bright orange "Polynesian" print, contribute to the group's unified identity. All eyes are on the leader (to the right) as he turns to check the alignment of his troupe, another sign of unity and a crucial component of a successful performance. (Photograph by L. M. Carucci)

access to a full variety of styles and colors, their choices reflect a narrow range of local predilection: black is the preferred color for suits or sports coats (their category includes navy blues), though brilliant solid colors are occasionally purchased; brown and grey are never considered desirable. For those who can afford to supplement their zoris (termed "flip-flops" by some Americans) with shoes, black patent leather is most highly treasured. In 1977 one *jepta* decided to innovate on the standard attire: they settled on all-white uniforms with black shoes and belts rather than the usual black and white.

As with women's dress, the availability of new options on Āne-wetak has altered social practice. Yet the alterations are equally predictable. With better access to yard goods, most *jepta* now color coordinate men's shirts with women's dresses. Although bright prints increase a songfest group's ability to represent cohesiveness, the staple to the bright complement of color has remained unchanged—black or white trousers with black belts and shoes.

The meaningful aspects of this color symbolism are integral parts of the message of *Kūrijmōj*. Attractiveness and irresistibility are the desired qualities, and the brilliant color contrasts of so-called Polynesian prints best capture these characteristics on Āne-wetak, where such clothes can be made in common for all *jepta* members. In lieu of such supplies, bright contrasts are manufactured from black and white or, in the case of women, bright colors and white. Although this is the most manifest level of representation, the male/female contrast is also worthy of analytical attention. With increase and renewal as overall celebratory themes, it is not surprising that women opt for reds and greens. These are colors with female properties—women's reproductive properties in the case of red, and the productivity of nature in the case of green. In daily contexts, red is associated with the blood of menstruation and with female sexual parts. Equally, pandanus and breadfruit are female fruits that, at increasing metaphoric remove, point to female sexuality and reproductivity. The female associations of these symbols are manifest in many stories, including a classic tale about the trickster Etao and a primordial woman gathering pandanus (Carucci 1980b: 241–42). Green, symbolic of growing land products, is the color most manifest in living versions of those plants. Greens are said to be colors with depth or "wetness" (Conklin 1964: 189–92), having multifaceted "reflective" qualities that are frequently associated with rank and sacred force.

The men's black-and-white garb evokes the antitheses of day and night, life and death. The ceremonial overthrow of the old and its replacement by the new is the critical theme of *Kūrijmōj* that is reinforced by the absolute contrastive shades of male attire. Day, associated with the unfolding future, is the positive pole to be sought. Night, the negative pole of the ancient heathen past, is seen as a fear-inspiring arena to be left behind. Bringing the two spheres into a direct confrontation, much as black and white are impregnated above and below on the sides of men's canoes, creates the conditions for explosive, potentially transformative occurrences. This counterpositioning is used by canoe builders purposefully to create the conditions under which canoes "take flight."

Analogously, in *Kūrijmōj* the explosion of the tree is the sort of event that results from the bringing together of contraries. Although men's clothing is certainly not thought to cause the tree to explode, the evocative contrast of black and white contributes to the construction of conditions under which such explosive events are likely. *Kūrijmōj* is a ritual attempt to represent the sharp contrast between the old and the new. In addition to representation, the celebration uses the potent performative power generated by bringing opposite poles into contact to bridge the boundary between the past and the future. This boundary must be crossed to allow life's continuity on earth to be projected into the future. The contrastive shades of men's attire help fashion a context for the attainment of these symbolic ends. A series of closely associated aims is represented in a different genre through the words of a favorite Jitto-eņ song, *Rup Meram* (to cause light to explode, or to bring about the dawning of the era of light).

Nowadays, only men must wear belts at *Kūrijmōj,* but, as in the past, they remain a culturally overdetermined piece of attire. Owning a belt is a privilege, and belts are always in short supply. Tracing the passage of a belt between persons, from the time it reaches the island until it disintegrates from saltwater decay, produces a map of important endearments and solidarities. The attention belts receive is, undoubtedly, closely linked to nineteenth-century Marshallese reliance on belts as primary markers of rank and prestige. People claim that everyday belts of that era were made from pandanus, whereas belts of finer quality were woven from hibiscus bark or stripped coconut fronds. Both of the latter are still used for fine weaving on Wūjlañ because they are stronger and whiter than are strips of pandanus. Fineness of weave, like whiteness, lends increased value to woven objects.

The coloration and design of nineteenth-century belts were markers of social rank. I have not found any historical documents that record the details of specific belt patterns, but Wūjlañ people say that black, white, and red, in special combinations, were used to delineate the rank of the belt's owner. Different patterns and styles of manufacture also separated male and female belts. These complex woven belts have not been made for some time, though a commoditized version that became popular during Japanese times can still be found in handicraft shops today.

Imported belts, though lacking the elaboration of the nineteenth-century variety, carry their own sense of significance. Black belts are now the most popular, though white belts obtained from the Āne-wetak post exchange were also highly valued on Wūjlañ in the late 1970s, and one red belt received from an enlisted man on Āne-wetak instantly became the most desired belt among young Wūjlañ men. On the other hand, brown belts, which were in abundant supply on Āne-wetak, were not purchased, and one brown belt obtained through a trade on Āne-wetak was brought to me to exchange within a day of the time it reached Wūjlañ. My own tattered black belt was deemed much more desirable than the unused and much more durable brown belt.

Belts are such important pieces of attire that they receive their own array of designata to describe their modes of attachment to the body. As with many other critical activities and pieces of identity-invested attire, the noun for the object, belt in this case, is reduplicated to ask something like, "Where is the belt you are 'wearing as a belt'?" The question "Where is the belt you are wearing?" is unacceptable because it demeans the element of shared identity that links the wearer and the object (which is an alternate representation of the wearer). As objects separated out from other apparel and treated as special sorts of things, belts become primary targets during *tōbtōb,* the game in which onlookers tug the clothes of performers on December 25. Chiefly capes, tattoos, and headgear, along with objects that contact the head or the active sexual organs (personal sleeping mats), receive lexical attentions comparable to belts, but they do not play a central role in *Kūrijmōj*.

Shoes *(juuj)* are also considered markers of privilege and importance. They separate the everyday apparel, generally zoris, from sacred church wear and are particularly representative of the sorts of valuables provided by sacred foreigners. Like belts, shoes are "worn as shoes" (the reduplication of the final segment transforming category into process: *juujjuuj*). Like the other objects, it is possible to ask, "Where are the shoes you were traveling around in?" but incorrect to say, "The shoes you were 'wearing.'"[3]

Obtaining a pair of shoes for the festivities of December 25 is as critical as finding a belt to wear, because both are public demonstrations of social position and value. Fit and style are less critical than is the fact of wearing shoes, and many participants appear with oversized footwear ranging from recent Honolulu fashion to polished army boots. Shoes are special not only because they are rare but also because they elevate a person above the surface of the earth. They separate the wearer from potential sources of pollution and help the ceremonial self attain a state of purity.

One demeaning form of impurity comes from stepping in some sort of fecal remains. Though the ground is itself "dirty," it becomes particularly polluted through the absorption of feces. For the same reason, all fecal matter is immediately removed from the household grounds, the area termed *eoonļā* (on the small white stones). As mentioned, one part of the preparation for *Kūrijmōj* involves renewing these beach stones.[4] Soil pollution also endangers patients involved in local medical treatments. Those being cared for wear shoes to maintain purity. Pregnant women in the care of medical practitioners must be particularly careful to wear zoris at all times outside the house.

These restrictions are based on a theory of categorical dissimilarity rather than on a germ theory of disease. Excrement is dangerous and polluting because it represents the remains or residues of another living being. Feces have come into contact with the internal facets of another creature and transmit the worst of that being's essence to the person who touches them. There are no prohibitions against such contact between parents and offspring, for they are "one and the same," but among the members of one clan and another or between humans and other sorts of beings, animals or superhuman beings, such dangerous substances can be lethal. Feces in the bush are avoided because their source is not known. In short, feces mark species, and the fecal remains of high chiefs or skilled magicians are particularly dangerous for commoners to touch. They incorporate something of the sacred, mana-infested substance of these foreign beings and inherently conflict with the incarnate materials of commoners. In a reciprocal way, commoners' feces are polluting to chiefs because they are mundane and earthly. Likewise, animal remains pollute humans by bringing them into contact with creatures of a different order.

Kūrijmōj participants wear shoes to attain a state of purity by becoming presentable and unafflicted in the eyes of God. People who wear shoes partake only of their own substance; they are neither polluted by feces from below nor endangered from above. Much as ancient Pacific Islanders carried royalty around on a platform perched on the shoulders of bearers as a mark of not only purity but also separation, so shoes maintain the purity of the human typological order. Royal platforms doubly elevated great chiefs and chiefesses by placing them above the heads of the common people and kept them from contact with the ground. Shoes at *Kūrijmōj* construct purity by clarifying the boundaries around different human types. These ordered differences are important to the pursuit of renewal, for they represent the universe at the moment of its inception. In other words, pure types recreate the primordial order, with its lack of ambiguity. These types become a representation of the renewed state of existence people desire for the coming year. At the same time, that very newness is attractive, an additional attribute of concern to *jepta* members as they attempt to draw the attention of members of other *jepta* and of God.

Sunglasses, semantically connected with faces, are the newest piece of personal attire to be added to the celebration. Like the objects described above, they are not simply "worn" but "worn as glasses," as "part of the face." Sunglasses are particularly popular for public events because they cover the eyes, a part of a person closely connected with one's emotive characteristics. As noted, young participants are especially embarrassed to enact the ritual roles required at *Kūrijmōj,* and sunglasses serve to situationally alter the persona. At the same time, sunglasses allow Marshall Islanders to look like Americans. For travelers who have just returned from Hawai'i or the mainland United States, glasses are a marker of difference, of being well traveled, knowledgeable, and, therefore, attractive. Glasses of certain styles contribute to this public refashioning. Wearing the wire-rimmed aviators' style, for example, is an important way to represent similarities with empowered American servicemen who, not unlike empowered chiefs and deities, are associated with unlimited access to wealth and prosperity. The difference between wire-rimmed and black plastic glasses is critical to local people's representational sensibilities: black plastic shades are available in Mājuro, whereas "real glasses" must come from the United States.

Associated with objects of dress are other pieces of attire that convey meanings equally as important to Wūjlañ people as belts, hats, shoes, and glasses. The lei *(ṃarṃar)* and head wreath *(ut)* are among these. Like the special display items discussed above, leis and head wreaths must be used in both a nominal and a verbal sense: "Where is the head lei you were 'wearing as a head wreath'?" or, "Where is the lei you were 'wearing as a lei'?" Because the noun *(m̧arm̧ar)* is already constructed by reduplication (indicating a multiplicity of small parts), it is made into a verb through the addition of the suffix *-iki* rather than through reduplication. Special categorical possessives are also used to speak of head wreaths or leis: "Where is your head ornament-type head lei?" or "Where is your lei of the necklace category?" As with the body adornments already discussed, the special linguistic attention given to these objects indicates their importance within a Marshallese hierarchy of values. Those elements of greatest concern to local people, core elements of their identity, are highly overrepresented in the celebration of *Kūrijmōj*.

The head wreath encircles the most highly ranked part of the body, and therein lies its value. The custom that requires commoners to place themselves below the level of the chief's head also codes the cultural value of the head. The location of sleeping platforms on the high-ranked windward or ocean side of the house has a similar intent, and the recent decline of this practice concerns older residents. It is proper to sleep with one's head toward the windward part of the sleeping platform, and the household head should sleep with his or her head in the most windward and most oceanward location. People also claim that, in premission times, the head of a grave was placed toward the windward end of an islet. Like a few other important body parts, the importance of the head is partly coded in its treatment as a "possession-class" of its own—it takes a suffix to indicate whose head is being discussed. Along with the face and sexual parts, the head (home of thought processes) is one of the most discussed body parts. The ranking of the head is also evident in its incorporation in fundamental concepts of social hierarchy, most notably the term *bōrwaj* (roof peak, household, or family head).

The head wreath not only encircles the highest-ranked part of the body, it also requires braiding and, therefore, may incorporate hidden magical potency or force. This magic is literally woven into head wreaths by their makers, who capture the essence of chanted charms during the braiding process. A number of forms of magic are possible, including those that increase one's own desirability, those that attract another person to whom the wreath is given, and those that are imbued with magic intended to harm the person who wears the wreath. To wear a wreath made by another requires trust in one's relationship with the gift giver. I was often warned about accepting such wreaths without consideration, for, as with food prepared by strangers, wreaths may be objects of sympathetic magic that transmit intended consequences directly from the giver to the receiver.

The lei has less importance on Wūjlañ than it does in other parts of the Pacific, and it is worn less frequently. Perhaps a shortage of large flowers on the atoll makes it a rarity. Nonetheless, the lei conveys critical symbolic value. Like the head wreath, the lei is discussed in terms of its considerable beauty. Most of the leis constructed on Wūjlañ Atoll are made of shells rather than of flowers, but this does not reflect a cultural preference. People remember earlier times on Āne-wetak, where ample supplies of plumeria were available, when flower neck leis were made more often. Whereas the head wreath sits atop the most highly ranked part of the body, the lei surrounds the throat, the seat of the emotions, with a cultural significance similar to the heart in English. The lei is given as a show of affection. Being close to a person's throat, the lei represents a gift of love.

Both the head wreath and the lei are considered things of beauty. Fashioned from flowers, they are objects of desire that convey their message through the beauty of the flowers. During the present era, Marshallese culture is not particularly oriented toward artistic display. Nonetheless, it would be mistaken to say that Marshall Islanders have no appreciation of art. Their categories of classification just differ. If we look at the collections and renderings of the nineteenth century, many practices that had developed substantial artistic variety and elaboration were thought by the missionaries to be heathen customs with potentially disruptive potential. Tattoos, dance, elaborate rituals and ritual objects, and other objects and practices thought to have local religious significance were radically transformed within a few years of missionization.

Wūjlañ people often questioned why Americans value locally produced handicraft items and what the Americans would do with the shells Wūjlañ people exchanged with servicemen on Āne-wetak. They had little empathy for the answer I found most obvious: "They are things to create beauty." I later told them they were "objects to use for recollection," and the idea of memorabilia struck them as more sensible, reminiscent of the way some local people save mementos of World War II, or the way sunglasses or photographs legitimize people's attempt to portray themselves as well traveled by evoking connections with the places they have been.

In spite of the current lack of Marshallese interest in display art, complex ritual forms like *Kūrijmōj* and the construction of personal beauty are local varieties of performed art. Head wreaths and leis are naturally imbued with beauty, and, by wearing such an object, the power of that beauty is transferred to and becomes an inherent part of the person.

Part of the culturally coded attractiveness of the head wreath or lei lies in the fragrance of the flowers. Much more acutely attuned to the signification value of smells than Americans, Marshallese linguistically recognize a wide array of scents. Takaji Abo and his coauthors list more than fifty different types of smells as separate lexical items in Marshallese; about one-third of these items are applied to body odors and human smells (Abo, Bender, et al. 1976: 460). In addition to the terms listed, the Wūjlañ people use a number of dialect-specific terms to refer to various body odors and smells. These terms are employed commonly in deprecatory forms of joking, though, at times, a certain sincerity underlies these negative opinions of others. People frequently respond to jokes aimed at them with a return comment such as, "You have a bad smell," or with more specific references to unpleasant smells like,

"You smell of feces" (or "You are covered with feces"), or "You smell of unwashed sexual organs." This designation is fashioned into a term of reference to discuss third parties, either jokingly or disparagingly: "that unwashed sexual organ." All of these terms are used humorously when referring to babies and toddlers but are applied with mixed intent to adults.

The converse of this speaking style is found in phrases that express the intrinsic value with which fragrant objects are imbued. Good-smelling objects may include the fragrances of flowers, perfumes, and humans. The good smell of cooking or of cooked foods is closer in meaning to "delicious," because *ennọ* means good tasting as well as good smelling or, as Takaji Abo and Byron Bender would have it, savory (Abo, Bender, et al. 1976: 448). The fragrance and beauty of a lei or head wreath carry the message of desirability and lend the object irresistibility. This desirability, indexed by the beauty and the fragrance of the flowers, is transferred to the recipient when a lei or head wreath is given to another person.

The irresistibility of the object may be further increased through magic. Magic is incorporated through incantation or special treatment of the gift, and on Wūjlañ, where people claim that no one knows any magic (at least of the detrimental sort), the rites and ritual treatments vary a good deal from person to person. Because of the disclaimer, the physical treatments and accompanying incantations are more closely guarded than are the ingredients in Chanel perfumes. Nonetheless, formulae for love potions that cause little damage are occasionally discussed. One commonly used formula (which has several variations) to attract would-be paramours was given to me by a young single man. He claimed that it was to be used by men only. The man should go to the ocean side of the island and walk up and down the shore (some say in a leeward direction) in search of a type of red surf-polished stone. The stone must be of a solid, smooth consistency, far less common than the bits of pitted coral frequently encountered on the beach. Three of these stones need to be gathered and transported to the man's sleeping location without anyone's knowledge. There the stones are placed in a special concoction that includes coconut oil and a strong perfume and are kept for three days. (One man I consulted claimed that the magical effects would be increased if the container was placed under one's pillow and "slept with" for the three-day period.)

After three days the man removes the smallest of the stones and places it in his shirt pocket. He positions himself in an opportune location and waits for his lover to pass (some say she must be traveling in a windward direction). As she walks by, he tosses the red stone in front of her (on her windward side). If all of the conditions have been followed, if the accompanying eating prohibitions and sexual prohibitions have been obeyed, and if the man concocted a strong potion, the woman may be irresistibly attracted. If she is not immediately love struck, the remaining two stones should be treated in the same manner on the subsequent two days. When the largest stone has been tossed on the third day, the woman will be drawn to the magician. She will be irresistibly attracted even if it is against her wishes and even if she did not notice the red stones that were tossed in front of her.

Numerous symbolic attributes empower this formula: the redness of the stone, which is associated with women's sexuality; the shininess of the stone, which connotes power and attractiveness; gathering the stone on the ocean side (the male sphere) in a leeward direction (the "female" inclination), which links the actor with his intent; the three stones kept for three days (three being of extraordinary power in magical contexts because the opposition is imbalanced, the action unresolved); transporting the stones to the sleeping place and lying with them (the same actions desired of the woman); and tossing the stones in front of the woman while she is traveling in a windward direction (front and windward, often equated, are associated with males). Not only is the woman moving in a male direction, but her downwind position means that she will be overwhelmed by the fragrant potency of the magic. Thus a core attribute of the formula lies in its fragrance. The scent has its own force, and its attractiveness travels unseen through the air. Lacking a concrete, identifiable form, the smell transmits its potent, magical message. One Wūjlañ resident told me that to make this magic irresistible everything had to be performed "just right." At the same time, this young woman said that "the strength of the magic," its essence, was "a fragment of its fragrance," a desirable scent so strong and potent that it would be carried, airborne and spiritlike, into the woman's body. The woman "could never not take it" (come under its control).

For December 25, each woman prepares several head wreaths or leis. These are worn by all of the women and by many of the men. Those who do not wear wreaths or leis go out of their way to find a bottle of perfume or cologne to splash over themselves prior to the celebration. Although cologne lacks the visible beauty and encircling qualities associated with the flower wreaths and leis, it still carries the irresistible fraction of fragrant attraction. Both men and women increase their attractiveness by using such scents. Members of each *jepta* also bring perfumes, fragrant hair grease (pomade or scented coconut oil), hair spray, baby powder, and other fragrant substances with which to douse members of other groups. These scenting and beautifying acts occur while members of a group are performing. Usually the women of the group run into the audience (composed of members of the other two *jepta*) and shower the men with the scents. Some considerable amount is also spread by the men and women of one group on same-gender members of other *jepta*. This act spreads the quality of desirability and irresistibility to all participants, regardless of age or gender. Most fragrances are transferred from women to men, secondarily from men to women, and thirdly from men to men or women to women.

Spreading all of these fragrances is important. People's concern with personal cleanliness is carried to an extreme in order to prepare the participants for December 25. These preparations ritually renew through creating characteristics that epitomize youth, beauty, and sexual attractiveness. Desirable fragrances are a core part of being attractive and personally beautiful, and the perfumes, leis, and head wreaths each help to enhance that beauty and desirability. A person who is scented and made beautiful is attractive not only to members of the other *jepta* but also to God and the deities. These two presentations of person are equally important because humans and deities jointly witness and engage in exchanges with the ritual performers. Part of the success of the performance requires the ritual attainment of youth, purity, and attractiveness as symbolic devices that help secure renewal, community growth, and regeneration of nature, that is, the desirable state of being people pray for throughout the celebration.

Perfumes, leis, and head wreaths not only prepare the members for ceremonial participation, they also help construct desired conditions. The fragrances that are spread about reiterate the centrality of sexual reproduction in the celebration and are weapons of mock warfare between the competing *jepta,* which, like a clan, must exchange its own members for spouses from other *jepta*. As Nancy Pollock notes (1969: 19), both men and women are trying to make themselves attractive so they can entice a man or a woman from another group. The fragrances are magnets that ensure successful attractions. But when fragrances are distributed in the ritual encounters of December 25, there are no constraints. The medium of attractiveness, unleashed and unbounded, proves overwhelming and, thus, ensures that reproduction and regeneration must occur.

Women from each *jepta* compete to control the medium of attractiveness during the performance of each songfest group. As *jepta* members douse audience members with perfume, audience members commonly respond in kind. Female performers, however, often direct their scented sprays on certain men from each opposing group to make them irresistible. Throughout the preceding weeks, these select men have become the specific objects of their ritual affection. Symbolic unions with those particular men recapture the irresistible sense of desirability reminiscent of early adolescence. Such renewed desirability among adults caricatures adolescent attractiveness and is considered humorous. At the same time, irresistible desirability must be infused into the culminating phase of the ritual because such emotive states inevitably lead to sexual activity that must take place to perpetuate life on earth. At the same time, such beauty cannot help but attract the deities, who must bless earthly unions to ensure their reproductive success. Therefore, the fragrant deluges help create irresistibility that will lead to conditions of continued reproductivity.

Humor is a critical way for any group to weave happiness into its performance, and humor is commonly produced through ritual inversion. In daily life, the men of a clan have overt responsibility for all marriage negotiations on behalf of members of their group. If a man comes to ask for a woman, he should ask the woman's mother's older brother and, nowadays, the woman's father and mother as well. If he is insecure, he is accompanied by his own mother's brother or by his father. On December 25, however, the female members of a *jepta* are the core actors in the ceremonial constitution of intergroup unions. They are the ones who make members of other groups irresistible to members of their own group. Although the inversion of the day-to-day pattern is humorous, it equally reflects the fact that women are thought to be more closely linked to human reproductivity than are men.

In parallel fashion, the women of Naṃo, like those on Wūjlañ, wash their husbands' clothes (along with their own) to make them attractive to opposite-sex members of other *jepta* (Pollock 1969). In the melee of a group's performance on December 25, Wūjlañ women drag women they have doused with perfume from the audience during their performance and present them to the men of their own group. These actions ritually fulfill the parodied unions that will ensure fertility and increase for the coming year.

There is always retaliation for the highly scented dousings of the audience, and these counterattacks only heighten the attractiveness between ritual sexual partners. As the "collective effervescence" further negates the constraints of mundane activity, women in the audience respond to the fragrant showerings by running into the midst of a performing *jepta* and bodily carrying the song leader from the premises. Further negating their feminine character, the women capture not only a symbolic marriage mate but also the head male, representative of all others in the group and also the person integral to the group's successful performance! The performers must continue singing leaderless. The audience roars with laughter at the coup, at the women's display of male strength in battle, and at the attempt of the performers to continue leaderless. Any errors in the subsequent performance are met with applause, and the clapping increases as further flaws become apparent.

These battle tactics are supported by banter that accompanies dousings of hair tonics and perfumes: "You have really damaged that person now" or "They have been obliterated now" are representative comments. The comments typify the karatelike battles of young boys in the village, but the former is also a sexual metaphor, indicative of the time when a youth is first introduced to adulthood through the loss of his or her virginity at the hands of an experienced adult.

The excess in the distribution of fragrances and their control by women has a further significance. Fragrances transfer their potencies in magical ways through the air, the invisible medium inhabited by superhuman beings. Just such an intangible superhuman potency—the life-giving potency inherent in plants, fish, birds, and humans—is one of the most desired consequences of the celebration. The fragrances index the magical qualities that are controlled by superhuman beings and mediated by women. Women are the logical mediators because their attractiveness is innate, whereas men must make themselves attractive.

The associations between women, the control of inherent reproductive force, certain sexual qualities, and sharing the productive potential of that force with men in exchange for qualities they control (as warriors, public negotiators, and providers for families) are replicated in the relationship between gods and humans. These are women's godlike qualities (and the womanlike qualities of gods). In the ritual relationship between gods and humans on December 25, women distribute hair tonics and perfumes that make humans irresistible to one another, because their relationship to men in Marshallese cosmology is analogous to that between gods and humans. Women are, therefore, central to the celebration: they are the only symbolically appropriate mediators who can ensure the renewal of life. Their cultural characteristics must be tapped as a symbolic resource in order to ritually secure the regeneration of human society, the return of the long days, and the ripening of the pandanus and breadfruit, all events that take place as a result of Jebrọ's rule of the heavens and of Christ's governance of moral humans in the Marshall Islands.

In a group's dance performances, body movements always arouse the crowd. The movements of ancient dances are said to have captured and demonstrated desire and reproductive potency, and today's forms carry the same message, if much more subtly and in a less-elaborated array of forms. The sexual suggestiveness of the subdued, ritually nuanced dances of *Kūrijmōj* is thoroughly reinforced by the messages of attractiveness coded in costume, leis, and clothing color. Along with these signifiers, hair greases and perfumes promote symbolic intercourse between humans and deities, audience and performing *jepta,* by making participants mutually irresistible.

The mystically transmitted quality of the fragrances is supplemented by the process of "making" one's hair. The preferred hair grease, pomade, incorporates a desirable fragrance with a shininess that is even more reflective than that attained by the use of coconut oil. Reflectiveness is highly valued, as evidenced in discussions of well-kept skin, teeth, and hair. Shininess is a characteristic antithetical to "dried-out" grey-brown, the color Wūjlañ people find totally unattractive, and although shininess is not solely attributed to a particular color, it is often noted as a positive quality of blue-green. The highly valued highlights of beautiful Marshallese hair are said to be blue-green, associated with the reflective qualities of various leaves and with lagoon waters. The deep sea becomes the precise analogue of Marshallese hair. It is classified as black, rather than blue, but it has blue-green highlights that are reflected in the light of early morning.[5]

For December 25, the desirable highlights of hair are heightened. Oiling makes hair shiny and reflective and gives it the same live, vibrant element inherent in the living colors of plants and in the protected waters of the lagoon. People say that Marshallese hair has this blue-green sheen when washed and rinsed in coconut milk or greased with pomade or coconut oil. A story of ancient life on Āne-wetak uses the shininess of teeth and the reflective qualities of hair to construct images of irresistibility. The story describes the most desirable maiden of Āne-wetak in the time of Kawewa, an early nineteenth-century warrior and chief. When the maiden smiled, her teeth glistened like the hair on her head. The high chief found the maiden irresistible, and her power over him was fashioned through metaphors that associated attractiveness and reflectiveness. Her irresistibility, demonstrated in her radiant beauty (and condensed in symbols of hair and teeth), ensured her union with the chief. Analogous powers of attraction are sought when participants in *Kūrijmōj* coat their hair with pomade or scented coconut oil. The mystical attraction of the fragrance is reinforced by the potency of shininess.[6]

One ritual practice on December 25 appears to contradict the attempt to imbue hair with reflectivity, but in Wūjlañ eyes the acts are mutually reinforcing. During the *jepta* performances the heads of members of other groups are whitened, most commonly with baby powder. The same thing occurs during *kalbuuj,* when prisoners are returned to their own *jepta.* In both of these instances, I believe that the significance of the act is clarified by an understanding of Marshallese valuations of hair color and by the relationship of the powdered performers to the overall aims of the ritual. Baby powder replaces the desirable living attributes of blue-green shininess with blondness. And blond hair, no matter how white, is termed by Marshallese red, because its highlights are red. Only foreigners, and some half-caste Marshallese, have red hair.

As I have demonstrated, the ritual interactions of *Kūrijmōj* often metaphorically represent sexual attraction and reproductive activities between members of different *jepta,* but the ritual also directs its imagery of attraction toward foreigners. In *kalbuuj,* I noted that the prisoners were returned as foreign beings, not as the captured spouses, and that their hair had been "reddened" with baby powder. The celebration must also engage sacred beings in the network of exchange, for ritual play among humans is not adequate to gain access to the life's force controlled only by God. The heads of participants are reddened on December 25, I believe, to represent the presence of these sacred, foreign guests. In both cases, local islanders are transformed into others who are imperative to the symbolic aims of the festivity. The excessive use of hair oils and perfumes makes others irresistible, whereas "reddening" the hair directs the message to foreigners or to visiting deities. In the latter case, the human witnesses to the performance of a songfest group come to represent the deified witnesses toward whom the entire celebration is directed.

Red hair is associated with foreigners, particularly with Americans who are intimately connected with the source of sacred force to which Wūjlañ people are attempting to gain access for earthly renewal (Carucci 1989). I have already noted how Wūjlañ people associate chiefs, foreigners, and deities in chapter 2, a pattern widespread (though not universal) throughout the Pacific (cf. Lawrence 1971; Sahlins 1981, 1985; Feinberg 1988). Baby powder, perhaps connected with infants through its intended function, provides a direct link with the returning deity Jebrọ, for as the ascendant deity arrives from afar, he brings the ripening of the pandanus and breadfruit (both red female-associated fruits that ripen seasonally) and the redness associated with pubescent women and fertility.

The union of those who inhabit the earth and the deities of the sky results in regeneration and renewal at *Kūrijmōj.* When Jebrọ dives into the western sea, another union is resymbolized in the events of summer. Fish become greasy as a result of having eaten the "excrement of Jebrọ." A direct transfer of substance takes place between the underside of the earth and the back side of Jebrǫ. The appearance of blue bubbles (ḷait) on the shore is one evidence that this transaction has taken place. Another evidence is linked with the appearance of the albatross, when the seas become red with plankton. The albatross travels in diving patterns and is said to never cross the lagoon reef to enter the atoll. According to some, Jebrǫ consumes the albatross as his own food, and the bird's diving patterns intertwine the heavens and earth in a manner unique to this time of the year. Following the appearance of the albatross, Jebrǫ stays below, and the reddening of all of the sea represents this time at which Jebrǫ and Lōktañūr, journeying along their subterranean (and suboceanic) path to the eastern horizon, come into direct contact with the earth. The reddening of the hair of other "foreign" *jepta* members evokes the red-haired foreign deities as well as the reddening, reproductive, and regenerative power that Jebrǫ will bring to earth.

In addition to the subsurface contact between Jebrǫ and the earth, the rainbow (literally, the path) is also said to mark the trail that connects Jebrǫ with the earth. The connections with plant growth by way of the rainfall-marking rainbow are more obvious than are the subsurface connections between Jebrǫ and rich, greasy fish. The rainbow is also said to be linked to the Milky Way (the heavenly path), and it is Jebrǫ who drags the star-filled phase of the heavens across the sky through his connection with the Milky Way. Although drought may seem like an anathema in the rain-prone Marshall Islands, precipitation is not equally distributed throughout the year. In particular, during the winter, drought can bring on a shortage of water. Drinking coconuts become the prime source liquid refreshment, and if coconut supplies are exhausted, famine and starvation result. This is particularly true in the northern portions of the Marshalls, where the environment is less verdant and where there is less rainfall (Mason 1947). The reliance on Jebrǫ to overcome the fear of famine and death is marked by Jebrǫ's path, which becomes visible after rains, by his connection to the star-filled path of the Milky Way, which coincides with the coming of summer, and by his reddening of the oceans and enrichment of the fish of the sea.

The attractiveness instilled in performers by oiling their hair applies to the skin as well. Reflective skin is particularly desirable, and the same term used to describe coating one's hair with oil applies to coating one's skin. People have a great respect for the residents of Kapingamarangi, an atoll in the neighboring Federated States of Micronesia, because of their beautiful skin, and Wūjlañ folks contend that the uninterrupted, glossy texture results from constantly rubbing their bodies with oils. Such grooming is said to rid the skin of all variations and of the imperfections caused by scarring. Āne-wetak people also say Chuukese have clean skin. But Chuukese are thought of ambivalently, in part because their fine complexions result from their "despicable" consumption of tainted fish (another source of "grease"). The practice, it is said, makes one's skin heal quickly and without scarring.

Through the aforementioned forms of adornment, the body is transformed into a valuable symbol of attraction, desire, and renewal. Each performer must be clean bodied, with reflective skin and hair, bedecked with leis and wreaths, showered with perfume, or spritzed with hair spray. Along with the movements of the dance, these elements ensure that messages of allure and enticement are not overlooked. These themes are critical because life's force, productive and reproductive potency, can only be attained by ordinary humans through the power of ritual. Only in this way can God's attention be gained. Only through these mechanisms can humans convince the deities to assist them in their search to transform representations into events.

SIGNIFICANCES OF SETTING

Cleanliness extends beyond the *jepta* to include the entire village, each household, and the central church grounds. As noted, each location is cleaned and polished prior to December 25. The community's secular leaders and the chiefs see to it that the cleanup is thorough and complete. In addition to being clean, the church must be decorated for December 25. Decorations are not complex, but their character is informative. For the main celebration, palm fronds are made into large fleur-de-lis designs and hung from columns in the central part of the church, in the entryway, or in windows. The columns are then connected with strings of coconut-leaf rings interlaced into long chains. On Āne-wetak, where coconut fronds are at a premium, these decorations have been supplemented with plastic and tinseled strings of American-style Christmas ornaments.

The palm frond occupies a particular semiotic space in Christian theology that shares some features with Wūjlañ usages but does not exhaust its implications in the celebration of *Kūrijmōj*. The palm is a central motif that surrounds the Sunday preceding Christ's death and serves as a welcoming carpet on his final epic journey. In Christian theology, the palm continues to be associated with welcoming, giving, and alms. Wūjlañ frond use at *Kūrijmōj* is certainly a symbol of welcome. Like Hawai'ian *kahili,* the fronds delimit sacred and important pathways. In other respects, the palm occupies its own semiotic position in a calendrical ritual that is rather different from Western Christian interpretations. Wūjlañ palms are never seen on Palm Sunday, as is typical in Christian celebrations, but several of the ideas associated with a Palm Sunday welcoming preceding Christ's death, along with an abstract connectedness between life and death, form part of *Kūrijmōj*. Indeed, Easter's unelaborated form on Wūjlañ and Āne-wetak must be understood in relation to the encompassing representational aims of *Kūrijmōj*. On Easter, community members regroup into their *Kūrijmōj jepta,* sing songs, and prepare food, but the event is not invested with the energy of *Kūrijmōj*. Indeed, much of Easter is irrelevant, because *Kūrijmōj* brings the return of the ascendant deity, Christ, and his concomitant promise of ongoing life. As a boundary marker of sacred space and as a symbol of welcoming and of giving, the palm's appearance at *Kūrijmōj* suits local sensibilities about the value of the celebration.

In addition to welcome, palm fronds have other associations: high rank, purity, and male inseminational force. Physical evidences of these qualities are found in the coconut, which is above the land and has pure white fruits (Carucci 1987a). One recognition of this purity is the frequent use of immature coconut liquid as the elixir in prescriptions for local ailments. These undeveloped coconuts, picked before the meat has begun to appear, are always pure unless they have been magically damaged by evil spirits. Moreover, palm trees are much taller than pandanus, breadfruit, and other productive trees. In a cultural sense, it is natural that palms rank at the apex of the land-based fruits. In this atoll world, "being at the highest point here on earth" is an expression used to describe the tallest coconut trees and the skilled climbers who reach these vantage points.

To draw on the representational associations with high and low, palm fronds are arranged so that each fleur points upward, toward the social space inhabited by God and the ancient deities. "People of this world" are opposed in their fundamental character to the deities, who are represented iconically as sky dwellers, but who, in spirit form, move freely among all spaces, visible and invisible. Coconut-frond chains are strung overhead and never come into contact with the earth in order to ensure their symbolic purity. In 1977 I entered a household in which young women and girls were transforming coconut fronds into fleurs-de-lis and linked chains. As they worked with the decorations, a child was being chastised because he moved one fleur-de-lis from a mat to a sleeping platform: "It is dirty there; return it." The child proceeded to pull the decoration out of the house onto the paving stones of the house plot. The overseer then yelled, "Iiio! It is damaged. You (children) play with it and then throw it out." Though the decoration was not physically harmed, it had become polluted and lost its ritual value.

Only new fronds are used to make these decorations. These fronds are whiter than are fully developed fronds, a characteristic of purity that adds to their rank. The same type of immature fronds are used to make the fine handicraft items that are of greater value than similar items constructed of pandanus.

A TREE IS A "TREE"—OR IS IT?

The high point of a songfest group's presentation on December 25 comes with the "tree." This *wōjke* is the focal event of a group's performance. It condenses much of the imagery associated with renewal, with Jebrọ, and with Christ. As the central icon, the tree not only contains representations of wealth that sustain life, it re-creates the cataclysm that unites high and low, sacred and profane. In the explosion, the well-being of humankind is secured through a demonstration of human generosity that, by creating in God feelings of indebtedness, comes close to a guarantee of the conditions of renewal that humans desire.

Trees often take the form of bombs or missiles, iconic signifiers of con-

Figure 15. The young men of Meden prepare to explode their *wōjke* (tree) in the church on Āne-wetak in 1982. Wires are attached by the team on the left to cause the tree to explode magically moments later. Mixed tinsel and coconut-frond streamers adorn the church. (Photograph by L. M. Carucci)

centrated potency or force. An awe-inspiring tree creates and represents a group's ritual success, just as the best songs, dances, and speeches contribute to the performance by "capturing the throat" of the audience. Each of these features, along with overwhelming quantities of food and uncountably large contributions of wealth, are representations of the core forces and principles in operation during *Kūrijmōj*. The tree unifies these manifestations of force in a visible icon of demonstrably productive potency. It becomes the most didactic symbol of group strength and the metonym that condenses most concisely the aims of *Kūrijmōj*. If the tree fails to explode, the anticlimactic culmination of a group's performance may be taken as a bad omen. In contrast, successfully detonated trees are greeted with more enthusiasm and applause than are stunning singing performances or overwhelming amounts of food. Therefore, the way the tree is presented and its mode of operation are as important to the meanings as is its form.

The tree represents a coherent force, mystical in form and directed to a particular end. The mystical element is designed into in the tree by its builders, who must explode the device surreptitiously from a distance. Significant effort goes into the device's design, and the most highly acclaimed trees are those that incorporate ingenuity. Their logic of operation must be difficult for the audience to deduce. The most successful tree exploded during my years on Wūjlañ was discussed frequently for weeks. At the time, people said, "We do not know how [the designer of the tree] caused it to explode; it is a thing of amazement." Fifteen years later the tree was still recalled as a thing that created amazement.

The tree's mystical form is equally supported by the skit that is used to "reveal the tree" to the audience. These skits are either silent and vaudeville-like, with overemphasized communicative gestures, or conducted in English or Japanese gibberish. Both communicative modes are thought to be humorous, and the laughter certainly contributes to the aim of making *Kūrijmōj* a time of happiness. But, perhaps more importantly, the secret performative codes maintain the mystery that is associated with the tree, with its mode of detonation, and with the imagery of sacred, productive, force that it depicts in metonymic form.

The physical form of the tree indexically captures local memories of the most potent and powerful objects in the world. Āne-wetak people witnessed bombs in prolific and destructive display during the World War II battles on Āne-wetak Atoll, and many lost their lives during the battle (Carucci 1989). The war is now memorialized each year with a special day of remembrance when songs and stories of the era reconstruct an emotion-laden time. Earlier memories of the war are recorded in songs written down by Jack Tobin in the 1950s (1967: 28–29). Wūjlañ people also witnessed some of the most powerful aboveground nuclear explosions conducted in the 1940s and 1950s. During one such blast (the 1952 test of the first thermonuclear device), people were taken out to sea on a military vessel, far to the southeast of their atoll residence. Though nearly three hundred miles from Āne-wetak, people recall the test in dramatic detail. In one man's version:

> All of the sky in the north was so bright. There was a cloud much higher than the other clouds, and it was red and yellow and violet. It was so bright that one could never watch it. And then, after a little time, there was a sound, like thunder but greater yet; it was Āne-wetak and we knew that it was gone. Our thought was that we never would again see our homeland. (Wūjlañ Field Notes 1976–1978)

In the Marshallese view, the concentrated force of these explosions is divinely inspired, because no human could generate such power without supernatural assistance. How did the Americans come to control such apocalyptic force? For Wūjlañ residents, this was explained through adventures of Etao, the sly cultural trickster. According to these tales, Etao traveled the entire Marshall Islands Chain, coming from the islands to the west to Wūjlañ and Āne-wetak, thence to Pikinni, and from Pikinni through the remainder of the Rālik and Ratak Chains. At each atoll Etao performed various sly maneuvers: on Wūjlañ he made the arrowroot bitter, and on Āne-wetak he stole a bag of arrowroot that the chief was using for a pillow, leaving traces of it to cloud the waters and direct sailors between Āne-wetak and Pikinni (Carucci 1980b: chap. 4). After tricking the chief of Mājro to trade a very swift canoe for a beautiful and highly polished canoe of his own (but made of *Pemphis acidula,* a hard and heavy wood that sank upon setting sail), the trickster fled to the islands to the south (Kiribati) via Arņo and Mile. There Etao continued his exploits by convincing a unwary chief to bake himself in an earthen oven while the trickster made off with his daughters. As always, Etao narrowly escaped capture and sure death. After leaving Kiribati, Etao again fled. Some say that he escaped to the south, traveling via the Ellis or Tokelau islands to Fiji. Others say that Etao stowed away aboard an American ship. They captured him in a bottle, but in exchange for his freedom and for asylum, Etao confided in them about his great magical powers and agreed to tell the leaders of the American nation the secrets of this force. In this way, the Americans learned about the sacred force controlled by Etao, and they used the knowledge he shared with them to make the United States into the greatest nation on this earth. With the sacred force Etao conveyed, they were able to make bombs, airplanes, missiles, and satellites, so now they are the most powerful nation on earth (Carucci 1989).

The same magical qualities conveyed to the Americans through Etao, unfathomable and uncontrolled forces, are symbolized in the tree, an object that epitomizes the regenerative power that is the raison d'être for *Kūrijmōj*. Like the sacred, life-giving force that women bring into being through birthing (marked by the continuous-clan pathway), like the sacred force of the wind captured in the sails of a man's sailing canoe, the potent, explosive force of the tree represents the reproductive and regenerative forces that cause cyclical renewal on earth.

Kūrijmōj provides Wūjlañ and Āne-wetak people with a ritual means of controlling superhuman forces. Such control is always dangerous, for it must involve contact with the sacred. But there are limited options. Through exchange and liminal inversion, the deities are entertained. Reproductive continuity of clans, ostensibly controlled by women, ultimately depends on deified blessings, because women alone cannot avoid clan extinction. Men's provisioning role, particularly in relation to the sea, is equally dependent on God's good will. The fallacious idea that "providing for" is truly controlled by men is humorously noted as women co-opt men's roles during *karate*. Likewise, the role of male respected elders as the public speakers for female-headed clans is replaced by the central public performances of women during *Kūrijmōj*. All of these unsettling parodies are dangerous but, at the same time, productive.

People claim that men have always enacted the skit that allows each group to detonate its tree. Most skits on Wūjlañ have military themes; after all, male soldiers during World War II were those who "made war." Yet other themes are possible, as in ancient times, when men and women fought together in wars against other Marshallese (cf. Finsch 1893: 35). In 1977 an innovative pattern was introduced. Jitto-eņ chose to have a woman, dressed as an astronaut, participate in the skit. It was the most laughter-provoking skit of the festivities and contributed substantially to the success of the Jitto-eņ tree. Nonetheless, the event became a source of controversy when the woman died in childbirth two years later. Some believed the events were connected and suggested that the woman had "gone ahead and elevated herself too highly." "Humans should never attempt to grab hold of heaven, for they will be damaged." Therefore, even though the liminal practices of *Kūrijmōj* are the only means humans have for transforming the conditions of their current lives, these practices are dangerous. Only the deities know when ritual practices exceed necessary limits. At such times, God will demonstrate that the limits have been surpassed.

More typically, women encircle the arena while men enact the skit that leads to a tree's detonation. The circular organization is critical here, representing both the value of the center and the protection associated with surroundedness. Metaphors of sexuality and the family are also conjured up in the skits as women play the protective, enveloping role while men enact active, display-oriented roles. Just as a woman surrounds the child in her womb, the tree envelops the valued treasure that represents the wealth of renewal for humankind. Equally, at the time of detonation, women encircle and support the men as they make the tree work, just as women surround the men during sexual intercourse or as they sit in the surrounding audience as the headmen of clans and households stand in the center of council meetings to speak on behalf of their families or clans.

Even though inversion provides a transformative mechanism in the tree's detonation, many of the symbolic actions separate those things that are, for local people, properly kept separate. As a core symbol, the tree represents sacred productive and reproductive force. On Wūjlañ, both are social processes that rely on the complementary opposition of male and female. In order for a tree to fulfill its potential, to magically reveal enormous wealth, then to encumber the deities by giving this primary gift to them, the tree must rely on the productively balanced and reproductively successful division between male and female.

Because the tree is constructed to capture the essence of magical force, the logic of its detonation remains opaque. Trees detonated by hand are not considered to be very successful, for they fail to adequately represent the mystical qualities of life-giving force sought in the ritual. This force is, ultimately, controlled by God, but, at the same time, the path that provides humans likely access to it is through the younger-sibling deities Jebrǫ and Christ. Both of these entities are the mediators who, through love and caring, take care of ordinary humans as a corollary of their structural position in a suprahuman family of orientation.

Not unlike the World War II pilots who described their airplanes and the bombs they dropped as women, sweethearts, and offspring, one group of young men busy constructing their group's tree began to joke about it in ways that provided support for the idea that reproductive force was, somehow, captured in the tree. They talked about the tree as a newly pubescent woman in whom several of the young men had an interest. Their *jepta* theme was "the star" (of Bethlehem), and their tree would eventually be a painted, plywood-paneled box topped by a star, the sides of which would fall off to reveal the branching framework covered with money and other gifts within. At this point, it was simply a box of painted wood. Nevertheless, the young men constructed vivid images of their fantasied paramour's most desirable features, mainly her genital region, in analogical parallel with the tree that was being built. The young men temporarily attached makeshift parts to the torso to represent arms, breasts, and a head. In their impromptu, private performance the interior of the tree, the part that encompassed the tree's explosive force and the treasure, represented the woman's womb—the site of primary interest to the young men and the site of sacred reproductive force. Their laughter intensified as the workers danced around the tree, singing the most popular song of that *Kūrijmōj,* a song from the songfest group that the young girl would likely join the coming year: *Rup Meram* (the explosion of the light, or the coming of salvation). One of the young men patiently explained to me the irony in their dark and light construction: while they sang of explosions of light, it was really the "coming of darkness" the young men desired, mission-inspired talk for the young woman's sexual fall from grace. In fact, for these young men, the image of an explosion of light seemed far more appropriate to represent the cataclysmic experiences to be shared by the young girl and her first paramour.

The sacred character of the tree is not only constituted analogically in the features of its construction but also fashioned from human interactions in relation to it. Like the sacred maidens of old on Āne-wetak and elsewhere in the Pacific (cf. Hecht 1979), the tree must be kept in isolation. Only the young men of the *jepta* are permitted to see it until it is tested or tried out at a secret practice of the entire group. It is then returned to seclusion until its presentation on December 25. Although trees seldom go unseen, because members of other groups try to secretly spy on them, attempts are made to maintain the appearance of obscurity and secrecy. The tree remains in a hidden spot within the practice house of the *jepta* or within the house of one of the builders. When it is not being worked on, the tree is draped with muslin. During construction someone watches to see that no outsiders view the tree, especially women or members of another *jepta*. On December 25 the tree remains draped in white cloth until it is unveiled in the church by the men of the *jepta*.

Equally important, trees contain all of the requisite elements of cataclysmic display. As a group begins to sing and dance, young children gather around because they know that the skit and the tree will follow, but, with the explosion, cataclysm is realized in praxis. In the midst of blinding light and loud explosion, the treasure inside the tree comes into view. Yet the mystical means of causing the explosion is as important to the performance as is its content. All are components that represent the power of God. The wealth contained within represents the inexhaustible supply of goods available to God and the power to transmit this prosperity to the members of the community. The explosion uses incalculable intensities of light, heat, and sound as ritual representations of the earth-building and earth-shattering forces controlled by

God, and the mystical method of explosion captures something of God's ultimate control of magic as well as the *jepta*'s successful use of these powers for its own purposes. As the gifts within the tree are revealed and as they are dedicated to God, the conditions of indebtedness that will ensure prosperity for the coming year are put in place. The gifts of wealth not only recognize the high position of the deities, they force the deities to continue the exchange with reciprocal gifts of their own. One speaker dedicated the gifts of his *jepta* to God by calling them "objects to speed things up," as if writing a preface to a treatise that would spell out future good fortunes (Carucci 1980b). Reciprocal obligations placed on the generous and loving deities (Jebrọ and Christ) by the wealth that emerges from the tree guarantee that they will watch over the people in the coming months. Contact with the deities need not be lengthy, for their true position is "high up." Their attentions are required only momentarily, during the culminating liminal moments around December 25. Indeed, more prolonged contact with such high-ranked beings would be dangerous.

One important feature of the celebrations that residents say has changed since the time of Ernej (the locally born Wūjlañ pastor who is viewed in ideal terms) is the manner in which wealth is redistributed. The greatest concentration of wealth is contained within the tree. Like the Kwakiutl potlatch, *Kūrijmōj* involves an ever-expanding collective display of valuables that participants contend is out of control yet seem to lack the power to change. In olden times, people say that part of the collected wealth of renewal celebrations went to the deities and to the men who watched the deities *(rūkaanijnij)* and that another portion went to the chiefs and their families but that a significant segment was returned to the people. In Ernej's time this was still true.

Today, however, this arrangement has changed: all of the valuables within the tree are kept by the minister. Yet, as mentioned elsewhere, no matter how deplorable the people consider the minister's hoarding, they give the wealth "freely" in order to ensure that the higher purposes of the celebration are accomplished. These goods "belong to God," and, as one woman noted, "whoever receives these works [prestations] is all the same, for it is the will of God." At the same time, as part of the present egalitarian critique of chiefs and others in positions of power (Carucci in press), participants think that today's ministers, like Ernej, should redistribute the goods they receive. Such generosity would greatly increase the minister's rank within the community and would represent to all participants the spirit of giving on which the celebration is based. Indeed, in Wūjlañ people's interpretations of the Bible, giving freely without expectation of reward is an anomalous idea, because giving freely always carries its own reward: the increased rank of the giver. This is why God, like any deity, must reciprocate in greater measure the gifts of each *jepta* at *Kūrijmōj*. Likewise, the minister, in order to truly instantiate the position of honor he is given in the community, should return gifts to the community that outweigh those presented to him. Since the return to Āne-wetak, the contents of each tree may approach US$1,000, and a minister on the atoll may easily increase his wealth by US$20,000 by the end of the celebration. As prestations have increased in quantity, it is not surprising that the semipublic pleas for reciprocation have increased in frequency.[7]

Not unlike the motifs attributed to Melanesian Cargo (Burridge 1960; Worsley 1968; Lawrence 1971; Lindstrom 1993), *Kūrijmōj* builds partly on the recollections of war. The tree represents these military themes in a condensed, symbolic form. On Wūjlañ and Āne-wetak it reconstructs moments from World War II and the era of nuclear testing, events that are spoken of as continuous by local people (Carucci 1989). The tree condenses experiences and reminiscences of this era into a ritual representation of potent display with cataclysmic potential followed by a period of good times. Indeed, local historical experiences are discussed in analogous terms. After the battle of Āne-wetak people were displaced from their homes and moved by the United States Navy to concentrated settlements on the northern islets of the atoll. Yet local people were so grateful to be alive that they remember these times in positive terms. Indeed, in contrast to the Japanese military personnel, who threatened to kill them, the Americans were, they believe, kind and generous, a portrayal supported by the unlimited distribution of goods that continued through the navy era.

The period of nuclear testing was followed by times of extraordinary deprivation on Wūjlañ—a phase when Wūjlañ residents seriously questioned the chiefly intentions of governments and God. By the late 1960s, they boycotted attempts by Marshall Islands officials to continue to force them to live in poverty (*Micronesian Reporter* 1968). Soon afterward, they began to question the United States' use of their homeland. But the experiences of the community during the era of suffering on Wūjlañ are described as being equivalent to those of the lost tribes of Israel. Whereas the most recent phases of this encounter with outsiders are tinged with increasingly bold interactions mediated by foreign lawyers, the locally inspired strategies prior to about 1970 are symbolic attempts to draw on local sources of potency to bring about a state of atollwide well-being and increase.

Kūrijmōj, Wūjlañ style, was largely produced during this era. Not unlike the symbolically sequenced interactions described by Peter Lawrence for Madang as Cargo, Wūjlañ *Kūrijmōj* foresees a transformation of current modes of living and a pathway to good times in the future. The valuables in the Wūjlañ *Kūrijmōj* tree are only metonymic representations of the goods and welfare sought in the new year. Good fortune is the aim, but there is no set format in which the wealth must appear. On Wūjlañ, reproductive success and a plethora of provisions are seen as gifts from God worthy of thanks in the prayers of the Sabbath. But the wealth of provisions during the navy era and recent compensations for nuclear testing on Āne-wetak are also described as responses to the community's pleas to God.[8] These good fortunes are conditional: they exist as part of a larger exchange relationship with the deities. If God is pleased with the activities of *Kūrijmōj* and if people live upstanding lives, goods will be provided. The period of doubt and questioning that follows December 25 represents the community's fear that the aims of *Kūrijmōj* will not be realized due to the community's own shortcomings. If these shortcomings are witnessed by God or by any of a number of superhuman entities, they will act through "evil spirits" to display their displeasure with the ordinary people. In such instances, misfortunes will interrupt the fortuitous flow of fortune.

Because of the acquisitiveness that is said to occupy people's thoughts these days (as opposed to times past), Wūjlañ and Āne-wetak people are concerned that their quest for future well-being will not be realized. The pastor, an outsider, cannot ruin the community's ritual search for life, but all gifts at *Kūrijmōj* should be presented as "the possession-class things of God." When a pastor receives these gifts, it is only in his role as an interpreter of God's word. Since God knows the minister's intent, if the prestations are coveted by the minister, he places himself at great risk. God sanctions flawed human actions, and illness and death are punishments for personal disingenuousness. Indeed, one former Wūjlañ pastor is said to have died as a result of his greed. Similarly, community members must give freely, or invite God's wrath. Communitywide wrongs may be sanctioned by God's own action, and the results come in forms such as typhoons. For smaller offenses, God seeks retribution through lower order "policemen" (Carucci 1987b). These enforcement personnel, or "demons,"[9] are always present at *Kūrijmōj*. They bear witness to positive signs of welcome, generosity, cleanliness, and happiness and to negative practices such as drinking and fighting. Their persistent oversight makes the ceremonial atmosphere even more highly charged with excitement and danger, a setting in which the cataclysmic nature of the explosion of the tree is suited to its ends.

The light and sound of the tree's explosion mediate between sacred, superhuman beings and common people. Like free-flowing body substances, uncontrolled light and sound are part of the creational force represented in the explosion of the *wōjke*. Unconstrained light and sound are both markers of openings in the interstices of heaven and earth and are semiotic devices used to open the communicative channels between these domains. At the same time, in constrained but continual doses, both noise and light are associated with life. Therefore, they are antithetical to the presence of the demons. Even a small amount of light is thought to keep demons away. When kerosene is depleted, everyone makes coconut oil in order to keep a light burning throughout the night. Likewise, lights are used to travel through bush lands to fend off dangerous (often foreign) supernatural spirits. Pregnant and nursing women must be even more careful. Well-lit houses are imperative when they and their children sleep.

Community members constantly worried that I would be bothered by these spirits because I elected to sleep without a light. When my adoptive brother's son slept in my house for a few days, he was appalled by the dozens of spirits that could be seen around the perimeter of the roof when the light was extinguished. After two worry-filled nights, he insisted on lighting a lamp to illuminate the house at night while he resided there. Townsfolk became even more concerned when I moved to a small house in the land parcels a short distance from the village. The site was extraordinarily dangerous because it was near a cemetery. Some concerned relatives brought me a lamp to use during the nights spent in the cabin.

Sound also marks the channel between the superhuman and human spheres at the same time that, in controlled quantities, it serves as a deterrent to supernatural entities. Thus thunder, though infrequent, is associated with downpours. When its clap is heard, weather forecasters commonly say that "the heavens are open." On the other hand, fishermen who travel into the bush at night are most comfortable in large, rowdy groups. This is particularly important in *Āne-kōn̄ēn̄e,* the leewardmost end of Wōjlan̄ islet, because foreign spirits from the west appear with frequency on the leeward tip of Wūjlan̄ Atoll and the leeward part of the islet.[10] Therefore, the ritual uses of sound and light are multiple. With the explosion of the tree, the communicational channels between heaven and earth are opened. A week later, on New Year's Eve, the repetitious and sleep-disturbing sound of children's singing combines with the continual light of lamps to chase supernatural spirits from the scene. Sound and light entirely eliminate nighttime, for night is associated with superhuman beings, with death, and with the past.[11]

THE DEFIANCE OF DEATH THROUGH DANCES OF LIFE

Another central feature of the activities of December 25 are dances, the *beet* and the *m̧aaj,* which I described in chapter 1. These dances are compromise forms between the mission-tabued ancient dances and the subdued line dances of Japanese origin. On Āne-wetak, ancient dances are claimed to have been integral parts of sacred ritual performances. They were important tools of attraction that helped humans perpetuate life on earth, and, though radically refashioned, they continue to promote this aim today. The dances of *Kūrijmōj* have doubly empowered themselves by incorporating new symbolic forms as well, particularly the imagery from Japanese and American military formations. The *beet* and the *m̧aaj* give atoll residents access to the empowering potentials of dance and, at the same time, accommodate their own ideas about the strictures of the church. *Kūrijmōj* dances maintain their position as an acceptable performative form through separation from "true" Marshallese dances. They fit none of the common categories of dance: *ikkure* (dance as a subtype of play), *kwōjkwōj* (dances with rapid hip movements), *dun̄* (sexually explicit dances), *tuuj* (rock-and-roll dancing), and so forth. Yet people recognize a commonality between *Kūrijmōj* dances and these more animated forms. When speaking of the most skilled performers at *Kūrijmōj* people say, "[So-and-so] really knows how to dance."

In many parts of the Pacific, including Āne-wetak and Wūjlan̄, skilled dancers occupied respected positions in premission times. Otto von Kotzebue (1830) notes that the chief of Wōjjā had his best dancers perform during a welcome feast on his second voyage to the atoll. As with warriors, seafarers, and other positions of skill, renowned dancers received special recognition by their chiefs, and dancers of old are still discussed by residents of Āne-wetak Atoll. Although today's skilled dancers hold no specialized positions, their abilities are recognized in community commentary.

Both the *m̧aaj* and the *beet* capture and construct important facets of remembered history. As a concomitant of the military theme that opposes one *jepta* to another, the *m̧aaj* gives the members of a group a fashionable way of entering the performative arena. Highly stylized and reminiscent of the entry dances captured in the film *Trobriand Cricket,* the *m̧aaj* and the *beet* incorporate both men and women. Ancient dances separated males and females, but in the *Kūrijmōj* performances, gender identity is subtly marked by movements that segment men and women using linear or concentric patterns that maintain an opposition between them. Both men and women perform synchronized steps alongside the opposite-sex group, yet males and females never touch or directly mix. The linear organization of today's dances is reminiscent of men's dances described in historical texts (Finsch 1893: 27 et seq.; Kramer and Nevermann n.d.: chap. 4) and of the reconstructed steps in the film *Mokil.* Nevertheless, today's Marshall Islanders claim that Mājeej residents created the *beet* during the 1930s, as an adaptation of Japanese dance forms. The *m̧aaj* is said to have been added after the war, but military review steps appear to have affected the *beet* as well, altering the fluid, unbroken sequences of *bon* dancing.

Equally important to the *beet* and the *m̧aaj* are thematic foci that draw on people's constructions of the ancient past. Ancient men's dances are said to have modeled the themes of parable-like stories that concentrated on warfare, on interpersonal relations and trials of nature, and on love and sexual exploits and desires. The reconstruction in the film *Mokil* represents a rough approximation of descriptions and enactments of the Wūjlan̄ war dance. In like regard, women's dances brought stories to life through the fluid and dynamic representations of body motion.

Female dances were of two major types. Sitting dances stressed movements of the head and arms, whereas hulalike dances included hip movements and more provocative themes. People say that sitting dances were performed to the meter of a discordant monotone chant, whereas the hula-style dances were accompanied by drumming and chanting. The sitting dances have become a humorous marker of ancient times for the men of the community, who claim that women had no idea of how to sing ("properly") before the missionaries' arrival. Their rhythmic chants in high, scratchy voices (a prominent ritual form of public singing rarely heard now) are thought to be nearly unbearable. The hulalike dances draw a much more mixed response. Even though knowledgeable old residents claim that the themes of these dances varied, the most sexually provocative ones have been elevated to the level of a generic stereotype for the entire category. In most public contexts, committed Christians view the genre with disdain, but young single men and women revel in its display. Hulas belonged to certain performers, and the performances were shrouded with secrecy. Commoners could observe hulas during special ritual events, but at other times they were performed only at the request of persons of rank. Barren women could not view such dances at all, but, for most women, instruction in hula-type dances, it is claimed, were part of adolescent training. Such training groups were the women's counterpart of men's military groups (see Carucci 1992).

All these forms of dance have been slow to emerge from their underground forms. Only the most bold Wūjlañ and Āne-wetak people dance in the hula style in semipublic settings. Such performances draw many smiles and snickers, and female performers are often labeled, somewhat playfully, as Etao—tricksterlike, or a really ill-behaved person. Although men are not so readily chastised for their Etao-like imitations of ancient dance (Carucci 1983), they, too, clearly approach the margins of the acceptable.

Some people note that women's seated dances began with a metered entry step prior to the main performance, and, according to their accounts, a related closing step accompanied the dancers' departure. These transitional forms are analogous to the *m̧aaj* in *Kūrijmōj,* though today's *m̧aaj* also reflects elements fashioned after the military parade ground and is most often performed to the beat of a song accompanied by a ukelele or a guitar. Often the leader of the *m̧aaj* backs into the church, shouting commands and reminding lackadaisical dancers toward the back of the dance troupe of the proper step. The guitarist or ukelele player walks to the side. The *m̧aaj* is not central to a group's performance, but it allows a group to enter the performative arena in a stylized manner and, often, to exit with equal aplomb. Nevertheless, some groups do not exit. They simply disband after the final gifts are given to the minister. The best groups design a *m̧aaj* that captures some of the foot movements of their *beet* and incorporates them into a processional and recessional step.

In contrast, the *beet* represents a *jepta*'s real dancing expertise. Years later, steps from well-known *beet* can be recalled, and fragments can be reenacted, but no one remembers a *m̧aaj* for very long. People say that one intent of the *beet* is to "make happiness" within the community. The *beet* stresses complex, skilled movements. Whereas the *m̧aaj* displays lines, male and female, in balanced synchrony, the *beet* interweaves lines of dancers of opposite gender using synchronic and harmonic movements. Even though the dancers do not touch, the *beet* uses diversified and animated movements, backward and sideways as well as forward, to elaborate on the woven-line performance. This weaving together of males and females presents an image of formal and reserved seduction, paired and balanced but very subdued, like the paired vintage folk dances of Europe.

In spite of the *beet*'s subdued character, the audience responds wildly to the movements of the dancers. Some say that the *beet* is "just like" the hula-type dances performed on ritual occasions of the past century but refashioned to align with the rules of the church. Indeed, the missionary tabu of dancing is still a concern to local people, and the boldness of any form of dance within the church is marked by the fact that the *beet* is not performed on

Epoon, the motherland of the Marshallese Protestant Mission. Nevertheless, diversity of motion and variation in rhythm have been increasingly infused into the *beet* in the past twenty years. The six dances I witnessed in the 1970s played heavily on the balanced, interweaving movements of males and females but had a limited array of movements that people considered sexually provocative. By 1982, however, Io̧lap performed a Marshallese *beet* called *Mojān dikdik* (very small motions). In this *beet,* the incanted words *Mojān dikdik* are accompanied by a series of rapid hip rotations. This performance dazzled the crowd, drawing shouts of approval, clapping, and shrieks of laughter. Women rushed from the audience to carry male performers from the scene, and men ran up to tug on the dresses of women dancers. It was a rousing success—and the *beet* was the gift of the assistant minister's wife!

Therefore, in spite of the claim by some longtime church members that animated dances have no place in *Kūrijmōj,* each newly choreographed *beet* moves in that direction. Indeed, the *beet* of the 1970s already had the ability to conjure up the stereotypical sexual foci of ancient hulas even though their form was more mundane. At that time "Etao's dance" alongside the *beet* made the sublimated theme apparent (Carucci 1980b). Such enactments of Etao, the sly island trickster, are performed impromptu, alongside a group's dancing of the *beet.* In contrast with the ordinary dancers, however, Etao dances with excessive sexual explicitness to stress the lacuna of the staid mission-constrained form. The crowd finds this mime of Etao's actions hilarious. It is a sure way to ensure happiness (Carucci 1983), and the *jepta* that has a skilled, sly dancer to perform by its side is very apt to win the dance part of the performance.

Etao dancers are frequently members of the *jepta* that is presenting, but on occasion a member of another *jepta* will mime the performers. Such outside impersonators are always persons who are publicly acknowledged metaphoric lovers or spouses of the opposite group. They have joked continually with the performing group during the weeks of *karate, kalbuuj,* and *kaṃōḷo,* and they skillfully mime the movements of the group with which they are enamored. In either case, the trickster simultaneously replicates and parodies notable movements of the *beet,* transforming them into seductive folly. The trickster's parody innovates in richly metaphoric ways on the basic footwork, arm motions, or clapping patterns of the *beet,* making them small, or overwhelming, in contrast to a particular dancer's self-conscious style. Simultaneously, the Etao performer introduces slight, seductive hip movements or bold, rapid ones to draw public attention to the sexually explicit themes attributed to dances of old.[12] Etao thus acts out covert aspects of the dance, those tabued by church doctrine, yet the very themes of human reproductivity that are integral to *Kūrijmōj.* Waves of applause and animated commentary point out the attraction to that which is simultaneously tabu and confirm the importance of dance, its own movements, and the parodies of these forms, as body behavioral representations of the themes of *Kūrijmōj.*

The trickster teeters on the edge of the past and the present, drawing into the *beet* of the present day the potencies of attraction inherent in dances of the remembered past. These prohibited actions of the skilled hula dancer, now stereotyped as seductive and sexual in character, provide the potency to unite male performers with female, the members of one *jepta* with those of another, and ordinary humans with the gods. The representation of irresistibility does not end here. The audience responds by attacking the Etao dancer first, tugging on each piece of clothing as a representation of irresistibility and desire. But Etao only embellishes on movements of other dancers. Once claim is laid to Etao's clothes, members of the audience tug the clothing of the other dancers. The performers' attractiveness is recognized, the interweaving of male and female is realized, and the perpetuation of human existence on the earth is ensured. After the performance, the exchanged clothes are worn as mementos that remind participants of the celebration and of the humorous and irresistible actions that made *Kūrijmōj* such a success.

Another represented component of creative force is apocalyptic and transformative power. Indeed, sexual energy itself has such power, as evidenced by local people's use of the motions of sexual intercourse as an appropriate imagery to describe the fire plow's ability to create fire out of nothingness.[13] But the military motions of the *beet* and the *ṃaaj,* the practiced line formations, point to an additional choreographed form of potency. Indeed, these movements bring to people's minds recollections of World War II and of the continued military presence after the war, during the time of nuclear testing. These memories are the most apocalyptic experiences of the recent remembered past, and the dance, along with the explosion of the tree, places this force at the disposal of local people. Āne-wetak and Wūjlañ people believe that such energy must have a superhuman source and that, indeed, it was Etao who brought such energy to earth and subsequently shared knowledge of it with the most empowered of earthly beings, the Americans (Carucci 1989). But local people also think that the powers of destruction and those of construction are one, but directed differently. This they were told by the Americans at the beginning of the nuclear-testing era: the detonation of nuclear devices would lead to continued peace for all of humankind (compare with Kiste 1974, on Pikinni). What better way to secure peace and future goodwill than through military parades and exploding Christmas trees?

Like each supporting symbolic device of *Kūrijmōj,* the dance is a minor representation within a complex, ever-changing, collective form. In and of itself, its meanings are minute, but the incremental accretion of such representational elements makes the celebration a tremendously empowering tool that allows local people to reconfirm the taken-for-granted order in the universe, to represent important life-sustaining processes and interrelationships, and then to seek the perpetuation of this order and the continuity of these processes beyond the present day.

CHAPTER SEVEN

Ritual Performance, Local Identity, and the Construction of Meaning

Core Themes and Innovative Applications

I have demonstrated how central the celebration of *Kūrijmōj* is to the people of Wūjlañ and Āne-wetak Atolls. Not only does it constitute one-third of each year's activities, it is a primary tool in terms of which the continuity of life on earth is pursued and local identity is defined. In spite of local claims about the uniqueness of Wūjlañ *Kūrijmōj,* many of its features are shared with other locations and other times. Indeed, as a celebration of renewal, *Kūrijmōj* has deep temporal roots that link its celebration with other calendrical celebrations throughout the Pacific. At one level, then, Wūjlañ symbols and ritual practices represent that part of identity that is shared with many other Pacific people. Although symbolic actions are polysemic representations that simultaneously situate identities at many levels, I separate these levels from one another in the following sections for purposes of presentational clarity.

WŪJLAÑ PRACTICE AS A MARKER OF PACIFIC PERSONHOOD

Kūrijmōj delineates Pacific components of Wūjlañ personhood in a number of ways, both conscious and subconscious. Indeed, these elements of identity are not of great concern to Wūjlañ and Āne-wetak people because they view *Kūrijmōj* as a local atoll celebration, to be compared and contrasted with Marshall Islands' and other nearby celebrations. At the same time, as Āne-wetak people (and Marshall Islanders more generally) renegotiate their national and atoll identities with other new Pacific Island states and in opposition to the United States and Japan, I believe that common Pacific practices will be used to forge new senses of oneness. Perhaps the most important Austronesian or Pacific element of *Kūrijmōj* centers on the analogy drawn between the ascendance of Christ and the rising of Pleiades (in the Marshall Islands, Jebrọ).

As I have indicated, however, Wūjlañ people differ in their ability to recognize and/or rationalize the commonalities. Why, then, is it so important? First, because some of the most astute storytellers, who leave indelible imprints on the cultural consciousnesses of tomorrow, recognize the critical ways in which the Marshallese starscape relates to yearly renewal and to *Kūrijmōj*. Second, as the strength of the missionary era dissipates, along with the passing of the final cohort of Āne-wetak people who saw the first mission teachers, local people will rethink their religious views, innovating on current understandings of ritual practice. Āne-wetak people have already begun to resituate (Congregationalist) Christianity in opposition to Assembly of God advocates. They rely less frequently on their own heathen past to position themselves as Christians. As religious sects proliferate and as Pacific states search for a common ground, this rethinking will continue. In particular, I believe that the "otherness" of many Āne-wetak people's conceptions of their own past will become less important to the Christian segment of the community, because the competition for local souls has changed its focus. Whereas Christianity was once threatened by the heathen past, today's sects compete with one another on the basis of funding and on their beliefs about ABCFM-inspired tabus—such as smoking, drinking, and dancing. From this increasingly multiflavored stew of identity components, at least some segments of the Wūjlañ/Āne-wetak community, I believe, will perpetuate and elaborate on the belief that Jebrọ and Christ are cut from the same mold.

Elsewhere (Carucci 1980b), I have noted other features of Wūjlañ *Kūrijmōj* that explore Pacific tropes, particular themes held in common with the well-known Trobriand *milamala* and the *makahiki* of Hawai'i. The similarities between Trobrianders' sweeping the village of the ancestors at the end of *milamala* (Malinowski 1954: 186) and Wūjlañ youths "making night into day" with noise and illumination on New Year's Eve are hardly random. In both cases, spirits of great potency, necessary to each celebration's ritual aims but equally dangerous to daily life, are driven back to their distanced everyday domain.

Equally, the frolic and water splashing that occur in *karate* and the Hawai'ian *hiuwai* that was part of the *makahiki* draw on related sets of cultural possibilities. Although social personae differ, both forms of water splashing are representations of sexual interactions in search of fertility. When I mentioned such similarities to Wūjlañ and Āne-wetak people, they said, "Oh, of course, we are all one and the same, people of the Pacific region, with just one grandparent." Presented with evidence of common epistemology, Āne-wetak people immediately enveloped the information within their own theories of shared identity.

Analogous forms of belief and ritual practice in Pacific renewal celebrations are hardly surprising, because these societies share many linguistic and cultural traits. Such affinities result from a relatively brief settlement histories—if archaeologists are correct, about two thousand years in the Marshall Islands (Rosendahl 1979; Dye 1981). More important, however, they represent the perduring character of cultural logics and the ability of Wūjlañ people to refashion their culture in new and viable forms without abandoning the conceptual outlines of a central episteme (Foucault 1970). As Marshall Sahlins says of Hawai'ians, "the more things changed, the more they remained the same." In many senses, this is true of Wūjlañ. In spite of local people's concerted attempt, at different historical moments, to reconstruct themselves along the lines of their various colonizers (and thereby appropriate their powers), they have continued to reformulate ideas of a consistent cultural character as they expand the map of their own episteme to include new, uncharted sectors.

The Pacific-wide tropes of *Kūrijmōj* have varied significance to Wūjlañ and Āne-wetak people depending on who they are in the community at the time. Most Wūjlañ and Āne-wetak people recognize the wide Oceanic distribution and salience of the Antares/Pleiades/Orion triad, in which Pleiades (the younger sibling Jebrọ in the Marshall Islands) is associated with themes of kindness and yearly renewal (for example, Makemson 1941; Malinowski 1965; Valeri 1985). On the other hand, only the most knowledgeable storytellers of today drew my attention to the analogies between Christ and Jebrọ. Local Christians of the 1970s and 1980s, still shuddering under the specter of heathen belief, would never do so. Nevertheless, the cultural milieu continues to shift, and I expect that my storytellers' views will become more salient as rifts in established religious and cultural identities begin to appear.

THE RELATIVIZED OPPOSITION OF REGIONAL TROPES

By using *Kūrijmōj* as a core signifier for local atoll identity, regional continuities with related people, like the Pacific commonalities, are understressed. When asked directly, Wūjlañ people note that songs, dances, and even the general feast form are largely shared with neighbors. Nevertheless, placing themselves in the center of their universe, Wūjlañ people see the common features of their neighbors' practices as degenerate replicas of their own. This is more true of local people's view of Marshall Islanders than of Eastern Caroline Islanders. Current political relations drive this symbolic posturing because local people work much harder at distancing themselves from Marshallese than from Pohnpei, Kosrae, N̄atrik, or Mōkil. Wūjlañ people readily admit, therefore, that certain songs and dances were inspired by Carolinian composers and choreographers. They even note similarities between their own feasting format and that of the Eastern Carolines (see Peterson 1979; Lieber 1984; Poyer 1993: 162–65, 183 et seq.). At the same time, the shared features of Wūjlañ and Marshall Islander's *Kūrijmōj* are understressed or even denied. These constructed contrasts were not unrelated to other causes of the day: first, Wūjlañ people's decision to appeal for a separate trust agreement with the United States rather than affiliate with the proposed Republic of the Marshall Islands early in the 1980s; second, Wūjlañ people's use of *riMajel* (Marshallese people) to describe a group of others, distinct from "us." In only a very restricted number of higher-order contrasts did Wūjlañ people of that era categorize themselves as Marshall Islanders.

Nevertheless, the common themes of Marshall Islands practice are readily apparent. As political winds shift, these too may become tomorrow's markers of shared identity. For example, on Naṃo, site of the best documented of the Marshallese *Kūrijmōj* celebrations (Pollock 1969), the atoll divides into *jepta* that, in some idealized form, represent residence groups. Because Naṃo Atoll residents live largely on three islets of the atoll, intraislet competitions occupy the early phases of the celebration. But during December, when the atoll population coalesces, each islet segment learns the songs of the other segments, so that by December 25 a higher level integration takes place. The Jittōk-eṇ and Jitto-eṇ halves of Ṃajkōn islet combine, and Ṃajkōn competes directly with Mae and Naṃo islets. The festivities of December 25 take place on Ṃajkōn with Jittōk-eṇ hosting the Mae islet visitors and Jitto-eṇ hosting the Naṃo islet visitors. Formal ownership rights are suspended, and Ṃajkōn becomes a common gathering ground for host and visitor groups as they prepare for December 25 (Pollock 1969).

As is the case throughout the Wūjlañ and Āne-wetak festivities, Nancy Pollock notes that the activities are part of a search for happiness of a worldly order, "but it eases into the wide-ranging theological idea without undue pressure" (1969: 15). In ways quite reminiscent of Wūjlañ, *Kūrijmōj* involves ritual cleanliness, a suspension of daily labors, and a "relaxation in the rules governing interaction between the sexes" (Pollock 1969: 18). No games on Naṃo parallel *karate* and *kalbuuj,* but nearby Lae (in *Kapinmeto,* the central-western Rālik Chain of the Marshall Islands) has coined a ritual form not unlike *karate.* As William Alexander describes it, after a fishing trip or food-gathering activity by one of the halves of the village, the members of that *jepta* will travel to the other group, "smearing pomade on the laughing victims, dousing them, and not incidentally, leaving a portion of the catch at each household. Within a few days the victims will retaliate" (Alexander 1978: 109). Although the specific forms vary, the constituent elements of competitive attack and reciprocal counterattack rooted in representations of generosity, beauty, attractiveness, sexual license, and of ceremonial bathing are as evident on Lae as they are on Wūjlañ.

To return to Pollock's more complete descriptions, many of the highly elaborated Wūjlañ and Āne-wetak ritual scenarios are compressed and focused around December 25 on Naṃo. This is equally true on Mājuro, where I was surprised at the simplicity of the *Kūrijmōj* celebrations in comparison with those on Wūjlañ and Āne-wetak. On Naṃo, a shortened series of singing presentations is followed by the placing of small gifts around the base of a plastic Christmas tree. The piñatalike *wōjke* of Wūjlañ and Āne-wetak derivation, overloaded with every dollar the *jepta* can collect, is unknown, though Alexander describes a related form of tree from Ebeye, on Kuwajleen Atoll (Alexander 1979). As with *karate* and *kalbuuj,* Āne-wetak people use their elaborate explosive piñatalike trees as markers of distinctive identity at both the atoll and *jepta* level. When the plastic tree made an appearance on Āne-wetak in 1990, it was introduced by the least-competitive group and drew derisive comments from members of the other *jepta*.

The gifts given by each member of the community on Naṃo are followed by the distribution of small amounts of change from the group leader to each member of the *jepta*. These are deposited in front of the minister. Small items (matches, soap, gum, or candy) are then given to *jepta* members, who toss them into the air so that they hit the ceiling and drop into an onlooker's grasp. As we have seen, this social practice, known as *penuk* or *pānuk* (pile up, or gather) (Abo, Bender, et al. 1976: 236), became a popular part of the celebration on Āne-wetak in the late 1980s. After each Naṃo *jepta* has performed and distributed *pānuk,* many of the scarce matches are "wasted" by children. Pollock notes the incongruity of this action in light of the perpetual shortage of matches and suggests that it is a form of conspicuous consumption, an informal part of the ritual sequence. Indeed, conspicuous consumption, especially of food, is important, but, if my interpretation is correct, lighting matches, which on Wūjlañ is manifest in the great conflagration that causes the tree to explode, is a critical representation of renewal. The act ritually rekindles a spark that doubly represents fire, the source of heat and light (the sun), and the regenerative requirement to place the sun back on a northward track. As the ultimate source of heat, light, and growth, the sun must be enticed to move northward and provide the potency that will cause living things to regenerate. This occurs in the great conflagration of the Wūjlañ tree, which, with its explosive power, reveals the gifts for God and forces the deities, in order to retain their superior rank, to reciprocate with inflated quantities of similar items.

Matches, a condensed representation of "white people's magic," create heat and light out of nothingness (totally inorganic materials). Wūjlañ fire makers use the ritual efficacy of chants and rapid back-and-forth motions that are equated with the productive movements of sexual intercourse to bring fire forth using the fire plow:

Iit I oo.	Make fire here (in this spot).
Iit I kañal I oo.	Cause this *Pisonia grandis* to ignite.
Kijeek ueo.	The fire is right there.
	(see Lamberson 1982 for Āne-wetak plants and trees)

The conspicuous consumption of rare matches when building trees and the great conflagration when Wūjlañ trees are exploded are substantially different variants on this central theme.

Pollock's comments about the end of the Naṃo festivities on December 25 and the course of action in the week between then and New Year's Day are particularly valuable:

> The day's proceedings end with the Christmas tree being moved into the centre of the Church floor. Around the tree are placed the various large gifts going from community to community. In addition mats, coconut oil for cosmetic and medicinal purposes, and soap are placed around the tree by representatives from each of the three communities. These latter are the annual gifts to the Iroij *[irooj]*. They always take the form of mats, coconut oil and soap. The Iroij thanks the communities with some brief remarks, and some witticisms, and that concludes the order of proceedings for that day. Everyone is exhausted.
>
> . . . The period between Christmas and New Year is also the one in which there is a constant flow of goods from the people to the Iroij. These again are conveyed by community groups. . . . [E]ach community sends the first servings of whatever is being cooked to the Iroij's household. The representative of each community is in turn fed whatever the Iroij's household has available; this food is eaten there in the Iroij's house.
>
> In addition each community presents various forms of tribute *(ekkan)* to the Iroij at various times. All the community members line up, a leading woman in front, then the young girls, the older women, and finally the men. Each person carries a shallow basket containing a breadfruit, & a drinking coconut or two, or a stem of bananas between two people, and they proceed singing. The goods are laid on a big table outside the house beside the Iroij, and the bearers of the gift draw back and stand or sit. Speeches are exchanged on both sides, and the Iroij may give a 50 lb. bag of flour or sugar to one representative in the name of the whole group. Twice he [the chief] knew ahead of time that a group was coming to present ekkan to him, and he ordered rice and tea to be cooked. . . . Likewise when a man goes fishing during this ritual period, he is expected to bring the biggest and best fish of his catch to the Iroij. He in turn is fed at the time of presenting the gift.
>
> In addition to these gifts to the Iroij from all of his subjects, his Alabs also bring gifts to him. Twice these consisted of food and once of money. Also the Atoll Council officials (Magistrate, secretary, and policemen) were paid one third of their annual salary ($60 each) at a meeting of the Council. At that time, the magistrate who is also the Iroij reminded these men that they should give their Iroij $10 from this income.
>
> Besides gifts to the Iroij, each of the japtas *[jepta]* gives ekkan in cash to the Preacher and his family, and two japtas presented food gifts. The Preacher's family is also included in the distribution of each meal by each community in similar fashion to that of the Iroij. . . . (Pollock 1969: 23–25)

The description of these interactions with the *irooj,* at that time Lōjelañ Kabua, paramount chief of large segments of the Rālik Chain of the Marshall

Figure 16. A man husks coconuts in the bush lands of Jittōk-eṇ in 1977. Last-minute preparations for December 25 include additional bags of coconut to be made into copra for the minister. (Photograph by L. M. Carucci)

Islands, replicates many ideal-type descriptions of interactions among *irooj, a̧lap,* and *kajoor* (chiefs, land/extended family heads, and commoners) during German and Japanese times. There are significant similarities with tribute and first-fruits offerings to Hawai'ian chiefs (Carucci 1980a; Sahlins 1985; Valeri 1985) and elsewhere in the Pacific as well. The similarities and differences with Wūjlan̄ and Āne-wetak practices are also informative.

On Wūjlan̄ and Āne-wetak the gifts inside the tree go directly to the minister as God's earthly representative. As I have noted, people complain about this and contend that during the ideal times when Ernej was the minister, they used to be divided among members of the community. Nonetheless, in spite of threats to withhold the goods or insist on their redistribution, on Āne-wetak and Wūjlan̄ the minister is the beneficiary. Like other guests, the Wūjlan̄/Āne-wetak chiefs receive special treatment, but the minister here occupies the position of the *irooj* as chief intermediary with the deities.

These altered practices represent the deeply embedded Āne-wetak distrust of chiefs, the polyvocal accounts of who actually is a chief, and the seemingly paradoxical elevation and lowering of the very idea of chiefs in the consciousnesses of Wūjlan̄ and Āne-wetak people. Since Lōjelan̄'s death considerable controversy has also arisen in the Marshall Islands over the status of the Rālik chiefs, yet idealized views of how chiefs ought to act persist. Wūjlan̄ people have their own idealized view of chiefly practice, but it is rooted in their construction of ancient times and kept at considerable distance from chiefly demeanor in German, Japanese, or American times. As a result, two antithetical resolutions of the chiefly–commoner paradigm lead to similar forms of social practice. The common practice is that Wūjlan̄ and Āne-wetak chiefs must constantly strive not to be separate from or elevated above other atoll residents. The differing ideologies are, first, that high chiefs never existed on Āne-wetak and that today's chiefs are "overgrown" respected elders or that high chiefs once existed, but until the German era sacred chiefly essence was transmitted matrilineally. A famed atoll personage, Jianna, changed all of this when he returned to Āne-wetak from Wūjlan̄ and claimed the chieftainship and prerogatives of patrilineal transmission on the basis of what German administrators desired. So today's chiefs are just "overgrown" respected elders, the offspring of Jianna, who obscure the legitimate rights of living but hidden chiefs.

Another ideology is that Wūjlan̄ and Āne-wetak are the original sources of all Marshall Islands clans, including chiefly ones. Because of their long isolation, however, the local community is highly intermarried, whereas Marshall Islanders' diversity has led to the birthing of new clans. Nevertheless, all Āne-wetak people are really chiefs who can trace their connectedness directly to an extant chiefly line in four or five generations. Even though today's chiefs are extremely close to the empowered path along which sacred chiefly essence is transmitted, they are simply representatives among equals in a totally chiefly community.

In either case, the chiefs are indigenous rulers "of the Āne-wetak people only," in one instance because local chiefs are totally disempowered, in the other because everyone is highly empowered. In both scenarios the denial of special privilege occupies nearly as much of an Wūjlañ chief's time as does the representation of differential rank. In neither scenario is *ekkan* (first fruits, or a chiefly share of profits on copra) due a chief, even though other privileges accorded ranked personages are reserved for the preacher, visitors, and Wūjlañ chiefs. Unlike Lōjelañ, a truly foreign chief who visited Naṃo from Kuwajleen Atoll, indigenous Āne-wetak chiefs must maintain the modesty of their ranked position through an identification with local people and with the younger-brother line. Although Wūjlañ chiefs are able to manipulate a number of representations of sacred force, they cannot enact the roles of outsiders, whose distant positions of respect and fear can be used as claims to power among Marshallese paramount chiefs (cf. Carucci 1980a, 1988, in press).

THE LOCAL, THE CHRISTIAN, AND THE CONSTRUCTION OF MEANING THROUGH KŪRIJMŌJ

Although the general themes of *Kūrijmōj* align with Pacific and nearby atoll and island tropes, the detailed features of the celebration make the festivities truly unique. Wūjlañ and Āne-wetak people definitely recognize these innovative elements of *Kūrijmōj*. Indeed, they speak of the *Kūrijmōj* as one major marker of their communal identity and claim that their *Kūrijmōj* is better than any other in the Marshalls or Eastern Caroline Islands. Though they know less about festive forms elsewhere in the Pacific, Wūjlañ people also use comparisons of this emerging international celebration (Miller 1993) to discuss similarities and differences with people of other locations.

In essence, *Kūrijmōj* provides an enormous arena in terms of which specific meanings are constructed from a multiplicity of local representations of the world in order to further empower Wūjlañ people. An ongoing series of exchanges are central to Wūjlañ *Kūrijmōj,* and local people manipulate modes of exchange as sources of ritual power. The first exchange is an internal one that each *jepta* uses to attract and maintain its members, thereby constructing a cohesive sense of group identity. At a higher level, a set of external exchanges among *jepta* dominate intracommunity relationships throughout the festive period. In this ongoing competition among *jepta,* singing and dancing groups rely on representations of war and marriage to interact with opposite groups that are, likewise, patterned on a model of community cohesion rooted in matriclan opposition. At this level, each group enters the game equally ranked, and the idea is to win the competition among *jepta*. Simultaneously, the community as a whole, constituted by the complementary collectivity of *jepta,* engage in a higher-order exchange with the deities. Again, the aim is to win this encounter, an aim that is attainable by having "the best *Kūrijmōj* yet." A victory on this battlefield secures the continuity of life on earth, including the reproduction of clan lines, and the regeneration of products to sustain life for the coming year. The rules of engagement are different here, however, because the parties to the exchange are not equally ranked. Nevertheless, if *Kūrijmōj* is, indeed, the best yet, God will be impressed with the gifts the *jepta* have accumulated and will be required to reciprocate abundantly in order to demonstrate the legitimacy of his or her rank.

Kūrijmōj on Wūjlañ and Āne-wetak is so prolonged and complex that its meanings are multifaceted and multivocalic. One central theme among the people of Wūjlañ and Āne-wetak, as among Christians elsewhere, is a focus on giving in abundance and on the feasting of the poor by the rich (Miller 1993). In this small-scale setting, however, I do not see the latter phenomenon as liminal inversion but, rather, as a recognition of the status quo ante. Chiefs and deities (indeed, all who claim to be of high rank) hold their rank on two accounts. First, they have the ability to reciprocate with substantial generosity the prestations they receive; second, they do in fact reciprocate with generosity. As Annette Weiner would have it, in one sense it is true that the only "inalienable possessions" on Wūjlañ and Āne-wetak are the sources of sacred force held by deities and chiefs (Weiner 1992: 51 et seq.). At the same time, such symbolic instantiations of power only gain efficacy as realized practices within an established, if open-ended, system of exchange. At its most general level, *Kūrijmōj* is a ritual form of empowerment that allows earthly beings and commoners, respectively, to manipulate the system of exchange in order to entice sacred beings to share their productive and reproductive potencies with ordinary humans.

Other elements of ritual practice make the comparison between Wūjlañ *Kūrijmōj* and European and American Christmas valuable. In many senses, the ritual forms vary radically, but in other ways themes (and even motivations) overlap. As Lévi-Strauss notes of the Anglo-Saxon forms:

> The progress of autumn from its beginning until the solstice, which marks the salvation of light and life, is accompanied, in terms of rituals, by a dialectical process of which the principal stages are as follows: the return of the dead; their threatening and persecuting behavior; the establishment of a modus vivendi with the living made up of an exchange of services and presents; finally, the triumph of life when, at Christmas, the dead laden with presents leave the living in peace until the next autumn. (Lévi-Strauss 1993: 49)

Mission teachers had no difficulty persuading Āne-wetak people of the value of "the salvation of light and life," and, as with European forms of Christmas, the confrontation between life and death remains primary. The participation of the dead is equally unequivocal, but the historical changes that have affected interactions with the dead are different. Little of the uncertainty about the form and potency of the dead that concern Europeans enters into the Āne-wetak and Wūjlañ celebration. The entire pantheon of ancient and recent spirits, foreign and local, are critical to Wūjlañ *Kūrijmōj,* and interactions with these beings are wholeheartedly encouraged. Indeed, although the magic of European and American Christmas is commonly questioned by adults, certain belief in the magic of the living dead underlies the potency of the Wūjlañ form.

In both European and Wūjlañ forms, children are separated from adults as representations of renewal. But whereas Europeans and Americans make children into unequivocal others (Lévi-Strauss 1993: 49–51), Wūjlañ people fashion them into mediators between the living and the dead. In part, this is because the living dead need only be enticed to act as humans would like (kept at a distance or brought temporarily close), not brought to life. But equally, it is because Wūjlañ *Kūrijmōj* is about the perpetual existence of communal entities, atoll groups, clans, and extended families, not about the extension of individual lives into the uncertain future of death. After all, in spite of their claims, the realists are only relativists in disguise.

Daniel Miller also notes that one accomplishment of Christmas celebrations, as ritual constructions, is the focusing of attention on the family. Indeed, Christmas becomes the family-focused international rite of choice (Miller 1993). This may be true for other locations, but it is not entirely so for Wūjlañ and Āne-wetak. Here, as for the Eskimo, the celebration is primarily a community rite (cf. Bodenhorn 1993).

More accurately, *Kūrijmōj* constructs messages of empowerment for social actors at many different levels. Although the community level is central, the community itself is constituted by *jepta* that construct valued identities for themselves based on their ritual interactions. As I have indicated, however, the *jepta* are multifaceted in their form. At certain moments they draw on symbols of extended families to create a sense of internal cohesion. At other times they are representational analogues of clans: opposed groups that transform difference into unity as the celebration progresses. Furthermore, within each *jepta,* constituent households attain positions of renown based on their levels of and consistency of activity. The women's and children's groups are also critical representative units of the community, each with its own important symbolic contribution. Thus each major social unit—community, clan, extended family, and household—is represented during *Kūrijmōj,* and each forms a valued symbolic resource on which local people depend to elaborate on their ritual messages. Only in one sense is *Kūrijmōj* truly a family rite, but, in terms of a general theory of such events, perhaps this sense is the most critical one. On Wūjlañ, the family *(baaṃle)* and extended family *(bwij)* serve as the preferred metaphors of community solidarity. All Wūjlañ people are really "just one family." The salience of this statement and the degree to which local people believe it to be true help situate the differences between communities like Wūjlañ and other societies in which substantially different communities of residence are the norm.

In his analysis of American Christmas, James Carrier notes that the nature of the exchanges reveals a great deal about the meanings of the event (1993). Like Carrier, I have used Marcel Mauss as a guide through the many arenas of *Kūrijmōj*. Using this method, the communal nature of Wūjlañ *Kūrijmōj* is made as apparent as is the familial focus of American Christmas. Furthermore, whereas Americans are concerned with the contradictions between "affectionate giving" and the impersonal character of capitalist goods (Carrier 1993), Wūjlañ people are far more concerned with the contradiction between the ideally reciprocal relationship between chiefly–commoner giving and extant exchanges between the community and the minister. As I have indicated, these later exchanges are modeled on the chiefly–commoner pattern. But the chiefly pattern is also that of heavenly chiefs. Although the community grudgingly accepts stingy ministers, I believe that their stinginess poses a threat to the whole logic of *Kūrijmōj,* which depends on engaging the gods in exchanges to create conditions of indebtedness that must be remunerated with greater generosity (to maintain the rank of the deities) in the coming year. Stingy representatives of God on earth cannot help but create questions about God's generosity.

If one side of the Christmas coin uses metaphors of family-writ-large to valorize community unity, the other side of the unity coin is vested in symbols of opposition. The idea that *Kūrijmōj* on Wūjlañ and Āne-wetak is better than the same event in other parts of the Marshall Islands stands at the core of people's insecurity about their own atoll identity. Throughout their residence on Wūjlañ, Āne-wetak people were considered by Marshall Islanders to be unenlightened, backwoods people, not beings much like us. By having the most prolonged and "best" Christmas in the region, Wūjlañ and Āne-wetak people overcompensate for the regionally inspired community insecurities. Christmas, associated as it is with goodwill and generosity, proves the incorrectness of Marshall Islanders' assertions about Wūjlañ folks. Is it not true that the missionaries indicated it is God's position to judge the actions of earthly beings? Is it not true that God will straighten out incorrect assertions? It is only logical that God will find that those who work so hard at *Kūrijmōj* exemplify the core values of the celebration: generosity, love, and kindness.

In 1979, Wūjlañ people invited dignitaries and church members from around the Marshall Islands to help celebrate the dedication of a new church on the atoll. Again, in 1993, Āne-wetak people invited Marshall Islands leaders to celebrate the local liberation day marking the end of suffering on Āne-wetak during World War II—"The Time We Came out of the Holes." On these occasions, Āne-wetak people staged great, ostentatious parties with feasts, communal games, and gift giving as ways of displaying for Marshall Islanders what Āne-wetak and Wūjlañ people are really like—"our ways of moving," as they say. Like these occasional events, *Kūrijmōj* provides a comparative arena for the expression of lived identity. Like them, it offers an opportunity for the display of love and generosity. However, such special events occur once a decade, whereas *Kūrijmōj* takes place every year. It occupies so much time that it constantly risks becoming mundane, yet, at the same time, its frequent, recurring nature makes *Kūrijmōj* the core performative arena for the practiced proclamation of Wūjlañ and Āne-wetak identity.

So central is *Kūrijmōj* to life on Āne-wetak and Wūjlañ that it is not surprising that local people use it as a channel for the conscious and comparative expression of local identity. At the same time, however, this fact hardly exhausts the meanings of *Kūrijmōj*. On a larger scale, *Kūrijmōj* stands as a core representation of Christian identity; and, until the past five years, Christian identity was communal identity. This notion of Wūjlañ and Āne-wetak people as Christians was itself defined in oppositional terms. Along a temporal plane, it separated today's people who "live in the light" from the ancients who "lived in darkness." The damned–saved contrast was also readily extended to separate the present-day "we" from "they." It separated the Wūjlañ community, with all of its self-perceived moral correctness, from those stereotyped as pagans, like Yapese or New Guinea people. At the same time, it separated Wūjlañ people from other "non-Christian" groups, including Catholics. Each individual Wūjlañ person might or might not be a practicing ABCFM Protestant, but in local terms the community was "Christian."[1]

Only with the recent appearance of a small Assembly of God congregation on Āne-wetak has religion been tentatively excised from the communal regions of atoll identity. As I noted above, religious options will inevitably lead to a rethinking of issues of identity and to an elaborated format for the celebration of *Kūrijmōj*. In Mājuro, for example, *jepta* are fashioned along lines that are very different from those on Āne-wetak and Wūjlañ. Rather than incorporating the characteristics of clan and extended family, other forms of religious and political discourse are expressed in the interactions among Mājuro's *jepta*. In some instances, Mājuro *jepta* represent solidarities of local sections of the atoll. Other groups reflect the competition among religious factions or between young and old. Currently, the young Āne-wetak families who have been drawn into Assembly of God (often by educational opportunities for their children) have been excluded from participation in the atollwide celebration of *Kūrijmōj*. They stage their own small-scale *Kūrijmōj* rather than sponsor a denomination-specific *jepta,* as do many religious groups in Mājuro or Ebeye.

Even so, recent moves toward an acceptance of diversity can be noted. In 1989, the first year in which Assembly members tried to establish a church on Āne-wetak, the possible presence of a second church was perceived as a major threat to atollwide solidarity. Noting that Āne-wetak people had always been "one only" or "all part of the same extended family," questions were raised by core Congregational Church members as to whether a new church would be allowed. Eventually, however, a location for the new church was found (on the land parcel occupied by one of the new converts), and the ban on denominational diversity was dropped in favor of a policy of exclusion. This exclusionary policy has led to the current two-*Kūrijmōj* format, with Assembly members staging their own celebration. But paths of interpersonal relationship crosscut the two-church division, and some people, already too exhausted or too slow to make weekly services at the "real Church," may opt to attend a Sunday service with their Assembly of God relatives. Therefore, although the separate celebration of Assembly members points to their current marginalization on Āne-wetak, I believe the situation to be temporary. As other religious groups move to the outer islands, segmentation along religious lines will become commonplace, and the current sense that the Assembly people have broken the sacred trust of shared Āne-wetak identity undoubtedly will disappear. At that point, the exclusionary policy at *Kūrijmōj* may give way to a new celebratory framework. Today's religious rifts, so threatening to the long-established cohesion among the components of a conglomerate Āne-wetak identity, will be fashioned into new representational forms. Those forms, I believe, will accommodate the currently unbridgeable gaps between unity and diversity.

Indeed, some other principles of *jepta* organization evident in Mājuro are taking root on Āne-wetak. *Kane ekāāl* (the new sort [of people]) is an Āne-wetak *jepta* formed in the late 1980s that uses its newness as a source of differentiation from other *jepta*. Newness means largely "younger generation," and, indeed, many *Kane ekāāl* members come from the old Ioļap group, which was already dominated by younger members on Wūjlañ. Āne-wetak *jepta* identity has been undergoing other Mājuro-like reformulations as well. Even though atoll sections on Wūjlañ could be roughly aligned with *jepta* boundaries (Jittōk-eņ and Jitto-eņ), a great deal of flexibility in *jepta* membership was the norm. The return to Āne-wetak brought multiple changes. Āne-wetak islet songfest groups have increased in number, giving atoll residents additional options for *jepta* membership. At the same time, however, the Meden *jepta* found itself isolated on a separate islet, resulting in less flexibility for its residents. Members of the Meden *jepta* commit themselves to a three-month residence on Meden. Their geographical isolation places them in a position similar to those of songfest groups on Naṃo or those of olden times. In such cases, interactions among groups were limited until all groups came together on a central islet during December. In spite of the multidirectional changes in today's *jepta,* local people say that the alterations are motivated by a single logic. On Wūjlañ, *Kūrijmōj* focused on the community, and each *jepta* actively participated in ongoing communal interactions. This organizational framework was promoted by the patterns of residence, with everyone living in a central village on a single islet. Although people still speak of the community as primary, they also complain of rifts. They commonly complain that "the *jepta* now comes first," and they speak as if the change were contrary to the main celebratory intent—to "stand on behalf of all people of Āne-wetak."

Kūrijmōj stands for being Christian in the narrow sense of ABCFM Congregational Protestant, but it is used in its broadest sense to create a sense of similarity between Wūjlañ people and Americans. In the vessel the *Morning Star,* American missionaries first brought the Word to the Marshall Islands. As people throughout the Marshall Islands reminisce about their experiences during World War II, they use shared religious identity as a way of creating a sense of community with the Americans who arrived to defeat the Japanese troops (Carucci 1995c). In a similar way, the vast elaborations of *Kūrijmōj* are used by Wūjlañ and Āne-wetak people to represent just how similar they are to Americans—those primordial Christians who brought the Word of God to

Micronesia. Marshall Islanders and people from Pohnpei, Mōkil, and Piñlep form the comparative frame for Wūjlañ people. Because the celebrations on those islands are less elaborate than the celebrations on Wūjlañ, local people view the other islanders as less invested in Christian endeavor and, therefore, less like Americans. Kosrae and, perhaps, Epoon are seen as exceptions. These were the true primordial residence sites of the first Micronesian missionaries, and the depth of historical experience accumulated in a single place gives them precedence. N̄atrik is another exception, but the claims of its residents to Americanness are vested in representational pathways of interpersonal relationship (kinlike ties), not in special symbols of shared Christian identity.

As I have indicated, much of what people see as special about *Kūrijmōj* on Wūjlañ and Āne-wetak lies in the length of the celebration, in the frequency of songfest competitions *(kaṃōḷo),* and in *karate* and *kalbuuj*. These two ritual games, in particular, are core markers of unique Wūjlañ and Āne-wetak identity because they were developed on Wūjlañ in the 1950s and are celebrated only there. Nevertheless, the move to Āne-wetak has brought changes in these special markers of identity as well. In particular, with access to moneys from additional nuclear compensation funds, the people have placed greater emphasis on continual increase in the amount of money exchanged during *Kūrijmōj* and less on other forms of interaction and exchange. This conscious change, though not welcomed by everyone, has been determined by changed circumstances. The return to Āne-wetak brought radical changes to people's daily lives and equally significant changes to *Kūrijmōj*. The cleanup of radioactive wastes and World War II– and nuclear-testing–era debris left the atoll's residents largely dependent on imported foods. Only in recent years have modest quantities of coconut become available. Far less prolific and less dependable are the supplies of pandanus and breadfruit. On the other hand, with near-weekly Airline of the Marshall Islands flights and U.S. Department of Agriculture staples, the supply of basic foods is far more dependable.

Predictably, then, the number of songfest competitions has increased because ample food is available. The elaboration of foods, however—particularly foods of greatest value—has decreased. Some *jepta* stage *kaṃōḷo* solely with tea or coffee, rice, flour-based foods, and tinned meats. Ideally, some type of fish, or the rare pig or chicken, will form the complement, and wealthy *jepta* will give cola as the drink of preference. Because fishing is still common, *karate* has continued, altered only by the sorts of changes that have occurred with *kaṃōḷo*. Until recently, with islets stripped of all vegetation, pig food was at a premium, so it became common to have women *karate* with only canned meats to complement the cooked foods they give to the men. Chickens, either locally raised or imported in a semifrozen state on the airplane, have become the complement of preference (though the imported variety has added greatly to the frequency of food poisoning).

In contrast, in spite of its importance, *kalbuuj* has become a game of the past on Āne-wetak. Again the causes are largely pragmatic. *Kalbuuj,* the men's game against women, was never as attractive as was *karate*. This, I believe, is because, in a linguistically marked sense, *karate* pitted "unmarked" women over "marked" men, allowing them suddenly to "lord it over" the men in ways that local people found hilarious. In *karate,* women could gain control over the dangerous (but attractive) male domain, the bush lands. In *kalbuuj,* men simply controlled the domestic space that they entered daily anyway (though in a more circumscribed way than in *kalbuuj*). More pragmatically, however, *kalbuuj* often began when women went into the bush in small groups to collect pandanus fronds that would be woven into fine mats or handicraft items. These valuables added greatly to the symbolic value and balance of materials presented to the minister on December 25 (cf. Weiner 1992). Although pandanus were prolific in the 1970s on Wūjlañ, they were nonexistent on Āne-wetak in the 1980s. Moreover, on Āne-wetak the houses are distributed in the copra-era style that came into vogue in German times—with dwellings spread out along an islet on the various land parcels. As on Wūjlañ, it is rare for a woman to leave the domestic sphere on Āne-wetak. Even if she does, however, on Āne-wetak she would not cross the territory of an opposite *jepta* to collect pandanus fronds or other land products. These items are found on the land parcel where she resides. With new practical conditions, *kalbuuj* is not currently a dynamic ritual form. Symbolic symmetry alone could not provide local people with justification to rethink the rules that might govern this game under altered circumstances. When I asked about *kalbuuj* in the 1980s and 1990s, Āne-wetak people responded, rather unconvincingly, that the end of *kalbuuj* was saddening indeed but, at the same time, that it did not really matter, for *Kūrijmōj* on Āne-wetak was now bigger and better than ever. Most Āne-wetak residents share my sense of nostalgia for life on Wūjlañ, but they do not share any of my analytical views about the ways in which *Kūrijmōj* on Wūjlañ was part and parcel of that same way of life. For them, *Kūrijmōj* on Āne-wetak is better. To understand their view, I believe, it is necessary to consider some of the more fundamental meanings and symbolic aims of the festivity.

THE SOURCE OF THE FORCE IN KŪRIJMŌJ

Even though *Kūrijmōj* serves as a primary representation of what it means to be an Āne-wetak person, in and of itself, this does not fully answer, for the local resident or for the anthropologist or cultural historian, what *Kūrijmōj* is all about. Why does it exist? With each cultural actor, the answers to these questions vary, yet some answers are more thought provoking, more culturally and historically enriched, than others. As I have indicated throughout this book, I believe that the most provocative answers to these questions have to do with the renewal of human existence and with the regeneration of the products on which people and clans depend in order to remain alive. *Kūrijmōj* is the ritual tool par excellence that gives ordinary humans the symbolic power to try to influence cosmic events, that allows them to persuade God and/or the ancient deities to act on their behalf to make certain that these ultimate desirables are forthcoming in the new year. For precisely these reasons, Āne-wetak people have no nostalgia about Wūjlañ forms of *Kūrijmōj*. At a very real level, life on Āne-wetak, despite its endless problems, represents the fulfillment of the dreams of plenty that are the primary aim of *Kūrijmōj*.

I wish to preface my comments in this regard by separating an objectivist view from the intersubjectivist perspective that I have been pursuing throughout this work. In the objectivist view, life on Āne-wetak today has a plethora of social problems that were never apparent on Wūjlañ. People are less healthy, less active, less well nourished, more prone to violence, more dependent on alcohol, and more prone to suicide than they were on Wūjlañ. Their own sense of atoll and community identity is in question. Nevertheless, in 1982, when people were considering moving back to Wūjlañ, my older sibling (by adoption) rationalized his decision not to return to the atoll in the following terms:

> Wūjlañ? Why would one go back? There we were always hungry and there was never enough food, but on Āne-wetak, you can eat and eat to the limit. On Wūjlañ, if you got sick you would just get weaker and then weaker, until death, but on Āne-wetak, they will place a plane in flight and take you to the hospital and you will be alive. On Wūjlañ, we had to work every day fishing in the ocean and, in hard times, you would stay in the salt water so long that your hair would turn red and frizzled and, still, you might have bad luck and come home with only a couple of clams for your entire family. On Āne-wetak, the Americans send us food and, if it is gone, they will send more. . . . On Wūjlañ two clans died out . . . but now, on Āne-wetak, there are so many children that it is difficult to count them, and the extended families are getting stronger, not weaker. (Wūjlañ Field Notes 1982–1983)

In comparison with the subsistence conditions on Wūjlañ, life on Āne-wetak is nirvana. It has certain guarantees that were always highly contingent on Wūjlañ and, for my older sibling, these guarantees, as contingent on wavering political realities as they are, far outweigh any attractions that life on Wūjlañ still holds. Āne-wetak guarantees the basic necessities of life, those very items that *Kūrijmōj* seeks to fulfill.

Americans' sense of guilt about nuclear testing has resulted in the compensations that have created the temporary nirvana on Āne-wetak. Wūjlañ people, however, see the compensations in a far different way. Rather than consider nuclear trust funds as a way for Americans to recapture their own sense of moral purity in the international arena, Wūjlañ people see the nuclear tests as a demonstration of the American's sacred, godlike power, a power given to them by the Marshallese trickster, Etao (Carucci 1989). Concomitantly, the trust funds are just compensation on the part of a beneficent conqueror-chief for hardship created by local Marshall Islands leaders during the community's exile on Wūjlañ and compensation for damage to land that, as conquering chiefs, the United States had some right to use.

The 1980s and 1990s have brought modifications to these Wūjlañ formulations. As Āne-wetak people become accustomed to compensation moneys, their sense of dependence on them increases, as does their sense of having an inherent right to them. These changes only increase the complexity of the dilemma that the United States must now face. Having compensated Marshall Islanders for nuclear-related damages, the United States wants to see itself as free of further responsibility for nuclear claims (Section 177 of The Compact of Free Association 1982). In accord with local logic, however, America cannot eliminate the payment of future moneys without endangering its position on Āne-wetak as a good colonizer chief, the most powerful on earth. Just like celestial deities at *Kūrijmōj,* in order to legitimize its position the United States must continue to demonstrate its goodwill by generously sharing its inexhaustible supply of goods.

Therefore, for many of those who lived most of their lives on Wūjlañ, the return to a bountiful life on Āne-wetak represents the fulfillment of the pleas for well-being that are made at *Kūrijmōj.* But *Kūrijmōj* has a generative capacity that far exceeds current political arrangements. As a ritual form, *Kūrijmōj* is a continually regenerative tool, not the fruit of the process of renewal. Although many features of the ritual itself are innovative, representing selective slices of "invented tradition," at its core it is a celebration of renewal and regeneration with ancient roots and a perduring character. And although not all Wūjlañ and Āne-wetak people are eager to discuss these roots and some have little knowledge of them, for other residents the very potency of the ritual lies in the continuity of its character. To be strong, it must be connected to the source. That source is not only the *Morning Star,* the first arrival of Christianity, but also the first appearance of life on Āne-wetak and Wūjlañ Atolls. These perduring meanings are the ones that my knowledgeable consultant had in mind when, in 1976, he took me out to tell me the story of Jebrọ and Lōktañūr when I asked about the meanings of *Kūrijmōj.* In this age of polysemy, his story does not deny that the celebration is about "happiness," about "giving to the point of impossibility," or about "love." It is about all of these things. Nevertheless, his story tells us that not all meanings are created equal and that not all have equal weight (see Eco 1990). In Pierre Bourdieu's terms, authority (James Clifford's ability to author) is differentially distributed in a way that simultaneously reflects and constitutes a certain ranked order within a particular cultural domain (Bourdieu 1991; Clifford 1983). My knowledgeable informant was one of the two most highly respected storytellers of his day. The fact that he was not a committed Christian meant that he had little fear of blasphemy. He could construct his pasts in ways that committed church members never could, for he was only lightly encumbered with the weight of missionary repressions. Nevertheless, both of the distinguished storytellers had the community's respect, not only for their incredible memories and yarn-spinning abilities but because people considered the central messages of their stories to be true. They were the legitimized experts because, in day-to-day practice, they exuded all of the qualities required of "most knowledgeable persons."

There are other measures of this expertise, as well. First, the explanatory frame provided by Jebro̜ and Lōktañūr is all-encompassing. In contrast, the Christian scenarios see all correlative conceptual forms as competing and mistaken. The stories of Jebro̜ and Christ are said to be "one only"—suited to different times and unique geophysical circumstances but conveying analogous messages of love, compassion, and generosity—by the knowledgeable storytellers. On the other hand, missionaries taught Marshall Islanders that local beliefs were idolatry, a belief in false gods, and fear of reprisal prevents most church members from elaborating on the details of ancient beliefs.

At the same time, social practice also points to the critical importance of perduring ritual forms. Nowhere is this more obvious than where church repression comes into greatest conflict with local belief. *Karate, kalbuuj,* and the dances of *Kūrijmōj* all contain metaphoric sexual materials that are highly tabu (in terms of church doctrine) but absolutely imperative to the community's requests for the renewal of life. The juxtaposition of attraction and tabu are evidenced by the snickers, the youthful embarrassment, and the alter-ego performances of Etao. Yet, lacking access to emotionally satisfying alternative Christian practices, Wūjlañ *Kūrijmōj* draws on its own ritual recollections to create the dances and forms of sexual play that are central to the celebration's intent. These ritual forms rely on people's reminiscences of the ancient communal religious dances, the *kiye,* and on selective and evocative historical themes like the Spanish jail or Japanese self-defense to construct empowering ritual forms for the present day. The model of ritual practice that seeks its source in New England Christianity, the ideology that was brought to the Marshall Islands by the *Morning Star,* cannot explain the dances, *karate, kalbuuj,* or other forms of emergent local practice. The model that sees both Wūjlañ Christianity and the celebration of *Kūrijmōj* as local cultural products, fashioned from a bricolage of readily available representational tools from a variety of sources but with a local history and local trajectory in mind, cannot help but account for the nuanced ritual forms of *Kūrijmōj.*

For all Wūjlañ and Āne-wetak people, then, *Kūrijmōj* is, ostensibly, a celebration of the birth of Christ. Yet, unlike the American form that has elaborated on the themes of past European practice, on Christ's birth, and on the family (Miller 1993), the Wūjlañ form celebrates the coming of the Word of God to Micronesia, to the Marshall Islands, and to Āne-wetak. The use of the missionary vessel, the *Morning Star,* condenses these events into a single recollection of inordinate potency and power. The coming of the missionaries, however, is associated with the replacement of an ancient history of conflict and warring with spears and lances (the era of darkness) by a new era (the era of light). In the new era, humans learn to war only with love, a love that is brought to earth by Christ.

For the most knowledgeable storytellers on Wūjlañ, Christ represents love's second coming. Love's first conjunction with hierarchy was with Jebro̜, the youngest-sibling son of the primordial chiefly matriarch of the Marshall Islands. It is this story, analogous to the Christian story (with Christ as the younger-sibling offspring of God), that allows local people to explore more elaborate elements of local cosmology. Whereas Christ brings the era of love, Jebrǫ, the pragmatist, brings the regeneration of nature, the generous gifts of harvest fruits to people for whom the fear of starvation is very real. Whereas Christ brings promises of everlasting life to individuals, Jebrǫ guarantees only the promise of continuing life to clan lines and extended families. And whereas Christ is generosity and love generically extended, Jebrǫ is the detailed imperatives of life locally elaborated. Unlike other places in the Marshalls, on Wūjlañ Jebrǫ's selfish brother, Tūṃur, shares the rule of the heavens with him, marking the emphasis on sharing on the atoll vis-à-vis more hierarchically oriented social spheres in the region. Like a caring father, Jebrǫ rules the skies during the most tumultuous periods of the year, when humans need careful oversight. During the summer months, when Tūṃur rules the skies, Jebrǫ physically transfers to earth the enrichment that foods must contain to support human existence.

In many cases these themes translate into the practice of *Kūrijmōj* very consciously and iconically. In other instances, less representationally explicit forms of ritual action come into play. Most obviously, people note that *Kūrijmōj* is about love, caring, and generosity, and these are the "tools of warfare" that are employed in all of the encounters of *Kūrijmōj*. Food is one primary mechanism of exchange, and as I indicated in chapter 3, generosity and caring are marked by giving in abundance and by giving that which is most highly ranked. It would be naive, however, to think that these gifts are given without expectation of a return. Indeed, as discussed in chapter 2, they are given in order to elicit a return on two levels, one earthly, one godly. At the earthly level, foods, song presentations, speeches, and other items are given in abundance to other *jepta* with a dual intent: to continue the exchange and the intermingling of members of the separate *jepta* to form an interdependent and sustainable community, and to win the exchange. Because all parties to the exchange are equally ranked initially, winning can only be accomplished by giving more and more highly ranked valuables, thereby increasing one's rank through indebtedness.

At the celestial level, gifts are also given with the intention of creating indebtedness, but because God and the ancient deities are inherently more highly ranked than are mortal humans, they must reciprocate in greater measure any gift they receive. Therefore, in this circumstance of unequal rank, indebtedness is used as a ritual tool to guarantee that renewal and regeneration will be forthcoming in the new year. Most of December, December 25 itself, and New Year's Day are oriented toward this end. Each *jepta* gives increasingly generous gifts to the minister (God's earthly representative) up through December 25, relying on the logic of extreme generosity and indebtedness to win the battle with the deities for regenerational potency. A wide variety of symbolic mechanisms is used to make people irresistible during this period (see chapter 6), to attract deities to the scene as well as promote interactions

Figure 17. Jittōk-eņ and Jitto-eņ in the first game on New Year's Day in 1977. The entire community gathers along the baselines as the church and council-house grounds are transformed into a softball diamond for this important competition. (Photograph by L. M. Carucci)

among members of the various *jepta*. God and the deities are thought to be present to witness the celebrations of December 25; and, after the apocalyptic events that accompany the explosion of the trees, an apprehensive interlude fills the temporal landscape between December 25 and New Year's Eve. At that time, the necessary but dangerous sacred beings are chased from the village by the noise and light that "eliminate the nighttime" on New Year's Eve. The representative purities of proper moral action follow during the first week of the New Year, demonstrating to the now-distant deities that humans are upholding their agreement to conduct their lives with propriety. These are the major ritual acts directed toward God and the deities during *Kūrijmōj*, but a modest form of apprehension reminiscent of the time after December 25 infuses daily life in the new year as the outcomes of each activity are scanned for signs of God's beneficent hand or for the marks of disapproval contained in typhoons, famines, or unusual deaths. The entire next year is the period for God's remunerations, but if *Kūrijmōj* provides a time for humans to actively encourage the exchange, the outcomes of everyday life can influence its tenor and direction as well.

The renewal theme is equally evident in people's attempt to make *Kūrijmōj* a time of happiness. This aim is accomplished along two primary avenues. The return to childhood is the first, a theme that also symbolizes one component of the successful achievement of the search for renewal. Happiness means a life of plenty, unencumbered by constraints of work and family responsibility. Indeed, much of the attractiveness of life on postrepatriation Āne-wetak and the assimilation of the Āne-wetak return into *Kūrijmōj* as a mark of correct community activity can be understood in relation to local conceptions of happiness. The second way in which happiness is pursued is through ritual games. These games include a variety of contests among *jepta,* each of which has an equal opportunity to win. Softball and volleyball, pursued actively in the week after *Kūrijmōj* and culminating on New Year's Day, are one such form; the songfest encounters between *jepta* are another. But the most distinctively Wūjlañ games are the sexually evocative encounters during *kalbuuj* and *karate.*

As Charles Peirce notes, certain sorts of signifiers (icons) exist simply to represent themselves, but the ritual activities of *Kūrijmōj* are of a much different order. Ritual signifiers, as Stanley Tambiah would have it, exist because they accomplish something. And although what they accomplish is not pushed into being solely through the form of signification (Bourdieu 1991: 107–16, contra Austin 1962), *kalbuuj* and *karate* carry evidence of ritual intent in their ritual forms. As I have indicated, *karate* allows a *jepta* to win inter-*jepta* battles by co-opting the best planned *kaṃọ̄lo* in its reliance on high-ranked foods provided by males, whereas *kalbuuj* disrupts plans to produce critical female goods that form part of a songfest group's presentations at *Kūrijmōj.* Like the other ritual forms of *Kūrijmōj,* these wins are accomplished surreptitiously, employing an exchange format of extreme generosity to create feelings of indebtedness that must be repaid. Both games employ sexually explicit domestic metaphors to force cross-gender interactions among the *jepta* through parodies of male–female interdependence. Innuendos about sexual interdependence are the most humorous element of these parodies. The games, in other words, create the conditions for resolution among *jepta* in the same way that opposite-clan identity is transposed into a tenuous unity each time a spousal pair establishes a new household in order to perpetuate the society as a whole. Dual metaphors of work are used to represent the fundamental interdependence on which the community is based. *Karate* inverts and parodies men's labors in the bush as they stand opposed to women's food-transforming and domestic labors, whereas *kalbuuj* toys with the opposition between women's collecting and weaving labors and men's public manipulations of the products of those labors. Although the inversions make for great humor, the ritual activities that are considered even more hilarious deal with the sexual "work" that is so highly tabued by the mission but so critical to the perpetuation of human existence. Sexual parodies by themselves, however, do not guarantee the renewal of life on earth. Their appearance during *Kūrijmōj* promotes cross-gender, cross-*jepta* mixing as a representation and plea to the deities to bless those unions and make their metaphoric counterparts productive.

In addition to these core ritual forms, I have given equal attention to the nuanced way in which a variety of symbolic devices are employed to bring the celebration of *Kūrijmōj* into being and to make it meaningful. Each encounter relies heavily on a generic feasting format that is most frequently employed, in slightly altered form, in first-birthday celebrations. Each encounter builds into its ritual form important spatial representations of center and periphery, windward and leeward, left and right, as ways of creating and perpetuating taken-for-granted aspects of the local worldview but, equally, as devices to send messages about relative valuations of objects and social persona. And all of the activities focused on December 25, along with many earlier on, employ symbols of attractiveness and irresistibility to promote the intertwining of members of the various *jepta* as well as to attract the deities and engage them in an ongoing exchange.

I have analyzed some of the core performances of December 25—in particular, the dances and the explosion of the tree—in some depth in order to indicate how the symbolics of the senses construct important symbolic messages on Wūjlañ and Āne-wetak. As with the other ritual forms of *Kūrijmōj,* these symbols do not exist in a vacuum. They place the taken-for-granted characteristics of the universe in local people's hands in order to give them ritual access to powers and processes beyond their immediate control. In the case of the dances, the provocative sexual themes that are expressed subtly in the *beet* are made explicit in the playful antics of Etao. In the case of the tree, the greatest powers in the universe, simultaneously destructive and creative but entirely mysterious, are brought into play to reveal the sacred wealth within the "Christmas tree."

Ultimately, it is representations of well-being, reciprocated manyfold by high-ranked sacred beings who, like Christ and Jebrọ, must be generous to be deserving of their high position, that stand as the core symbols of *Kūrijmōj.* These objects are displayed following the explosion of a successful tree. Like all elements of the celebration, the meaning of "well-being" changed as people moved from their state of relative impoverishment on Wūjlañ to their current state of relative wealth on Āne-wetak. Once filled with single dollars, detergent, bar soap, and boxes of matches yet to be ignited, each a representation of newness, cleanliness, and generative potential, the trees are now filled primarily with cash. Once accompanied by other gifts of copra, mats, coconut oil, and symbolically important poverty staples like arrowroot, given to the minister for redistribution, the gifts within the tree are now supplemented with ever-larger (but less differentiated) quantities of money and food, no longer redistributed. Such is the character of life on Āne-wetak. Less marginal than life on Wūjlañ, it is also less differentiated.

Just as the community seeks an innovative form, so the celebration of *Kūrijmōj* and the historically grounded construction of atoll identity of which it is a part must seek innovative forms. Such ritual refashionings are constantly taking place on Wūjlañ and Āne-wetak. These components of *Kūrijmōj* are not practices without pasts, they are practices whose pasts are rewritten in the present tense with an eye ever fixed on the fulfillment of tomorrow's needs and desires.

NOTES

INTRODUCTION

1. Throughout the text I use the newly adopted official spelling of Marshallese words. Although I have some disagreements with the overly phonetic character of this style of spelling in relation to current recognition and use (particularly in regard to the descending diacriticals, which most Marshallese readers do not generally recognize or consider necessary), I adopt it in hopes that if it is generally accepted by Marshall Islanders, this work will be more readable by future generations of Rālik, Ratak, Wūjlañ, and Āne-wetak readers.

2. Kiste (1976: 64) reports 141, including the missionary (Klancy), his wife, and child. All others were Āne-wetak people.

3. By July 1978 there were 540 people with Āne-wetak parentage. By July 1982 the population had increased to 704, and by September 1990 it numbered 1,012. During this time the median age continually decreased, and in 1990 more than 68 percent of the population was less than twenty years old.

4. Sherry Ortner (1973) and others have discussed ways to separate key symbols from one another. My guiding principles derive from emotional investment and frequency of use. Thus the games of *Kūrijmōj* (chapter 4) are clearly of importance because they are discussed nearly conterminously with *Kūrijmōj*. In a different way, discussions of extended-family solidarity and of the uses of family as metaphors for songfest group solidarity (chapters 2 and 4) are reiterated with frequency and with such emotional energy that the family, too, is valued as a core symbol out of which

daily life is constructed and in terms of which it is expressed. Nevertheless, the anthropologist's choice of key symbols, though necessary and inevitable, is clearly one primary location in which the authority of texts becomes inscribed (Clifford 1983). The format of this book is intended to make those processes of legitimation apparent.

CHAPTER 1: KŪRIJMŌJ ON WŪJLAÑ

1. After Āne-wetak was replanted in 1979, the first breadfruit harvested *(akeo)* were consumed in 1989. By 1992, enough breadfruit were harvested to allow each person about half a fruit every other month, but the insufficient height of maturing coconut trees could not withstand the typhoon that devastated Wūjlañ and gave Āne-wetak a glancing blow late that year. With neither the protection of mature coconut trees nor a buffer of brush trees along the shore, breadfruit production suffered significantly.

2. In addition to these three stations, signals from as far away as Japan, the United States mainland, the Philippines, and Australia can be monitored at night.

3. With increased moneys available on Āne-wetak, these special goods are now commonplace. The resulting devaluation is compensated for by increasing the range of items and the quantities of each valued item.

4. For a discussion of the way in which accomplishment and renown are associated with travels to distant lands, see Carucci 1995.

5. Pubescent girls and boys may well be described as "more of a young woman," "becoming a young woman," or "becoming a young man," but they will be lumped into a category with other children until they have "entered the darkness" through sexual experiences.

CHAPTER 2: FUNDAMENTAL PRINCIPLES

1. In many cases, Annette Weiner (1992) refers more to the traces of identity that link a manufacturer or giver to a particular object than to the truly inalienable character of those objects. This, I believe, only reinforces the way in which the shared identities of person and prestation take on value in the context of exchange.

2. *Kūrijmōj* is used in both a nominal and verbal sense and thus not only signifies the various time sequences of celebration discussed in chapter 1 but also is used as an indexical reminder that humans act to make *Kūrijmōj* happen. The same is true with *maan iiō* (the face of the year), which is used to signify not only a time of the year but also the activities, particularly the proper conduct, that must be enacted in order to bring the New Year into being. The lack of sharp segmentation between these words qua nouns and their existence as verbs point to the critical nature of *Kūrijmōj* as an event in the process of becoming. Indeed, *Kūrijmōj* is both the ritual process and the religious event that brings into being the conditions that will ensure the propagation of life.

3. Marshallese would say "closer" in time because, according to their cultural perspective, time is judged and coded spatially, in relation to the present. It lacks the linear, metered, and vectorially directed sequencing of the Euro-American model.

4. The way land is divided on Wūjlañ and Āne-wetak Atolls is one means whereby local people separate themselves from other parts of the Marshall Islands. In the Ratak and Rālik Chains, anthropologists contend that landholding is closely tied to matrilineal patterns of clan organization and segmentation (Tobin 1958, 1970; Kiste 1968; Rynkiewich 1972, 1976). On Āne-wetak and Wūjlañ, rights to land are claimed bilaterally. Nonetheless, in line with Tadao Yanaihara (1940), Michael Rynkiewich (1972 [for Arņo]), and Leonard Mason and Robert Kiste (1984 [for Kuwajleen]), all

claim that land is not really owned in the European sense (though elsewhere these authors use "ownership" to describe tenure). This suggests that many of the discrepancies between my account of Wūjlañ and accounts of other Marshall Islands locations are due to differences in interpretation. Wūjlañ and Āne-wetak lands are certainly not owned; they are brought into being through human labor in a fashion analogical to the way men and women bring humans into being through the shared "work" of coitus. One form of labor shapes the child's physical and social psychological form; the other determines the continuity of conditions of nurturance after nursing has ceased (cf. Labby 1976 [for Yap]). Both are equally critical to the continued existence of Wūjlañ and Āne-wetak people as living beings. Certainly, potential land links through males appear to operate differently in the Marshalls (these are "workers'" claims; in the ideal, males work the land for matriclans), but these variations do not deny overarching similarities in the way that clanship and "blood and mud" (Silverman 1971: 72) are used alternately to describe and legitimize discussions of identity.

5. Unlike Io̧ap, which was too surrounded to be an effective competitor, Meden was too isolated to be so. To participate fully in the celebration, Meden residents eventually had to move to "the hotel" (a former military dormitory refurbished in 1995 for the primary school) on Āne-wetak. There they lived in such a makeshift fashion, without the support of land and household, that they suffered an extreme competitive disadvantage. Nancy Pollock (1969) discusses groups from Nam̧o's outer islets with similar disadvantages.

6. By 1989 the groups on Āne-wetak had further diversified, and the youngest and most innovative was a group called Kane Ekāāl (those who are new). Although I have not studied them in detail, these groups are beginning to disregard residence as a way of constructing solidarity. Their new instantiation is much more similar to Mājro groups, where residence is rarely a major factor in group membership. Concomitantly, Āne-wetak people are beginning to glorify the Wūjlañ *jepta* as being more solidary units, and overlapping identity based on shared religious identity, shared land ties, and shared town membership all play a part in their glorified reminiscences about Wūjlañ.

7. I characterize the distinction between being married in a church and just being married (living together) as that of being *wed* as opposed to being *married*. Both are culturally acceptable marriages, but a church-wed couple is indissolubly united (it is a sin to separate), whereas a *koba* couple may separate and remarry without cultural sanction. Once children have been born to a married couple, the couple is more likely to be church wed than is the case prior to the birth of children.

8. A thorough discussion of intentionality is beyond the scope of this book. Let it suffice to say that the notion of intentionality, or willing, does not always reside within a single, socially constituted individual. Certain rules specify action for conglomerate beings, and each member of such a plurality does not necessarily have a say in the plurality of which he or she is a part. Such is especially true in situations that involve pluralities, whose constituents may be supernatural beings. It may also be the case in more down-to-earth relationships.

9. If a man from one group is trying to recruit another man who has not declared an affiliation with a *jepta,* he will stress the dancing and singing abilities of the women from his *jepta*. In an alternation of poetic and graphic terms, a man might describe the sound of the women's voices as "sounds of heaven," the movement of their hips as being irresistible in their backward motion, with speed and rolling motions. The latter descriptions of dance movements simultaneously portray the movements of sexual intercourse. As the descriptions become more detailed, suggestions will be made that the potential member will have the opportunity to be in the middle

of the bush collecting coconuts or gathering pandanus leaves with specific women who are thought to be of interest. All of these daydream scenarios are made in a joking manner, yet they are effective recruiting procedures.

10. Although Alexander Spoehr (1949a, 1949b) uses the language of segmentary lineages to describe the Marshall Islands (mainly Mājro), he also notes that cross-cutting elements of bilaterality make this language somewhat unsuited to the use of these terms. My own aim is not to classify interpersonal relationships as icons of a particular type but, rather, to depict the array of meanings that are of significance to local people and to show how the meanings are manipulated in encounters like *Kūrijmōj*.

11. J. A. Barnes (1962), along with many others, has noted the substantial differences between Pacific and African social organizational constructs.

12. By "actual" I here mean that the stories are "real" to the people; they are not metaphoric or a type of joking.

13. Some recorded texts claim that there are ten brothers; others say that there are twelve. An account given by La Bedbedin of Ron̄lap lists the first four siblings along with Jebrọ: Tūm̧ur, Mājdikdik, Mājlep, Mājetadik, (other sons), and Jebrọ (Knight 1980: 1). Augustin Kramer and Hans Nevermann (n.d.) collected an earlier Ron̄lap version in which Lōktan̄ūr (Lektangir) has only five sons (see note 15 below). Another version of recent vintage claims that there were ten siblings: Tūm̧ur, Ļomijdikdik, Labwal, Ad, Mājlep, Daam-kobban, Ditata, Lok, Jāpe, and Jebrọ (spellings altered) (Downing, Spennemann, and Bennett 1992: 21).

14. Buoj refers to a gathering location, the spot where waves intersect, and the chiefly residence.

15. An early-twentieth-century version contends that she asked each brother to help her construct the sail prior to the race. Kramer and Nevermann do not record the event as a race, per se, but say simply that the first sibling to reach the eastern tip of Aelōn̄ļapļap from Wodja would become a great king. In the Murphy and Runeborg translation of Kramer and Nevermann:

> Lëoa and Lamedal of Bikini built the first boat out of hard *keno* wood. But they did not know yet how to make the sail; they merely paddled. First they travelled to Ailinginae (an *aolet* fish towed them), and stole *bob* [pandanus] fruit of the *robidjen* variety, and then went to Guadjlën [Kuwajleen] to the island of Arba [Arbwā]; here, too, they stole *bob* fruit of the anberia variety. Then they travelled to Rongrik. When they arrived, a man stood there in the entrance and killed the fish; then the boat drifted away. Therefore, then, they used the paddles and by that means managed to reach Wodja in Ailinglaplap Atoll.
>
> The woman, Lektangir lived there in a *këngi* tree; she had come from the sky, and she had five sons:
>
> 1. Demur; nowadays, the name of a small hill . . .
> 2. Mëdjilep
> 3. Tidada
> 4. Lodjalaplap (nowadays, one hole in the rock)
> 5. Djebro (nowadays 7 holes in the beach rocks of Wodja are still supposed to be reminiscent of him).
>
> All of them wanted to go to the east, for it was said that whoever got there first would become a great king. So they all made boats when they had seen that of the two strangers [Leoa and Lamedal from Bikini, the inventors of the first paddling canoe]. Their mother, however, made masts, sails and rigging, the

> deck houses, and an *adji* drum. Demur's boat was ready first. When he wanted to depart his mother said, "Take me with you!" She wanted to show him the art of sailing, but he was afraid and for that reason only wanted to paddle. He also did not want to take along his mother's big bundle for she was also the first to know how to plait mats.
>
> Then, Mëdjilep wanted to travel east, and again his mother wanted to come along, but he did not want that. The exact same happened with Tidada and Lodjalaplap. Only the fifth, Djebro, was willing to take his mother along with him. She came aboard, and said to him, "You will be king!" "Oh," he answered, "how is that possible? My four brothers have already left. I'll never overtake them." His mother said, "You'll see." She then raised the mast. "What is that?" Djebro cried angrily, but his mother soothed him and produced the rigging. Again he cried out in desperation, "What is that supposed to be?" She soothed him this time and attached the belaying pins, *djerukeli*. More angry outbursts from Djebro followed, which his mother knew how to best allay. When his mother finally brought the sail, the son became angry and anxious all over again; but when she showed him its use, he calmed down gradually. Then she instructed him in the use of rigging, hoisted the sail, brought the bow *djabrik* into the wind, and put Djebro in the stern of the boat, the *djablap,* where chiefs are accustomed to sit. There she taught him the use of the rudder. Then they set sail and the boat flew along rapidly, soon overtaking the other four boats. When they passed Demur, he shouted "Stop! I want to sail with you!" They took him aboard with them. But when he was in the middle of the boat, his mother said to Djebro, "Cast off the pennant, let it fall." Then the heavy sail fell on Demur and broke his back. He fell into the water and died. Djebro, however, was the first to reach the eastern land, Rear, and became king, whereas his brothers became commoners, *kadjur*. (Kramer and Nevermann n.d.: 31–33–VI)

16. I have made minor alterations to Gerald Knight's very literal translations, adding tense, number, and words like *the* to make this long quotation more readable in English without altering its content. Marshallese spellings have been altered, and parenthetical comments are also added on two occasions.

17. "Little death" is Knight's translation. Takaji Abo, Byron Bender, et al. (1976: 200) translate Mājlep as "big eye," though "large face" would be equally acceptable. Mājdikdik, logically paired with Mājlep, would, thereby, be "tiny eye" or "tiny face."

18. A minor confusion exists in this version, because Mājdikdik rises twice, before and after Mājlep.

19. I write here as though the Marshall Islands are separate from Wūjlañ and Āne-wetak, even though they are formally part of the current political entity, to reflect local conceptions. Typically, Wūjlañ and Āne-wetak people speak of the Marshalls as a separate place, inhabited by foreign people. Only in specific contexts do they include themselves as Marshall Islanders, usually in opposition to even more foreign sociopolitical groups.

CHAPTER 3: EATING THE FOOD OF MY ENEMIES

1. Otto von Kotzebue and the other members of his expedition may have been the first to begin to recognize the different roles of men and women in food procurement and consumption (Kotzebue 1821; Choris 1820–1822; Chamisso 1986).

CHAPTER 4: SPHERES OF SYMBOLIC ACTION

1. As I noted in chapter 1, *kwōjkwōj* also refers to hula-type dances that were a part of the social and religious festival called *kiye*. Considering these dances lewd, missionaries felt a need to separate Christian and heathen forms of communion.

2. Images of the newly emergent Micronesian states are changing, but these new states constantly battle the images of insignificance made notorious by former Secretary of State Henry Kissinger. In speaking of Micronesians in the 1970s, as a representative of the nation that was given trust responsibility for the region by the United Nations, Kissinger is quoted as saying, "There are only ninety thousand people out there. Who gives a damn?" (Cooley 1974; CBS 1979). All too often, such attitudes of marginality express precisely the manner in which the islands of the Western Pacific have been dealt with by Americans (Kiste 1993).

3. Today's games of war are distant relatives of the ancient wrestling matches and spear-throwing contests that typified similar festive occasions throughout the Pacific. Now, softball and volleyball games, as well as footraces, take the place of the ancient contests.

4. In daily life men may become irresistible by having the quality magically instilled. This does not contradict the statement made above, which is based on another "social fact" of Marshallese culture: men have sexual needs; women have desires but no such physiological needs.

5. On outer islands like Wūjlañ, the sharp division between men's attire and that of women disappears after dark. Evening wear consists rather universally of a wraparound waist covering *(ļōbļaba)* and no top. Such attire is donned after showering, around dusk. Men wear large bath towels wrapped around the waist; women commonly fold down dress tops and secure them around the waist.

CHAPTER 5: SUPPORTIVE DEVICES: SPATIAL AND SOCIAL LOGISTICS

1. In this man's view, wind direction remained a relevant dimension of rank in spite of the indoor setting. Although his rationalizations conflict with those about interactions within the church, the contrast confirms only the way in which rationalizations are fashioned in relation to the requirements of the situation. His statements do not disprove the applicability of any particular form of determining rank.

2. Jack Tobin describes three divisions of Āne-wetak Atoll that include Wurrin and Ānjepe (along with Āne-wetak) as coexisting entities, but all of the informed local historians I consulted insisted that Wurrin disappeared long before Ānjepe came into being.

CHAPTER 6: SUPPORTIVE DEVICES: THE SYMBOLICS OF THE SENSES IN KŪRIJMŌJ

1. In the songs that follow, "b," "t," "a," and "s" refer to the voices: bass, tenor, alto, soprano.

2. *Maroro* covers many hues for Marshallese, including greens, olives, chartreuse, aqua, and light and medium blues. Dark blues are called "black" and are not included in *maroro*. For purposes of celebration, the reflectiveness of highly saturated blue-greens—their brilliance—makes them desirable for celebration. In contrast, light shades of aqua, blue, and green are not highly reflective and are not of much value at *Kūrijmōj*.

3. In indigenizing the shoes and trousers that missionaries introduced as proper church attire, Āne-wetak people refashioned the categories to conform to their own semantic sensibilities. Not only is annunciation different, but meanings also differ.

Whereas English speakers wear "pairs" of shoes or trousers, Wūjlañ people wear "a" trouser and shoes (plural). Trouser(s) are singular objects; shoes are plural objects. One Wūjlañ resident, considering all of this quite obvious but questioning the logic of American English, said: "Well, we just watch and count, to know that one is one and two is two."

4. The expressed ideal is that all paving stones be replaced by new ones prior to the celebration, but a great deal of planning and labor is required to accomplish this end. Most often, only the cookhouse stones and those in the living quarters (if there are any) are replaced. Interior stones are then moved to the household grounds to renew the "truly dirty" stones that delineate the living space. On Āne-wetak and on Mājuro, renewing paving stones has become a simplified "high-tech" operation, assisted by shovels and imported pickup trucks. Ironically, the quality of the paving stones has deteriorated, for the purest white stones are no longer hand selected.

5. White and black are also thought to be particularly reflective. In contrast, red is described as brilliant rather than shiny or reflective, and desirable shades of red and yellow may qualify as bright or loud. These qualities of radiance are important, but they do not code the same meanings or evoke the same emotions as the reflective quality of oiled skin and hair. Lightness in weight, shade, or saturation is the antithesis of both brightness and reflectiveness, and Āne-wetak people find such shades of less value than highly saturated colors. Brent Berlin and Paul Kay (1969) would classify the Wūjlañ color schema as basic, but it seems to be based on characteristics reminiscent of Harold Conklin's descriptions of Hanunoo (1964). Color terms include *maroro* (blue-green), *būrōrō* (red, orange, violet), *kilmeej* (black), and *mouj* (white), though now *ia̧lo* is used to describe some shades of yellow (along with *oran* [orange] and a few other English terms). Shades of brown and grey are called *m̧ōņakņak,* though people say that this term really means "dried out" (cf. Conklin 1964: 191). *M̧ōņakņak* refers to brown, dried-out objects, which have no reflective, living qualities. It represents the logical contrast to green, reflective objects that are imbued with the essence of life.

6. Marshallese have difficulty understanding why Americans, light skinned and possessing other stereotypical qualities of beauty, use no grease on their hair. Even the Japanese, they note, used hair oils. People claim that treating their hair and body with coconut oil is a practice from olden times and that the ancients relied on it to help infuse a person with desirability.

7. On Wūjlañ, the rationale for giving these moneys to the minister was based on the fact that (with the exception of Ernej) ministers were foreign residents, without access to their own land. With the return to Āne-wetak, people necessarily became more dependent on trust-fund payments and less reliant on sparse land products. Therefore, minister and commoner are, once again, "all the same." In recent years, *Kūrijmōj* inflation has also exceeded income, and, with no requirements for the ministers to reciprocate, complaints about their stinginess have increased. Only the most generous ministers reciprocate, commonly through interpersonal channels that link them to certain Āne-wetak families, or occasionally through a feast that the minister gives at his departure. But neither approach is viewed as an adequate reciprocation of the community's generosity at *Kūrijmōj.*

8. Other analogous events include the United States military ships and airplanes that frequent the atolls of Micronesia and leave a sundry collection of goods. People recall in amazement the early days of the American administration when airdrops of goods around Christmastime were commonplace. Two such drops occurred during my twenty-five-month residence on Wūjlañ in the 1970s. Although local people

make no direct associations between the gifts and the ritual pleas at *Kūrijmōj,* the airdrops are an example of good fortune and a sign of American generosity. Airdrops are signals to Wūjlañ people that they have "moved in good ways," that is, in ways acceptable to the deities.

9. The term is appropriate, inasmuch as the Greek *daemon* were supernatural mediators between gods and humans. Nevertheless, for missionaries, demons were the false gods of indigenous belief. Even today, this church-inspired view persists, giving a negative tinge to many people's views of their own local spirits.

10. One substantial danger for people on Wūjlañ comes from spirit entities just arrived from the Caroline Islands. Spirit beings seldom frequent densely populated areas, but the paucity of residents on leeward parts of Wūjlañ makes these locations dangerous. On Āne-wetak, the spirits of *liklaḷ,* the leeward islets, are also dangerous, as are those that inhabit Jeptaan. Jeptaan spirits are inordinately powerful because they are chiefly spirits and therefore, like those from the Caroline Islands, foreign. People also fear the leeward end of Āne-wetak islet, the site of many of the graves of persons of rank as well as the location of a Japanese graveyard (on the ocean side). On Wūjlañ, people have a substantial fear of Jitto-eņ. Part of their fear of the leeward half rests in the associations between the downwind, "female" half and the beings of the noncorporeal realm. Although all bush lands have certain dangers, because they lack living human residents, windward, masculine-coded lands do not possess the same danger as leeward lands. The leeward end not only lacks living humans, it is predisposed to danger by its association with spirit beings and magical machinations.

11. The use of continuous noise, accompanied by lamplight, and the constant movement of living humans is reminiscent of "sweeping the village" in the Trobriand *milamala* (see chapter 7) and of J. G. Frazer's discussions of the ritual use of sound (1890: chap. 24). In *Kūrijmōj,* these nonverbal communicative devices, analogue in character, mediate between the corporeal and noncorporeal worlds. The desired order of daily life is kept separate from the world of the dead by the controlled emission of sound and light. Apocalyptic events, in contrast, signaled by overwhelming quantities of sound and light, mark a disruption of the status quo ante.

12. Sexually provocative dances are metaphorically related to the motions of fire making and lovemmaking. The chants that go along with either fire making or lovemaking are commonly applied to the provocative dance performances as well. Activities in any of these domains may be described with the Wūjlañ terms *irir* (to move back and forth in a rapid manner) or *rōterōt* (to roughen the surface with a filing motion).

One humorous island story concerns the travels of a turn-of-the-century Āne-wetak chief who went to the government center and entered one of the supply stores to find a wood file. The Marshallese call such an object *lā.* Although *lā* is now heard on Āne-wetak, the common Wūjlañ word for this tool is *bael* (file). The Wūjlañ chief requested a *bael,* but the storekeeper did not understand him. The chief repeated his request, but there was still no understanding. The attendant then asked for what purpose the object was intended, because many objects are denoted by their use. The chief replied in a manner that presumed that the meaning of his utterance was blatantly obvious: *"Kōn ta? Rōterōte, iriiri"* (For what? To file, to file, or to scratch up the surface, to move back and forth in a continuous rapid fashion). *Bael, rōterōt,* and *irir* are all Wūjlañ expressions, supposedly unknown to Marshallese, so the attendant was totally dismayed by them. The chief left the store with his request unfulfilled. Wūjlañ people laugh heartily at this humorous tale, in large part because of the sexually suggestive filing movements of the storyteller.

The story, of course, plays on the sexual innuendos involved, and in some tellings the storekeeper who assisted the chief is said to have been a woman. At the same time, it plays on the lack of shared identity between Wūjlañ/Āne-wetak people and Marshall Islanders, because all of the terms are "Wūjlañ speech" used frequently to construct jokes. In part, the joke is one that Wūjlañ people make about themselves, because Marshallese say they do not know how to speak "proper" Marshallese. Of course, the antithetical statement is equally true, because the ability to speak Āne-wetakese or Wūjlañese is the element of shared identity that makes the story humorous and empowering. The story is also a way of separating life on Āne-wetak today from life in the old days.

As an addendum to the story, one young man told me, "We were really 'crazy' [uncultured]. We did not know about all kinds of things." In this view, the situation has changed. Most residents speak an acceptable Ratak or Rālik dialect while still maintaining a knowledge of the slowly articulated and guttural-toned local dialect. Other Marshallese, who commonly disparaged Wūjlañ people for their backward ways, now say that they have changed, yet most remain unaware of their recently attained sophistication. Both groups are held in contempt by Wūjlañ people for their attitudes of superiority (though one is more blatantly contentious than the other).

Both *rōterōt* and *irir* are also used in relation to the motion associated with sexual activity, and from the commonality of motion they are applied to dancing. Especially appropriate is the term *irir,* which denotes a faster, less abrasive motion. Such speed is associated not only with the possession of sexual acumen but also with the rapid motions of dancing. The term is the basis of the joking chant mentioned earlier, "Rub it [female] back and forth, for she has lost direction." Both terms are used in sexual contexts when discussing various sexual exploits or potential encounters: *Rōte rōte, irri irri.*

The terms are further incorporated in the chanting associated with making fire with a fire plow *(iit),* an action that involves rapid, back-and-forth movement of hands and arms, forcing a striker stick into a wood platform of the same, or a slightly softer, material. The commonality between making fire with the fire plow and sexual acuity becomes applicable to dancing and exploding the tree, for each focuses on the complementary movements of males and females and on the resultant productive activity.

13. Young and middle-aged men, often accompanied by chants of a metaphorical sexual nature, create fire with the fire plow using rapid back-and-forth motions of one small dowel-like stick held in both hands (hand-carved and brought to a rounded point) along the flattened and grooved portion of another stick, 3–10 cm. in diameter and at least 1/2 meter long, that is stabalized with the feet.

CHAPTER 7: RITUAL PERFORMANCE, LOCAL IDENTITY, AND THE CONSTRUCTION OF MEANING

1. In 1982, one young atoll resident spent a long time telling me about a bizarre new religion that had recently appeared in Mājuro. It was not a Christian group, or even Catholic, he said. After some time, I began to guess: "Shinto? Confucianism? Buddhism? Zoroastrianism?" "No, no, no, no." After some time he departed, still uncertain about the identity of the new sect. The next day he returned, however, noting that he had remembered the name. Leaving me baffled, but more certain than ever about the veracity of David M. Schneider's contentions about alternate worldviews, he noted with certitude: "Baptist."

GLOSSARY

aḷap a respected elder; the head of a *bwij*

aḷeḷap a fishing technique; the surround method

Āne-wetak Enewetak Atoll; also Eniwetok; the primordial residence location of the Āne-wetak people; the site of a World War II battle and of United States nuclear tests

anij a sacred spirit being; God

beet stylized line dances of *Kūrijmōj*

bōrwaj house rafter purlin; a household

bwij a bilateral extended family

Etao the sly culture hero of the Marshall Islands

Ioḷap "There in the Middle," one of three songfest groups on Wūjlañ Atoll

irooj a chief; God

Jebro the first Marshall Islands chief to rule an earthly domain; youngest of the siblings born to Lōktañūr

jepta a Christmas songfest group

Jitto-eṇ "Here, This Location Facing Leeward," one of three songfest groups on Wūjlañ Atoll

Jittōk-en "Here, This Location Facing Windward," one of three songfest groups on Wūjlañ Atoll

jowi a matriclan

kalbuuj game played on Wūjlañ during the celebration of *Kūrijmōj*

kaṃōḷo a songfest

karate a game played on Wūjlañ and Āne-wetak during the celebration of *Kūrijmōj*

katak evening song practices

keemem a first–birthday celebration

Kūrijmōj Christmas; the time between early October and mid-January

Kuwajleen also Kwajalein; a major atoll of the Central Rālik Chain; the site of a famous World War II battle and now of a United States military installation

Lōktañūr the chiefly ancestress of the Marshall Islands; mother of Jebrọ

ṃaaj "marching style" entry dances of *Kūrijmōj*

maan iiō "the front of the year"; the first week after New Year's Day, when ideal typical demeanor is required

maañ pandanus fronds

Mājro Majuro; capital of the Republic of the Marshall Islands and former District Center under the U.S. Administered Trust Territory

mōña food; to eat

mōṇōṇo happiness

Naan Aorōk "important words"; the children's songfest group

ni coconut, both the tree and the drinking–stage nut

pānuk small gifts thrown into the audience by a performing *jepta*

Pohnpei formerly Ponape; Eastern Carolines government center, which had governing authority over Wūjlañ and Āne-wetak during the Japanese era.

Rādikdoon the women's songfest group

Roñoul Ļalem Raan "The Twenty-Fifth Day"; December 25

tōbtōb "to tug on"; a Christmas game in which the clothes of opposite–sex, opposite–*jepta* members are stolen as they perform

wōjke a tree; also the piñatalike constructs magically exploded during *Kūrijmōj*

Wūjlañ Ujelang Atoll; primordial residence location of the Wūjlañ people and nuclear–testing relocation site for the Āne-wetak community (beginning in 1947)

BIBLIOGRAPHY

Abo, Takaji, Byron W. Bender, Alfred Capelle, and Tony DeBrum
1976 *Marshallese-English Dictionary.* Honolulu: University Press of Hawaii.

ABS
1971 *Mótón Kalimur eo Mokta kap Kalimur Ekál—Jeje ko re Kwojarjar.* Marshall Islands: The Bible Society in Micronesia.

Alexander, William
1978 Wage labor, urbanization and culture change in the Marshall Islands. Ph.D. diss., New School for Social Research.
1979 The destruction of paradise. *The Progressive,* February, 45–46.

Appleton, John N.
1834 Journal of a cruise in the 'Waverly' also called the 'Kaahumanu', Captain Cathcart, for the search for Captain Dowsett, lost in the South Seas, told by Mr. Appleton, second mate of the brig 'Waverly.' Manuscript, Bishop Museum Library, Honolulu.

Austin, J. L.
1962 *How to Do Things with Words.* New York: Oxford University Press.

Barnes, J. A.
1962 African models in the New Guinea highlands. *Man* 62: 5–9.

Bateson, Gregory
1958 *Naven.* Stanford, Calif.: Stanford University Press.

Beaglehole, Ernest and Pearl
1938 *Ethnology of Pukapuka.* Bernice P. Bishop Museum Bulletin 150. Honolulu: Bernice P. Bishop Museum Press.

Beckwith, Martha

1951 *The Kumulipo: A Hawaiian Creation Chant.* Chicago: University of Chicago Press.

Bender, Byron

1969 *Spoken Marshallese.* Honolulu: University of Hawaii Press.

Berlin, Brent, and Paul Kay

1969 *Basic Color Terms: Their Universality and Evolution.* Berkeley: University of California Press.

Bickett, Robert D.

1965 *History of the Air Force Western Test Range 1 January–31 December 1965.* Vol. 1, *Enewetak and Bikini Atolls.* Washington, D.C.: National Range Division, Air Force Systems Command, United States Air Force.

Bingham, Sybil

1821 Journal of Sybil Bingham. February 9. Manuscript, Hawaiian Mission Children's Society Library, Honolulu.

Bodenhorn, Barbara

1993 Christmas present: Christmas public. In *Unwrapping Christmas,* edited by Daniel Miller, pp. 193–216. Oxford: Clarendon Press.

Bourdieu, Pierre

1977 *Outline of a Theory of Practice.* Cambridge: Cambridge University Press.

1991 *Language and Symbolic Power.* Cambridge, Mass.: Harvard University Press.

Burridge, Kenelm O.

1960 *Mambu.* London: Methuen.

Carrier, James

1993 The rituals of Christmas giving. In *Unwrapping Christmas,* edited by Daniel Miller, pp. 55–74. Oxford: Clarendon Press.

Carucci, Laurence Marshall

1980a The Enewetak conception of chiefs and foreigners. Paper presented at ASAO Symposium, Language and Politics in Oceania, Galveston, Texas.

1980b The renewal of life: A ritual encounter in the Marshall Islands. Ph.D. diss., University of Chicago.

1983 Sly moves: A semiotic analysis of movement in Marshallese culture. In *Semiotics 1981,* edited by John N. Deely and Margot D. Lenhart, pp. 139–51. New York: Plenum Press.

1984 Food categories and nutrition in the outer Marshall Islands. Paper presented at Annual Meetings of the American Anthropological Association, Denver, Colorado.

1985 Conceptions of maturing and dying in the 'middle of heaven.' In *Aging and Its Transformations: Moving toward Death in Pacific Society,* edited by Dorothy A. Counts and David Counts, pp. 107–29. Washington, D.C.: University Press of America.

1987a Jekero: Symbolizing the transition to manhood in the Marshall Islands. *Micronesica* 20 (December).

1987b Kijen emaan ilo baat: Methods and meanings of smoking in Marshallese society. In *Drugs in Western Pacific Societies,* edited by Lamont Lindstrom, pp. 51–71. Lanham, Md.: University Press of America.

1988 Small fish in a big sea: Geographical dispersion and sociopolitical centralisation in the Marshall Islands. In *State and Society: Emergence and Development and Social Hierarchy and Political Centralisation,* edited by J. Gledhill, B. Bender, and M. Larsen, pp. 33–42. London: Unwin Hyman.

1989 The source of the force in Marshallese cosmology. In *The Pacific Theatre,* edited by Lamont Lindstrom and Geoffrey White, pp. 73–96. Honolulu: University of Hawaii Press.

1990 Negotiations of violence in the Marshallese household. *Pacific Studies* 13(3): 93–113.

1992 An atoll called desire: Women, wars, and the language of welcome on Arno atoll. In *Proceedings of the Montana Academy of Sciences,* vol. 52, pp. 119–28. Bozeman: Montana State University.

1993 Christmas on Ujelang: The politics of continuity in the context of change. In *Contemporary Pacific Societies: Studies in Development and Change,* edited by Victoria S. Lockwood, Thomas G. Harding, and Ben J. Wallace, pp. 304–20. Englewood Cliffs, N.J.: Prentice Hall.

1995a Symbolic imagery of Enewetak sailing canoes. In *Seafaring in the Contemporary Pacific Islands: Studies in Continuity and Change,* edited by Richard Feinberg, pp. 16–33. DeKalb: Northern Illinois University Press.

1995b Shifting stances, differing glances. Paper presented at ASAO Symposium, Families in the Field, Clearwater, Fla.

1995c From the spaces to the holes; Ralik-Ratak remembrances of World War II. *Isla* 3(#2): 279–312.

In press Irooj ro ad: Measures of chiefly ideology and practice in the Marshall Islands. In *Chiefs Today: Traditional Pacific Leadership and the Postcolonial State,* edited by Lamont Lindstrom and Geoffrey White. Stanford, Calif., and Honolulu: Stanford University Press and the East-West Center.

CBS

1979 Who gives a damn? *60 Minutes,* December 23, 1979.

Chamisso, Adelbert von, ed.

[1836] 1986 *A Voyage around the World with the Romanzov Exploring Expedition in the Years 1815–1818.* Honolulu: University of Hawaii Press.

Choris, Louis

1820–1822 *Voyage pittoresque autour du monde.* Paris: Firmin Didot.

Clifford, James

1983 On ethnographic authority. *Representations* 2(Spring): 132–43.

Compact of Free Association, The

1982 The Compact of Free Association between the Government of the United States of America and the Governments of Palau, the Marshall Islands, and the Federated States of Micronesia, including the Section 177 Agreement. Witnessed and signed at Honolulu, Hawai'i on May 30, 1982 by representatives of the United States and the Marshall Islands.

Conklin, Harold C.

1964 Hanunoo color categories. In *Language in Culture and Society,* edited by Dell Hymes, pp. 189–92. New York: Harper and Row.

Cooley, Charles H.

[1902] 1922 *Human Nature and the Social Order.* New York: Charles Scribner's Sons.

Cooley, Michael D.
1974 Enewetak: An inquiry into who gives a damn about what, and why. M.A. essay, Wesleyan University, Middletown, Conn.
Doi, Takeo
1973 *The Anatomy of Dependence.* New York: Kodansha.
Douglas, Mary
1966 *Purity and Danger.* London: Routledge and Kegan Paul.
Downing, Jane, Dirk H. R. Spennemann, and Margaret Bennett
1992 *Bwebwenatoon Etto: A Collection of Marshallese Legends and Traditions.* Majuro, Marshall Islands: Historic Preservation Office.
Durkheim, Émile, and Marcel Mauss
1963 *Primitive Classification.* Translated by Rodney Needham. Chicago: University of Chicago Press.
Dye, Thomas S.
1981 *Archaeological Survey and Test Excavation on Arno Atoll, Marshall Islands.* Honolulu: Department of Anthropology, Bernice Pauahi Bishop Museum.
Eco, Umberto
1990 *The Limits of Interpretation.* Bloomington: Indiana University Press.
Enewetak Master Plan
1973 Enewetak Atoll Master Plan for Island Rehabilitation and Resettlement. 2 vols. Trust Territory of the Pacific Islands (Saipan, Mariana Islands): Holmes and Narver, Inc.
Fabian, Johannes
1983 *Time and the Other: How Anthropology Makes Its Object.* New York: Columbia University Press.
1990 *Power and Performance: Ethnographic Explorations through Proverbial Wisdom and Theater in Shaba, Zaire.* Madison: University of Wisconsin Press.
Feinberg, Richard
1988 Socio-spatial symbolism and the logic of rank on two Polynesian outliers. *Ethnology* 27(3): 291–310.
Finsch, Otto
1893 Ethnologische Erfahrungen und Belegstücke aus der Südsee. 2. Marshall-Archipel. *Annalen des k. k. Naturhistorischen Hofmuseum.* (Vienna) 8: 119–82, 419–20.
Firth, Stewart
1987 *Nuclear Playground.* Honolulu: University of Hawaii Press.
Fortes, Meyer
1958 Introduction. In *The Developmental Cycle in Domestic Groups,* edited by Jack Goody, pp. 1–14. Cambridge: Cambridge University Press.
Foucault, Michel
1970 *The Order of Things: An Archaeology of the Human Sciences.* New York: Pantheon Books.
1980 *Power/Knowledge: Selected Interviews and Other Writings.* Edited by Colin Gordon. New York: Pantheon Books.
Frazer, J. G.
1890 *The Golden Bough: A Study in Comparative Religion.* 2 vols. London: Macmillan.
Geertz, Clifford
1966 Religion as a cultural system. In *Anthropological Approaches to the*

Study of Religion, edited by Michael Banton, pp. 1–46. London: Tavistock Publications.
1973 *The Interpretation of Cultures: Selected Essays.* New York: Basic Books, Inc.

Gill, William W.
1876 *Myths and Songs from the South Pacific.* London: H. S. King.

Gladwin, Thomas
1970 *East Is a Big Bird: Navigation and Logic on Puluwat Atoll.* Cambridge, Mass.: Harvard University Press.

Goodenough, Ward H.
1955 A problem in Malayo-Polynesian social organization. *American Anthropologist* 57: 71–83.
1986 Sky world and this world: The place of Kachaw in Micronesian cosmology. *American Anthropologist* 88(3): 551–68.

Gregor, Thomas
1977 *Mehinaku: The Drama of Daily Life in a Brazilian Indian Village.* Chicago: University of Chicago Press.

Grimble, Sir Arthur
1931 Gilbertese astronomy and astronomical observations. *Journal of Polynesian Society* 40: 197–224.

Hecht, Julia
1979 Women of rank in Polynesia. Paper presented at an Association for Social Anthropology in Oceania Working Session, Women in Oceania, Clearwater, Fla.

Hezel, Francis X.
1983 *The First Taint of Civilization: A History of the Caroline and Marshall Islands in Pre-Colonial Days, 1521–1885.* Honolulu: University of Hawaii Press.

Hocart, A. M.
1927 *Kingship.* London: Oxford University Press.
1936 *Kings and Councillors.* Cairo: Paul Barbey.
1952 *The Northern States of Fiji.* London: Royal Anthropological Institute of Great Britain and Ireland.
[1952] 1970 *The Life-Giving Myth and Other Essays.* Translated by Rodney Needham. London: Tavistock Publications.

HOE
n.d. History of Enjebi Island, Eniwetok Atoll. Manuscript, Mid-Pacific Research Laboratory, Enewetak, Marshall Islands.

Hough, Frank
1947 *The Island War.* New York: J. B. Lippincott.

Kahn, Miriam
1986 *Always Hungry, Never Greedy: Food and the Expression of Gender in a Melanesian Society.* New York: Cambridge University Press.

Kirch, Patrick
1984 *The Evolution of the Polynesian Chiefdoms.* Cambridge: Cambridge University Press.

Kiste, Robert C.
1967 Changing patterns of land tenure and social organization among the ex-Bikini Marshallese. Ph.D. diss., University of Oregon.
1968 *Kili Island: A Study of the Relocation of the Ex-Bikini Marshallese.*

Eugene: Department of Anthropology, University of Oregon.

1974 *The Bikinians: A Study in Forced Migration.* Menlo Park, Calif.: Cummings Publishing.

1976 The people of Enewetak Atoll vs. the U.S. Department of Defense. In *Ethics and Anthropology,* edited by M. A. Rynkiewich and J. P. Spradley, pp. 61–80. New York: John Wiley and Sons.

1993 New political statuses in American Micronesia. In *Contemporary Pacific Societies: Studies in Development and Change,* edited by Victoria S. Lockwood, Thomas G. Harding, and Ben J. Wallace, pp. 67–80. Englewood Cliffs, N.J.: Prentice Hall.

Kiste, Robert C., and M. A. Rynkiewich

1976 Incest and exogamy: A comparative study of two Marshall Island populations. *Journal of the Polynesian Society* 85: 209–26.

Knight, Gerald

1980 *Man This Reef.* Majuro, Marshall Islands: Micronitor News and Printing.

Kotzebue, Otto von

1821 *A Voyage of Discovery into the South Sea and Beering Straits . . . in the Years 1815–1818.* 3 vols. London: Longman and Brown.

1830 *A New Voyage round the World in the Years 1823, 24, 25, 26.* 2 vols. London: Henry Colburn and Richard Bentley.

Kramer, Augustin, and Hans Nevermann

n.d. *Ralik Ratak.* Edited by Elizabeth A. Murphy and Ruth E. Runeborg. Unpublished translation in Pacific Collection, Hamilton Library, University of Hawai'i, Honolulu. Standard translation in HRAF files from Ralik-Ratak (Marshall-Inseln) von Augustin Krämer und Hans Nevermann, 11. Band der "Ergebnisse Der Südsee-Expedition 1908–1910, hrsg.v. Georg Thilenius. Walter de Gruyter and Co., Berlin, New York (1938).

Labby, David

1976 *The Demystification of Yap: Dialectics of Culture on a Micronesian Island.* Chicago: University of Chicago Press.

Lamberson, Janet O.

1982 *A Guide to Terrestrial Plants of Enewetak Atoll.* Honolulu: Pacific Sciences Information Center, Bernice P. Bishop Museum.

Lawrence, Peter

1971 *Road Belong Cargo: A Study of the Cargo Movement in the Southern Madang District, New Guinea.* Prospect Heights, Ill.: Waveland Press.

Lévi-Strauss, Claude

1963 *Structural Anthropology.* New York: Basic Books.

1969 *The Raw and the Cooked.* New York: Harper and Row.

[1962] 1970 *The Savage Mind.* Chicago: University of Chicago Press.

1993 Father Christmas executed. In *Unwrapping Christmas,* edited by Daniel Miller, pp. 38–51. Oxford: Clarendon Press.

Lieber, Michael D.

1984 Strange feast: Negotiating identities on Ponape. *Journal of the Polynesian Society* 93: 141–89.

Lindstrom, Lamont

1993 *Cargo Cult: Strange Stories of Desire from Melanesia and Beyond.* Honolulu: University of Hawaii Press.

Lutz, Catherine
1988 *Unnatural Emotions.* Chicago: University of Chicago Press.

Maifeld, Mary H., and Laurence M. Carucci
1982 Field notes on Enewetak family food consumption, in the libraries of the researchers.

Makemson, Maude W.
1941 *The Morning Star Rises: An Account of Polynesian Astronomy.* New Haven, Conn.: Yale University Press.

Malinowski, Bronislaw
[1916] 1954 Baloma: The spirits of the dead in the Trobriand Islands. In *Magic, Science and Religion,* pp. 147–274. New York: Doubleday.
[1935] 1965 *Coral Gardens and Their Magic.* 2 vols. Bloomington: University of Indiana Press.
[1922] 1984 *Argonauts of the Western Pacific.* Prospect Heights, Ill.: Waveland Press.

Malo, David
1951 *Hawaiian Antiquities.* Honolulu: Bernice Pauahi Bishop Museum Press.

Marcus, George E., and Michael M. J. Fisher
1986 *Anthropology as Cultural Critique.* Chicago: University of Chicago Press.

Marshall, Mac
1979 *Weekend Warriors: Alcohol in a Micronesian Culture.* Palo Alto, Calif.: Mayfield Publishing.

Marx, Karl
[1852] 1963 *The Eighteenth Brumaire of Louis Bonaparte.* New York: International Publishers.

Mason, Leonard
1947 Economic and human resources—Marshall Islands. In *Economic Survey of Micronesia.* Washington, D.C.: U.S. Commercial Co.
1954 Relocation of the Bikini Marshallese: A study in group migrations. Ph.D. diss., Yale University.

Mason, Leonard, and Robert C. Kiste
1984 Considerations in respect to the Kwajalein Atoll compensation funds. Research report written for George Allen (Cadwalader, Wickersham and Taft) in fulfillment of Allen's request dated January 1984, in the files of Leonard Mason.

Mason, Leonard, and Alois Nagler
1943 *Social Organization in the Marshall Islands: Cross-Cultural Survey.* New Haven, Conn.: Institute of Human Relations, Yale University.

Mauss, Marcel
1967 *The Gift.* New York: W. W. Norton.

Meigs, Anna S.
1984 *Food, Sex, and Pollution: A New Guinea Religion.* New Brunswick, N.J.: Rutgers University Press.

Micronesian Reporter
1968 Saipan, Mariana Islands.

Miller, Daniel, ed.
1993 *Unwrapping Christmas.* Oxford: Clarendon Press.

Mintz, Sidney W.
1986 *Sweetness and Power: The Place of Sugar in Modern History*. New York: Penguin Books.

Morison, Samuel E.
1951 *History of the United States Naval Operations in World War II: Aleutians, Gilberts, and Marshalls, June 1942–April 1944*. Boston: Little, Brown.

Niditch, Susan
1985 *Chaos to Cosmos: Studies in Biblical Patterns of Creation*. Atlanta: Scholars Press.

Obeyesekere, Gananath
1992 *The Apotheosis of Captain Cook*. Princeton, N.J., and Honolulu: Princeton University Press and Bishop Museum Press.

Ortner, Sherry B.
1973 On key symbols. *American Anthropologist* 75: 1338–46.

Pacific Daily News
1973 Agana, Guam. May 30, May 31, August 1, August 29.

Pease, E.
1887 Letter, January 1887, to the ABCFM, Hawaiian Mission Children's Society archives, Honolulu.

Peirce, Charles S.
1932 *Collected Papers of C. S. Peirce*. Vol. 2. Cambridge, Mass.: Harvard University Press.

Peterson, Glenn
1979 External politics, internal economics, and Ponapean social formation. *American Ethnologist* 6: 25–40.
1990 *Lost in the Weeds: Theme and Variation in Pohnpei Political Mythology*. Occasional Paper 35. Honolulu: Center for Pacific Island Studies, University of Hawaii.

Pollock, Nancy
1969 A pragmatic view of Marshallese Christmas ritual. University of Hawaii Library prize paper for Pacific Research, University of Hawaii.
1970 Breadfruit and breadwinning on Namu Atoll, Marshall Islands. Ph.D. diss., University of Hawaii.

Poyer, Lin
1993 *The Ngatik Massacre: History and Identity on a Micronesian Atoll*. Washington, D.C.: Smithsonian Institution Press.

Radcliffe-Brown, A. R.
1924 The mother's brother in South Africa. *South African Journal of Science* 21: 542–55.
[1952] 1965 *Structure and Function in Primitive Society*. New York: The Free Press.

Rosaldo, Michelle Z.
1980 *Knowledge and Passion: Ilongot Notions of Self & Social Life*. New York: Cambridge University Press.

Rosaldo, Renato
1980 *Ilongot Headhunting 1883–1974: A Study in Society and History*. Stanford, Calif.: Stanford University Press.
1989 *Culture and Truth*. Boston: Beacon Press.

Rosendahl, Paul H.

1979 Archaeological survey in the Marshall and eastern Caroline Islands: A completion of fieldwork progress report on the Ketlon-BPBM Expedition to eastern Micronesia. Manuscript, Alele Museum, Majuro, Marshall Islands.

Rynkiewich, Michael

1972 Land tenure among Arno Marshallese. Ph.D. diss., University of Minnesota.

1976 Adoption and land tenure among Arno Marshallese. In *Transactions in Kinship,* edited by Ivan Brady, pp. 93–119. Honolulu: University Press of Hawaii.

Sahlins, Marshall

1981 *Historical Metaphors and Mythical Realities: Structure in the Early History of the Sandwich Island Kingdom.* Ann Arbor: University of Michigan Press.

1985 *Islands of History.* Chicago: University of Chicago Press.

1995 *How "Natives" Think: About Captain Cook, for Example.* Chicago: University of Chicago Press.

Schieffelin, Edward L.

1976 *The Sorrow of the Lonely and the Burning of the Dancers.* New York: St. Martin's Press.

Schneider, David M.

1984 *A Critique of the Study of Kinship.* Ann Arbor: University of Michigan Press.

Schrempp, Gregory A.

1992 *Magical Arrows: The Maori, the Greeks, and the Folklore of the Universe.* Madison: University of Wisconsin Press.

Sharp, Andrew

1960 *The Discovery of the Pacific Islands.* Oxford: Clarendon Press.

Shaw, Henry, Bernard C. Nalty, and Edwin Turnbladh

1966 *History of U.S. Marine Corps Operations in World War II.* Vol. 3, *Central Pacific Drive.* Washington, D.C.: Historical Branch, United States Marine Corps.

Shils, Edward

1970 Centre and periphery. In *Selected Essays by Edward Shils,* pp. 1–14. Chicago: Center for Organizational Studies, Department of Sociology, University of Chicago.

Shore, Bradd

1977 A Samoan theory of action: Social control and social order in a Polynesian paradox. Ph.D. diss., University of Chicago.

Silverman, Martin G.

1971 *Disconcerting Issue.* Chicago: University of Chicago Press.

Spoehr, Alexander

1949a The generation type kinship system in the Marshall and Gilbert Islands. *Southwestern Journal of Anthropology* 5: 107–17.

1949b *Majuro, a Village in the Marshall Islands.* Chicago: Chicago Natural History Museum.

Tambiah, Stanley J.

1973 The form and meaning of magical acts. In *Modes of Thought: Essays on*

Thinking in Western and Non-Western Societies, edited by R. Horton, pp. 199–229. London: Faber.

Tobin, Jack A.

1952 Ujelang diet notes, October 14–19, in the files of J. A. Tobin.

1958 Land tenure in the Marshall Islands. In *Land Tenure Patterns in the Trust Territory of the Pacific Islands,* Vol. 1, pp. 1–76. Guam, Mariana Islands: Office of the High Commissioner.

1967 The resettlement of the Enewetak people: A study of a displaced community in the Marshall Islands. Ph.D. diss., University of California, Berkeley.

1970 The legend of Lijibake. *Micronesian Reporter* 18(1): 16–17.

1973 Pacific Cratering Experiments (PACE) program hearings on Ujilang Atoll March 26–28, 1973. Typescript, Office of the District Administrator. Majuro, Marshall Islands, April 3.

Turner, Victor

1967 *The Forest of Symbols: Aspects of Ndembu Ritual.* Ithaca, N.Y.: Cornell University Press.

1969 *The Ritual Process: Structure and Anti-Structure.* Chicago: Aldine Publishing.

UBS

1979 *Nan ko Remmõn ñõn Armij Otemjej: Kallimur Ekãl kab Psalm ko.* Marshall Islands: United Bible Societies.

Valeri, Valerio

1985 *Kingship and Sacrifice: Ritual and Society in Ancient Hawaii.* Chicago: University of Chicago Press.

van Gennep, Arnold

[1908] 1960 *The Rites of Passage.* Chicago: University of Chicago Press.

Wasserman, Harvey, and Norman Solomon (with Robert Alvarez and Eleanor Walters)

1982 *Killing Our Own: The Disaster of America's Experiences with Atomic Radiation.* New York: Delacorte Press.

Weiner, Annette

1976 *Women of Value, Men of Renown: New Perspectives in Trobriand Exchange.* Austin: University of Texas Press.

1988 *The Trobrianders of Papua New Guinea.* New York: Holt, Rinehart and Winston.

1989 Why cloth? Wealth, gender, and power in Oceania. In *Cloth and Human Experience,* edited by Annette B. Weiner and Jane Schneider, pp. 33–72. Washington D.C.: Smithsonian Institution Press.

1992 *Inalienable Possessions: The Paradox of Keeping-While-Giving.* Berkeley: University of California Press.

Williamson, Robert W.

1933 *Religious and Cosmic Beliefs of Central Polynesia.* 2 vols. Cambridge: Cambridge University Press.

Worsley, Peter

1968 *The Trumpet Shall Sound: A Study of "Cargo" Cults in Melanesia.* New York: Schocken Books.

Wright, Ione S.

1951 *Voyages of Alvaro de Saavedra Cerón, 1527–1529.* University of Miami

Hispanic-American Studies, no. 11. Coral Gables, Fla.: University of Miami Press.

Wūjlañ Field Notes

1976–1978 Library of L. M. Carucci.

1982–1983 Library of L. M. Carucci.

1990–1991 Library of L. M. Carucci.

Yanaihara, Tadao

1940 *Pacific Islands under Japanese Mandate.* London: Oxford University Press.

INDEX

Clifford, James, 177, 184
Clothes, 28, 30–32, 34, 38, 73, 94, 98–99, 101, 103–5, 111, 130–35, 141, 149, 151, 158–59, 188; and cloth, 38, 130, 142; and color, 130–33, 142, 157; and gender identity, 104, 130–33, 158; and *jepta* unity, 130. *See also* Belts; Head wreaths; Leis; Shoes; Sunglasses
Coconuts, 5, 8, 11, 30, 68, 71, 83, 86, 93, 116–18, 142, 144, 146, 174, 184, 186; drinking (ni) of, 30–31, 77, 82, 144, 165; fronds and fibers of, 20, 26, 133, 145–46; and medicine, 109, 146; and oil, 28, 138–39, 142–43, 154, 165, 182, 189; and sennit (coir), 64; sprouted *(iu)*, 8, 29, 30, 38, 77, 116. *See also* Copra
Commoners. *See* Kajoor
Compensation, 10, 76, 153, 174, 176–77
Competition, 20, 24, 26, 29, 50, 52, 60, 68, 70, 84, 90, 92, 103, 115, 119, 128, 161, 168, 172, 174
Congregationalist, 161, 172
Copra, 5, 8, 12, 19, 28–29, 116, 118, 168, 175, 182
Cosmology, 15, 65, 71–72, 105, 107–8, 123, 142, 179
Cowries, 20
CROSSROADS, 7

Dance, 22–24, 40, 73, 89; of the ancient past, 32, 34, 64, 68, 142, 155–57, 178; of Etao, 32, 34, 158–59; gender specific, 156, 157; hula-style, 23, 34, 157, 159, 188; of *Kūrijmōj,* 20–23, 25, 27, 29, 31–36, 40, 50, 52, 54, 75, 104, 113, 142, 145, 147, 151, 157–59, 161–62, 168, 178, 182, 185; military form of, 155–56; ambivalence toward, 73, 157; and energy, empowerment, and renown, 142, 147, 155–56, 159; prohibition of, 73, 137, 157; and sexual attraction, 142, 159, 178, 190–91. *See also Beet; Kiye; Maaj*
Darkness, 38, 50–51, 67–68, 80, 85, 104, 127, 151, 172, 178, 184
Death, 60, 65–66, 85, 88, 90, 94, 96–97, 100, 125, 127, 129, 132, 144–45, 149, 154–55, 167, 169–70, 176, 180, 187
December, 3, 20, 26, 75–76, 78, 163, 173, 179; December 25, 20, 26–31, 33, 36–37, 54, 60, 73, 75, 78, 80, 84, 88, 94, 101, 105, 113–14, 119, 129–30, 134, 139–43, 145–46, 151–53, 155, 163, 165, 175, 179–80, 182
Deities, 22, 64, 73, 82, 96, 150, 169; ancient, 42, 62, 67, 70, 96, 121, 131, 152, 179; empowerment from, 61, 74, 77, 135, 179; human interactions with, 28, 40–41, 69–70, 77–79, 84, 96, 98, 102–5, 114, 121, 140, 142–46, 149–50, 152–53, 164, 167–68, 171, 175, 177, 179–82, 190; of love and generosity, 68, 70, 79, 98, 106, 143, 145, 150, 152. *See also* God
Direction(ality), 67, 96–97, 108–9, 112, 188; of change in *Kūrijmōj,* 158, 173, 180; egocentric code of, 108, 110–11; and gender, 102, 108–10, 139; and land code, 108–11; loss of, 102, 191; and sea code, 108–11, 113–14, 138–39; and surroundedness *(kōṇak),* 111–13, 120–21, 137, 150, 185
Diversity, 173
Doane, Edward, 62
Doi, Takeo, 111
Drunkenness and imbibing, 37, 50, 73, 154, 161
Durkheim, Emile, 15, 62, 73

Easter, 19, 40, 145
Ebeye (Epjā, Kuwajleen), 21, 164, 172
Eco, Umberto, 14, 177
Ekkan (first fruits), 82, 165, 168
Eḷae, 96–97
Elders, 10, 11, 85; and church, 90; respected, 57, 84, 89–90, 149, 167
Enewetak. *See* Āne-wetak
Episteme, 162
Epoon (Ebon), 8, 21, 109, 158, 174
Ernej, 152, 167, 189
Etao, 34, 62, 73, 132, 148–49, 157–59, 176, 178, 182

91–92. *See also* Regeneration; Renewal
Gladwin, Thomas, 110
God, 5, 33, 50, 62, 75, 87, 99, 135, 143, 179; gods, 19, 42, 62, 75, 86, 92, 96, 141–42, 178, 180, 190; god chiefs, 62, 64, 68, 112; and the ancient deities, 42, 77, 86, 121, 146, 175, 179; and chiefs/ministers, 36, 42, 84, 114, 154, 167, 171, 179; blessing and grace of, 57, 86, 153; interactions with, 17, 35, 46, 48, 51, 60–61, 69–70, 74, 78, 80, 98, 112, 135, 141, 145–46, 150, 152–53, 159, 164, 169, 171, 180, 190; man-god, 61–62, 190; possessions of, 54, 94, 98, 105, 114, 152, 154; prayers to, 76, 84; protection by, 36, 111, 180; retribution of, 154, 171; as sacred, magical, and life-giving force, 143, 150–52, 176; will of, 36, 149, 152; work of, 51, 94; and women, 72, 141. *See also* Chiefs; Deities
Goodenough, Ward, 34, 48, 57, 117
Gregor, Thomas, 72
Grimble, Sir Arthur, 110

Handicrafts, 19–20, 26, 28, 30, 100, 121, 133, 137, 146, 175
Happiness, 8, 15, 21, 24–25, 31, 36–38, 43, 51, 53, 60, 63–64, 73, 79–80, 92–95, 100, 103, 121, 140, 148, 154, 157–58, 163, 177, 180
Hawai'i, 3, 22, 25, 31, 62, 73, 85, 98–99, 135, 145
Head wreaths, 32, 130, 135–40, 145
Hocart, Arthur M., 61–62
Household, 98, 106, 116, 134, 146, 165, 181, 189; head *(bōrwaj)* of, 31, 89, 102, 136
humor, 8, 12, 16, 21, 26–27, 40, 53, 78, 80, 92, 98, 104, 138, 140–41, 148–49, 156, 159, 181, 190–91

Iakjo, 44, 49
Ial. *See* Rainbow
Ifaluk, 79
Indebtedness, 43, 56, 101, 104, 146, 152, 171, 179, 181
Interdependence, 77–78, 114, 179, 181
Interpersonal relationships, 48, 61, 86, 108, 156, 172, 174, 186. *See also* Kinship
Ioḷap, 24, 34, 37, 44, 46–47, 49–50, 52, 96, 113–15, 120–22, 126, 128, 173, 185
Irooj (Iroij). *See* Chiefs
Irresistibility, 32–35, 53, 59, 100, 102–3, 128–29, 132, 138–43, 159, 179, 182, 185, 188

Jali (Charley), 22–23
Japan, 3–5, 8–9, 14, 23–25, 57–58, 62, 93, 111, 133, 148, 153, 155–56, 161, 167, 173, 178, 184, 189–90
Jebrọ, 63, 73, 85, 106, 186; and the albatross, 144, 182; and Christ, 68, 70, 78, 86, 98, 127, 146, 150, 162, 178–79, 182; and enrichment of fish, 68, 86, 98, 143–44, 161, 179; interactions with, 96, 99, 127; and Lōktañūr, 63–65, 67–68, 85, 144, 177–78, 186; and love, generosity, and caring, 64–65, 98, 106, 127, 129, 152, 162, 178–79, 182; and the Milky Way, 85, 144; as Pleiades, 64, 66–67, 85, 161; and the rainbow, 85, 97, 144; and redness, 144; and renewal, 67–68, 86, 142–44, 146, 162, 179; and Tūṃur, 64–65, 86, 179, 186; and winter solstice, 68, 85, 97, 179
Jemāliwūt, 62
Jepta (songfest groups), 16–17, 22, 24, 31–32, 42, 44, 68, 73, 94, 115, 135, 172–73; and attraction, 135, 139–43, 163, 182; and *bwij*, 43, 49, 51, 56, 170; children's, 24, 52, 70; and clans, 26, 54, 56–57, 59, 71, 104–5, 113, 140, 170; and community solidarity, 17, 26, 29, 78, 84, 145, 170, 173, 179, 181; dances, 32–35, 157–59; and Easter, 145; exchanges, 16, 32, 37–38, 42, 59–60, 80, 84, 103–5, 140, 152, 164, 179; interactions with chiefs, deities, and ministers, 27, 38, 69, 78, 82, 84, 96, 98, 105, 142–44, 152, 164–65, 169;